Friedrich Nietzsche

PHILOSOPHICAL WRITINGS

The German Library: Volume 48

Volkmar Sander, General Editor

Friedrich Nietzsche

PHILOSOPHICAL WRITINGS

Edited by Reinhold Grimm
and Caroline Molina y Vedia

CONTINUUM · NEW YORK

1995
The Continuum Publishing Company
370 Lexington Avenue, New York, NY 10017

The German Library is published in cooperation
with Deutsches Haus, New York University.
This volume has been supported by Inter Nationes,
and a grant from Daimler-Benz-Fonds.

Printed in the United States of America

Library of Congress Cataloging-in-Publication Data

Nietzsche, Friedrich Wilhelm, 1844–1900.
  [Selections. 1995]
  Philosophical writings / Friedrich Nietzsche ;
edited by Reinhold Grimm and Caroline Molina y Vedia.
      p.   cm. — (German library ; v. 48)
  Includes bibliographical references.
  ISBN 0-8264-0278-X (alk. paper). — ISBN 0-8264-0279-8
(pbk. : alk. paper)
  1. Philosophy. I. Grimm, Reinhold. II. Molina y Vedia,
Caroline. III. Title. IV. Series.
B3312.E5N34   1995   95-2494
193—dc20   CIP

Acknowledgments will be found on pages 270–71,
which constitute an extension of the copyright page.

Contents*

Introduction: Reinhold Grimm   ix

PART I: ON TRAGEDY
The Birth of Tragedy; or, Greekness and Pessimism (1872/86)
Attempt at a Self-Criticism   3
Preface to Richard Wagner   12
[The Birth of Tragedy]   13

From *Ecce Homo: How One Becomes What One Is* (1888,
published posthumously)
The Birth of Tragedy   73

From the so-called *Will to Power*
Art in "The Birth of Tragedy" (1888)   78
Translated by Walter Kaufmann

PART II: ON TRUTH
From *Five Prefaces to Five Unwritten Books*
On the Pathos of Truth (1872)   83
Translated by Bruce Armstrong
On Truth and Falsity in Their Extramoral Sense (1873)   87
Translated by Maximilian A. Mügge

PART III: APHORISMS, ESSAYS, NOTES
From *Untimely Meditations* and Related Writings
On the Use and Disadvantage of History for Life (1874)
(Selection)   103
Translated by Adrian Collins

Schopenhauer as Educator (1874) (Selection)   104
Translated by J. W. Hillesheim and Malcolm R. Simpson
The Battle between Science and Wisdom (1875; fragmentary)
(Selections)   105
Translated by Bruce Armstrong
Richard Wagner in Bayreuth (1876) (Selections)   106
Translated by Anthony M. Ludovici

From *Human, All-Too-Human: A Book for Free Spirits* (1878)
Of First and Last Things (Selections)   109
Concerning the History of Moral Sentiments (Selections)   115
The Religious Life (Selections)   116
From the Soul of Artists and Authors (Selections)   117
Signs of Higher and Lower Culture (Selections)   120
Man in Society (Selection)   124
Man Alone by Himself (Selection)   124
Translated by Helen Zimmern

From *Human, All-Too-Human II*
Mixed Opinions and Maxims (1879) (Selections)   126
The Wanderer and His Shadow (1880) (Selections)   129
Translated by Paul V. Cohen

From *Dawn: Thoughts about Morality as a Prejudice* (1881)
(Selections)   134
Translated by J. M. Kennedy

From *The Gay Science* (1882/87)
Books I–III (Selections)   139
Sanctus Januarius (Selections)   148
We Fearless Ones (Selections)   151
Translated by Walter Kaufmann

From *Beyond Good and Evil:*
Prelude to a Philosophy of the Future (1886)
Preface   159
On the Prejudices of Philosophers (Selections)   161
The Free Spirit (Selections)   164
Maxims and Interludes (Selections)   168
Concerning the Natural History of Morals (Selections)   168

Contents · vii

We Scholars (Selections)   172
What Is Noble? (Selections)   176
Translated by Walter Kaufmann

From *On the Genealogy of Morals: A Polemic* (1887)
Preface (Selection)   180
What Is the Meaning of Ascetic Ideals? (Selections)   181
Translated by Walter Kaufmann and R. J. Hollingdale

From *The Case of Wagner: A Musician's Problem* (1888)
Preface   190
Translated by Walter Kaufmann

From *Twilight of the Idols; or,*
How One Philosophizes with a Hammer (1888)
Maxims and Arrows (Selection)   192
The Problem of Socrates   192
"Reason" in Philosophy   197
How the "True World" Finally Became a Fable:
The History of an Error   201
Skirmishes of an Untimely Man (Selections)   202
What I Owe to the Ancients   205
Translated by Walter Kaufmann

From *Nietzsche contra Wagner:*
From the Files of a Psychologist (1888)
We Antipodes   211
Epilogue   213
Translated by Walter Kaufmann

From *Ecce Homo: How One Becomes What One Is*
(1888, published posthumously)
Thus Spoke Zarathustra: A Book for All and None   216
Genealogy of Morals: A Polemic   227
Why I Am a Destiny   228
Translated by Walter Kaufmann and R. J. Hollingdale

From *The Antichrist: Curse upon Christianity*
(1888) (Selection)   236
Translated by Walter Kaufmann

From the so-called *Will to Power*
(Summer 1883–Spring/Summer 1888)   238
Translated by Walter Kaufman and R. J. Hollingdale

Notes   255

Sources of the Selections   266

---

*For precise information on the sources of all works in the
contents, please see Sources of the Selections, pages 266–67.

Introduction

More than a hundred years have elapsed since Friedrich Nietzsche (1844–1900) rose to fame from the lowlands of provincial academia. The 1880s mark the height of his short and hectic creative career as well as the beginning of his worldwide recognition and impact. His reputation sometimes bordered on notoriety, but Nietzsche's influence, despite appearances, has never diminished. Rather, it has grown and spread in a way and to an extent surpassed, or even attained, by very few of his contemporaries. Like Karl Marx, his unwitting antipode, whom he so closely resembled in his devastating attack on bourgeois society, and like Sigmund Freud, his clandestine disciple, for whose revolutionary insights he not only laid the groundwork, but which he actually preformulated in certain cases, Nietzsche belongs to that vast array of thinkers from the German-speaking countries who have shaped the reality no less than the myths of our age. He can indeed be said to have been one of the makers of the twentieth century, both in the realms of philosophy and literature, and beyond them.

Unlike Marx and socialism, however, or Freud and psychoanalysis, Nietzsche has suffered from excessive maltreatment, and his work has been misread and misunderstood almost continuously. In part, this was due to the machinations and forgeries of his sister, which led to false or unreliable texts and to the attempted appropriation of their author by the fascists; in part, it was due to weighty if questionable and perhaps intentionally distorting critiques propounded by Georg Lukács and similar ideologists. Yet these are but the extremes of a general tendency toward misrepresentation that has prevailed for decades. Nietzsche and his provocative writings—the much abused, much debated so-called *Will to*

Power in particular—must be rediscovered. In fact, it is only now, with a sound textual basis finally established by recent scholarship, that we can hope to succeed in putting his controversial image and heritage to rights.

In itself, Nietzsche's life was far from spectacular—except, of course, for his mental breakdown and the ensuing years of madness and glory. Born at Röcken, a small Saxon village, on 15 October 1844, the gifted son of a Lutheran pastor was destined to follow in his father's footsteps and thus was privileged to attend the *Fürstenschule* at Pforta, a highly renowned "ducal college" emphasizing the humanities. Upon his graduation, Nietzsche entered the University of Bonn and dutifully devoted himself to the study of theology and then of classical philology. But he soon decided to concentrate exclusively on the latter, and returned to his native Saxony with his distinguished teacher, F. W. Ritschl, in order to enroll at the University of Leipzig. It was there that he excelled to such a degree as to be offered a position at the Swiss University of Basel in 1869, before having received his doctorate. The following year, Nietzsche was promoted to *Ordinarius,* or full professor, and held this chair until 1879, when he requested, and was honorably granted, early retirement on account of poor health. Henceforth, he wandered restlessly between various places, mainly in Switzerland and northern Italy.

Nietzsche was a detached yet unremitting psychologist who in cold blood examined, indeed dissected, human values, ideals, and, especially, morality; he was also an impassioned censor and visionary of mankind's fate and task who proclaimed his verdicts and commandments in an ever shriller, ever more trenchant as well as prophetical tone. His often volcanic outbursts of productivity, which resulted not only in thousands of printed pages but also in thousands of drafts and notes, came to an abrupt end in 1889 when the migrant philosopher broke down, after weeks of euphoria and increasing megalomania, in a public square in Turin.[1] What little remained of Nietzsche's life was spent in insanity, silence, and seclusion. On 25 August 1900 he died in Weimar, where his sister had taken him along with the holdings of the Nietzsche Archive she had established (and was able to control, unfortunately, until her own death in 1935).

Nonetheless, her choice of Germany's cultural capital, the city of Goethe and Schiller, was not unjustified. Nietzsche's writings bear the stamp of the poet and literary genius as much as that of the analyst or latter-day prophet. The quintessence of his worldview, whether cloaked in rationalism or clad in vision and myth, is always an aesthetic and artistic one. Significantly, the event that proved most important for his life and work was—apart from his encounter with the philosophy of Arthur Schopenhauer—his acquaintance with Richard Wagner. The experience of Wagner's art and personality affected Nietzsche deeply, both during their initial friendly exchanges, when he hailed and celebrated the "master" as the greatest of modern tragedians, as the artist par excellence, and during their slow but irreparable estrangement, when he assailed and denounced Wagner as the incarnation of histrionics and hateful decadence. Students of Nietzsche should never forget that no fewer than three of his most expansive confessional utterances are centered on things Wagnerian and the far-reaching problems he felt they implied. His fairly balanced *Richard Wagner in Bayreuth,* which appeared as the fourth of his *Untimely Meditations* in 1876, as well as his diatribes *The Case of Wagner* and *Nietzsche contra Wagner* of 1888 and 1889, respectively, testify to his lifelong fascination—or, to be more exact, obsession.

Wagner and his music drama, in however exaggerated and arbitrary a way, also figure prominently, along with Aeschylus, Sophocles, Socrates, and Euripides, in the very first of Nietzsche's many volumes: namely *The Birth of Tragedy from the Spirit of Music.* Dating from 1872 and, with the addition of its author's self-criticism, from 1886, its combined versions constitute one of his most revealing and typical (and most influential) texts. Hardly ever, at least in terms of his own development, did Nietzsche compose and publish a more telling, more seminal, more anticipatory book. On the one hand, its mixed reception in 1872 gave him a foretaste of his lot as a writer and philosopher; on the other hand, its conceptual and visionary core already contained—as he himself noted in 1886—the unmistakable seeds of a fundamental dualism of stern analysis and frantic prophecy, or Nietzschean enlightenment and Nietzschean mythopoeia, that was to shape and permeate his oeuvre as a whole.

Nietzsche's duality as an artist-philosopher, couched in a paradoxical unity, was not only foreshadowed but is actually embodied, as in a Janus-faced emblem, in the two dominant agents of his *Birth of Tragedy.* They are not Wagnerian in nature, in spite of

Wagner's importance and prominence. Nor are they, as might be expected, those twin forces, the Apollonian and the Dionysian, that have gained an almost proverbial currency. Rather, they are an overpowering Dionysian drive, inclusive of the Apollonian, and an equally powerful Socratic drive, in Nietzschean contrast and combination. The former, which manifests itself in Attic tragedy as created by Aeschylus and Sophocles, is seen as leading to frenzy, ecstasy, and cruelty, as well as to an irrational communion, through art and myth, of actors and spectators. The latter, which manifests itself in the drama of Euripides, is defined as a scientific attitude rooted in rationalism, and as an urge toward theory and morals as well as an optimistic belief in man's perfectibility, in progress and human betterment. The selfsame duality of Dionysian and Socratic, clearly discernible in Nietzsche's youthful essay, is far more present in his mature writings; in fact, the totality of Nietzsche's worldview—with all its contradictoriness yet ultimate oneness—is informed by their basic opposition. These two key concepts, and the names and historical realities from which they were derived, are evoked by him repeatedly, either directly or in countless variations and under the most diverse guises.

Nietzsche's art and thought abound with Dionysian illuminations and Socratic insights, but also with a host of concomitant notions, many of which have become proverbial: for example, some of Nietzsche's titles, such as *The Gay Science* and *Beyond Good and Evil,* as well as such truly Nietzschean oracles and suggestive catchwords as "eternal recurrence" and "superman," or, as some scholars would have us translate *Übermensch,* "overman." Even quite colloquial and seemingly unspecific phrases and terms—as, for instance, "reason versus instinct," or "truth" and "falsity," or "perspective"—could be shown to be intimately connected with Nietzsche's universal duality. But most expressive of his Socratism and Dionysianism[2] are the programmatic headings of a whole variety of pertinent texts, such as "Socrates and Tragedy" and "The Dionysian Worldview," two lectures constituting earlier stages of parts of his *Birth of Tragedy;* "Socrates," a laconic aphorism from the second volume of his *Human, All-Too-Human* of 1879/80 and *Dionysus-Dithyrambs,* a cycle of poems completed shortly before his breakdown in 1889, but published, like several other works from that period, only afterward.

It is the aim of this volume to lay bare at least the essentials, both aesthetic and philosophical, of Nietzsche's complex worldview as it originated in and around his first book and gradually developed over the years. The selections have been arranged in chronological order, beginning with the decisive sections of the (final) version of *The Birth of Tragedy* (plus two related writings of 1872/73) and ending with excerpts from the so-called *Will to Power* ("so-called" because it was not composed by the author himself but compiled posthumously, from his notebooks of the 1880s, by his sister and her collaborators.) Of necessity, these texts are incomplete in more than one regard; however, with the exception of the first *Untimely Meditation* (Nietzsche's attack on F. D. Strauß, which as a personal satire can be dispensed with nowadays) and *Thus Spoke Zarathustra* (Nietzsche's magnum opus), all of the major works of the artist–philosopher are represented. They comprise, apart from those already mentioned: two remaining *Untimely Meditations* (*On the Use and Disadvantage of History for Life* and *Schopenhauer as Educator,* both of 1874); the first volume of *Human, All-Too-Human,* which dates from 1878; *Dawn* of 1881 and *On the Genealogy of Morals* of 1887; and, last though surely not least, *Twilight of the Idols, The Antichrist,* and *Ecce Homo*—the latter three an eruptive triad of works all written in 1888 and published in 1889, 1895, and 1908, respectively.

This collection, which might as well be entitled "The Birth of a Philosophy," contains a few slight overlappings and repetitions. But neither are these of the kind usually labeled "unavoidable" by embarrassed editors, nor are they due to any editorial oversight. Rather, they have been incorporated on purpose, for they belong without doubt to the characteristic features of Nietzsche's style of writing and thinking. However, his predilection for massive italicizing and extremely long paragraphs, while likewise typical of his rhetoric, is less relevant philosophically; and since a faithful rendition of such peculiarities would have been unacceptable in English, they have—in accordance with the usual practice of Nietzsche translators, notably Walter Kaufmann—been curtailed to a certain extent. Nothing else has been altered in the text. Even the customary editorial additions (indicated by square brackets) or editorial cuts (marked by three dots unless otherwise specified) have been kept to a minimum, the sole exception being the passages from the so-called *Will to Power,* where careful editing was not only mandatory, but was finally possible in a responsible way—without reflecting negatively on the fine scholarship of the original translation—thanks to the new critical edition provided by the late Mazzino Montinari and the late Giorgio Colli.[3] The previous numbering and, as far as feasible, presentation have been retained, however, because it was in this form that the Nietzschean notebooks exerted their influence. Moreover, no English translation of their authentic version is as yet available.[3a]

Concerning the general situation of what Bernard Shaw, almost a century ago, blithely announced as a "Nietzsche in English,"[4] it must be said that every translation used here had to be revised throughout, not just extensively but often drastically.[5] This holds true especially for the Levy translations, yet even the Kaufmann translations—not altogether independent of their predecessors, for all the criticism they level against them—are not perfect.[6] But who can claim perfection as a translator?

New and additional notes, editorial as well as explanatory, have been supplied wherever appropriate and necessary. Still, no attempts have been made at systematizing or harmonizing Nietzsche's work and development. His Dionysianism, in the long run, tended to outweigh his Socratism, yet the opposite tendency nevertheless persisted and actually prevailed on occasion. After all, the artist-philosopher was a philosopher-artist as well, and as much obsessed with Socrates as he was with Wagner. Not only did Nietzsche the Socratic decry the appearance of the Greek sage as a moment of abysmal "perversity"[7] in the history of mankind, but Nietzsche the Dionysian, the frenetic prophet[8] of tragedy and the tragic worldview, was also able to exclaim: "Oh, how weary I am of the tragic gestures and words!"[9]

With regard to the principles on which this anthology has been compiled, let a last dictum of Nietzsche's be our motto: "The selection that one makes with regard to my books sets me thinking."[10] May it have a similar effect on the reader!

R. G.

Notes

1. For details, see Anacleto Verrecchia, "Nietzsche's Breakdown in Turin," in *Nietzsche in Italy,* ed. Thomas Harrison (Stanford University: ANMA Libri, 1988) 105–12.

2. The coinage is Nietzsche's, though he actually uses the spelling *Dionysismus.*

3. Friedrich Nietzsche, *Werke: Kritische Gesamtausgabe,* ed. Giorgio Colli and Mazzino Montinari (Berlin/New York: Verlag de Gruyter, 1967); henceforth abbreviated *KGW.*

3a. Meanwhile, Stanford University Press has announced a forthcoming 20-volume edition of *The Complete Works of Friedrich Nietzsche,* edited by Ernst Behler, and based on the Colli–Montinari edition.

4. Shaw's review of the same title appeared in 1896; see his *Dramatic Opinions and Essays with an Apology* (New York, 1916) I: 382 ff.

5. "On Truth and Falsity in Their Extramoral Sense" as well as a few isolated passages have been translated for this volume by Bruce Armstrong.

6. For bibliographical details, see below pp. 266f.

7. Cf. *KGW,* VIII/3, 81.

8. Compare, among other things, two titles Nietzsche drafted in 1885: "Dionysus: Attempt at a Divine Way of Philosophizing" and "Dionysus: Book of Prophecy" (cf. *KGW,* VII/3, 203 and 242).

9. *KGW,* VII/1, 29.

10. *KGW,* VII/3, 344.

Part I

ON TRAGEDY

The Birth of Tragedy;
or, Greekness and Pessimism*

Attempt at a Self-Criticism (1886)

1.

Whatever may be at the bottom of this questionable book, it must have been an exceptionally significant and fascinating question, and deeply personal at that: the time in which it was written, in *spite* of which it was written, bears witness to that—the exciting time of the Franco-Prussian War of 1870–71. As the thunder of the battle of Wörth was rolling over Europe, the muser and riddle-friend who was to be the father of this book sat somewhere in an Alpine nook, very bemused and beriddled, hence very concerned and yet unconcerned, and wrote down his thoughts about the *Greeks*—the core of the strange and almost inaccessible book to which this belated preface (or postscript) shall now be added. A few weeks later—and he himself was to be found under the walls of Metz, still wedded to the question marks that he had placed after the alleged "cheerfulness" of the Greeks and of Greek art. Eventually, in that month of profoundest suspense when the peace treaty was being debated at Versailles, he, too, attained peace with himself and, slowly convalescing from an illness contracted at the front, completed the final draft of *The Birth of Tragedy out of the Spirit of Music.*—Out of music? Music and tragedy? Greeks

---

*In the first edition (1872) the title was *The Birth of Tragedy out of the Spirit of Music*. A second edition with very slight textual changes was printed in 1874 and appeared in 1878. In 1886, the remaining copies of both editions were reissued with the above title.

and the music of tragedy? Greeks and the art form of pessimism? The most perfectly developed, most beautiful, most envied type of humanity to date, those most apt to seduce us to life, the Greeks— how now? They of all people should have *needed* tragedy? Even more—art? For what—Greek art?

You will guess where the big question mark concerning the value of existence had thus been raised. Is pessimism *necessarily* a sign of decline, decay, degeneration, weary and weak instincts—as it once was in India and now is, to all appearances, among us, "modern" men and Europeans? Is there a pessimism of *strength*? An intellectual predilection for the hard, gruesome, evil, problematic aspect of existence, prompted by well-being, by overflowing health, by the *fullness* of existence? Is it perhaps possible to suffer precisely from overfullness? The sharp-eyed courage that tempts and attempts, that *craves* the frightful as the enemy, the worthy enemy, against whom one can test one's strength? From whom one can learn what it means "to be frightened"? What is the significance of the *tragic* myth among the Greeks of the best, the strongest, the most courageous period? And the tremendous phenomenon of the Dionysian—and, born from it, tragedy—what might they signify?—And again: that of which tragedy died, the Socratism of morality, the dialectics, temperance, and cheerfulness of the theoretical man—how now? might not this very Socratism be a sign of decline, of weariness, of infection, of the anarchical dissolution of the instincts? And the "Greek cheerfulness" of the later Greeks— merely the afterglow of the sunset? The Epicureans' resolve *against* pessimism—a mere precaution of the afflicted? And science itself, our science—indeed, what is the significance of all science, viewed as a symptom of life? For what—worse yet, *whence*—all science? How now? Is the resolve to be so scientific about everything perhaps a kind of fear of, an escape from, pessimism? A subtle last resort against—*truth*? And, morally speaking, a sort of cowardice and falseness? Amorally speaking, a ruse? O Socrates, Socrates, was that perhaps *your* secret? O enigmatic ironist, was that perhaps your—irony?

2.

What I then got hold of, something frightful and dangerous, a problem with horns but not necessarily a bull, in any case a *new* problem—today I should say that it was *the problem of science itself,* science considered for the first time as problematic, as questionable. But the book in which my youthful courage and suspicion found an outlet—what an *impossible* book had to result from a task so uncongenial to youth! Constructed from a lot of immature, overgreen personal experiences, all of them close to the limits of communication, presented in the context of *art*—for the problem of science cannot be recognized in the context of science—a book perhaps for artists who also have an analytic and retrospective penchant (in other words, an exceptional type of artist for whom one might have to look far and wide and really would not care to look); a book full of psychological innovations and artists' secrets, with an artists' metaphysics in the background; a youthful work full of the intrepid mood of youth, the moodiness of youth, independent, defiantly self-reliant even where it seems to bow before an authority and personal reverence; in sum, a first book, also in every bad sense of that label. In spite of the problem which seems congenial to old age, the book is marked by every defect of youth, above all with its "length in excess" and its "storm and stress." On the other hand, considering its success (especially with the great artist to whom it addressed itself as in a dialogue, Richard Wagner), it is a *proven* book, I mean one that in any case satisfied "the best minds of the time."[1] In view of that, it really ought to be treated with some consideration and taciturnity. Still, I do not want to suppress entirely how disagreeable it now seems to me, how strange it appears now, after sixteen years—before a much older, a hundred times more demanding, but by no means colder eye which has not become a stranger to the task which this audacious book dared to tackle for the first time: *to look at science in the perspective of the artist, but at art in that of life.*

3.

To say it once more: today I find it an impossible book. I deem it badly written, ponderous, embarrassing, image-mad and image-confused, sentimental, in places saccharine to the point of effeminacy, uneven in tempo, without the will to logical cleanliness, very convinced and therefore disdainful of proof, mistrustful even of the *propriety* of proof, a book for initiates, "music" for those dedicated to music, those who are closely related to begin with on the basis of shared and rare aesthetic experiences, a sign of recognition for close relatives *in artibus*[2]—an arrogant and rhapsodic book that sought to exclude right from the beginning the *profanum vulgus*[3] of "the educated" even more than "the mass" or "folk." Still, the effect of the book proved and proves that it has a knack for seeking out fellow-rhapsodizers and for luring them on to new secret paths and dancing places. What found expression here was anyway—this was admitted with as much curiosity as antipathy— a *strange* voice, the disciple of a still "unknown God," one who concealed himself for the time being under the scholar's hood, under the gravity and dialectical dourness of the German, even under the bad manners of the Wagnerian. Here was a spirit with strange, still nameless needs, a memory bursting with questions, experiences, concealed things after which the name of Dionysus was added as one more question mark. What spoke here—it was noted with suspicion—was something like a mystical, almost mae-nadic soul that stammered with difficulty and arbitrariness, as in a strange tongue, almost undecided whether it should communicate or conceal itself. It should have *sung,* this "new soul"—and not spoken![4] What I had to say then—too bad that I did not dare say it as a poet: perhaps I had the ability. Or at least as a philologist: after all, even today practically everything in this field remains to be discovered and dug up by philologists! Above all, the problem that there *is* a problem here—and that the Greeks, as long as we lack an answer to the question "what is Dionysian?" remain as totally uncomprehended and unimaginable as ever.

4.

Indeed, what is Dionysian?—This book contains an answer: one "who knows" is talking, the initiate and disciple of his god. *Now* I should perhaps speak more cautiously and less eloquently about such a difficult psychological question as that concerning the origin of tragedy among the Greeks. The question of the Greek's relation to pain, his degree of sensitivity, is basic: did this relation remain constant? Or did it change radically? The question is whether his ever stronger *craving for beauty,* for festivals, pleasures, new cults was rooted in some deficiency, privation, melancholy, pain? Sup-posing that this were true—and Pericles (or Thucydides) suggests as much in the great funeral oration—what, then, would be the origin of the opposite craving, which developed earlier in time, the *craving for the ugly;* the good, severe will of the older Greeks to pessimism, to the tragic myth, to the image of everything underlying existence that is frightful, evil, a riddle, destructive, fatal? What, then, would be the origin of tragedy? Perhaps *joy*, strength, overflowing health, overgreat fullness? And what, then, is the significance, physiologically speaking, of that madness out of which tragic and comic art developed—the Dionysian madness? How now? Is madness perhaps not necessarily the symptom of degeneration, decline, and the final stage of culture? Are there perhaps—a question for psychiatrists—neuroses of *health?* of the youth and youthfulness of a people? Where does that synthesis of god and billy goat in the satyr point? What experience of himself, what urge compelled the Greek to conceive the Dionysian enthusiast and primeval man as a satyr? And regarding the origin of the tragic chorus: did those centuries when the Greek body flourished and the Greek soul foamed over with health perhaps know endemic ecstasies? Visions and hallucinations that seized entire communities or assemblies at a cult? What if the Greeks, precisely in the abundance of their youth, had the will to the tragic and were pessimists? What if it was madness, to use one of Plato's phrases, that brought the greatest blessings upon Greece? On the other hand, conversely, could it be that the Greeks became more and more optimistic, superficial, and histrionic precisely in the period of dissolution and weakness—more and more ardent for logic and logicizing the world and thus more "cheerful" and "scientific"? How now? Could it be possible that, in spite of all "modern ideas" and the prejudices of a democratic taste, the triumph of *optimism,* the gradual prevalence of *rationality,* practical and theoretical *utilitarianism,* no less than democracy itself, which developed at the same time, might all have been symptoms of a decline of strength, of impending old age, and of physiological weariness? These, and not pessimism? Was Epicurus an optimist—precisely because he was *afflicted?*

It is apparent that it was a whole cluster of grave questions with which this book burdened itself. Let us add the gravest question of all. What, seen in the perspective of *life,* is the significance of morality?

5.

Already in the preface addressed to Richard Wagner, art, and *not* morality, is presented as the truly *metaphysical* activity of man. In the book itself the suggestive sentence is repeated several times, that the existence of the world is *justified* only as an aesthetic phenomenon. Indeed, the whole book knows only an artistic meaning and crypto-meaning behind all events—a "god," if you please, but certainly only an entirely reckless and amoral artist-god who wants to experience, whether he is building or destroying, in the good and in the bad, his own joy and glory—one who, creating worlds, frees himself from the *distress* of fullness and *overfullness* and from the *affliction* of the contradictions compressed in his soul. The world—at every moment the *attained* salvation of God, as the eternally changing, eternally new vision of the most deeply afflicted, discordant, and contradictory being who can find salvation only in *appearance:* you can call this whole artists' metaphysics arbitrary, idle, fantastic; what matters is that it betrays a spirit who will one day fight at any risk whatever the *moral* interpretation and significance of existence. Here, perhaps for the first time, a pessimism "beyond good and evil" is suggested. Here that "perversity of mind" gains speech and formulation against which Schopenhauer never wearied of hurling in advance his most irate curses and thunderbolts: a philosophy that dares to move, to demote, morality into the realm of appearance—and not merely among "appearances" or phenomena (in the sense assigned to these words by Idealistic philosophers), but among "deceptions," as semblance, delusion, error, interpretation, contrivance, art.

Perhaps the death of this *antimoral* propensity is best inferred from the careful and hostile silence with which Christianity is treated throughout the whole book—Christianity as the most prodigal elaboration of the moral theme to which humanity has ever been subjected. In truth, nothing could be more opposed to the purely aesthetic interpretation and justification of the world which are taught in this book than the Christian teaching, which is, and wants to be, *only* moral and which relegates art, *every* art, to the realm of *lies;* with its absolute standards, beginning with the truthfulness of God, it negates, damns, condemns art. Behind this mode of thought and valuation, which must be hostile to art if it is at all genuine, I never failed to sense a *hostility to life*—a furious, vengeful antipathy to life itself: for all of life is based on semblance, art, deception, points of view, and the necessity of perspectives and error. Christianity was from the beginning, essentially and fundamentally, life's nausea and disgust with life, merely concealed behind, masked by, dressed up as, faith in "another" or "better" life. Hatred of "the world," condemnations of the passions, fear of beauty and sensuality, a beyond invented the better to slander this life, at bottom a craving for nothingness, for the end, for respite, for "the sabbath of sabbaths"—all this always struck me, no less than the unconditional will of Christianity to recognize *only* moral values, as the most dangerous and uncanny form of all possible forms of a "will to decline"—at the very least a sign of abysmal sickness, weariness, discouragement, exhaustion, and the impoverishment of life. For, confronted with morality (especially Christian, or unconditional, morality), life *must* continually and inevitably be in the wrong, because life *is* something essentially amoral—and eventually, crushed by the weight of contempt and the eternal No, life *must* then be felt to be unworthy of desire and altogether worthless. Morality itself—how now? might not morality be "a will to negate life," a secret instinct of annihilation, a principle of decay, diminution, and denigration—the beginning of the end? Hence, the danger of dangers?

It was *against* morality that my instinct turned with this questionable book, long ago; it was an instinct that aligned itself with life and that discovered for itself a fundamentally opposite doctrine and valuation of life—purely artistic and *anti-Christian*. What to call it? As a philologist and man of words I baptized it, not without taking some liberty—for who could claim to know the rightful name of the Antichrist?—in the name of a Greek god: I called it Dionysian.

6.

Is it clear what task I first dared to touch with this book? How I regret now that in those days I still lacked the courage (or immodesty?) to permit myself in every way an individual language of my own for such individual views and audacities—and that instead I tried laboriously to express by means of Schopenhauerian and Kantian formulas strange and new valuations which were basically at odds with Kant's and Schopenhauer's spirit and taste! What, after all, did Schopenhauer think of tragedy?

"That which bestows on everything tragic its peculiar elevating force"—he says in *The World as Will and Representation*,[5] volume 2, p. 495—"is the discovery that the world, that life, can never give real satisfaction and hence is *not worthy* of our affection: this constitutes the tragic spirit—it leads to *resignation*."

Oh, how differently Dionysus spoke to me! Oh, how far removed I was from all this resignationism![6]—But there is something far worse in this book, something I now regret still more than that I obscured and spoiled Dionysian premonitions with Schopenhauerian formulations: namely, that I *spoiled* the grandiose *Greek problem,* as it had arisen before my eyes, by introducing the most modern problems! That I appended hopes where there was no ground for hope, where everything pointed all too plainly to an end! That on the basis of the latest German music I began to rave about "the German spirit" as if that were in the process even then of discovering and finding itself again—at a time when the German spirit, which not long before had still had the will to dominate Europe and the strength to lead Europe,[7] was just making its testament and *abdicating* forever, making its transition, under the pompous pretense of founding a *Reich,* to a leveling mediocrity, democracy, and "modern ideas"!

Indeed, meanwhile I have learned to consider this "German spirit" with a sufficient lack of hope or mercy; also, contemporary *German music,* which is romanticism through and through and the most un-Greek of all possible art forms—moreover, a first-rate poison for the nerves, doubly dangerous among a people who love drink and who honor lack of clarity as a virtue, for it has the double quality of a narcotic that both intoxicates and befogs.

To be sure, apart from all the hasty hopes and faulty applications to the present with which I spoiled my first book, there still remains the great Dionysian question mark I raised—regarding music as well: what would a music have to be like that would no longer be of romantic origin, like German music—but *Dionysian?*

7.

But, my dear sir, what in the world is romantic if *your* book isn't? Can deep hatred against "the Now," against "reality" and "modern ideas" be pushed further than you pushed it in your artists' metaphysics? believing sooner in the Nothing, sooner in the devil than in "the Now"? Is it not a deep bass of wrath and the lust for destruction that we hear humming underneath all of your contrapuntal vocal art and seduction of the ear, a furious resolve against everything that is "now," a will that is not too far removed from practical nihilism and seems to say: "sooner let nothing be true than that *you* should be right, than that *your* truth should be proved right!"

Listen yourself, my dear pessimist and art-deifier, but with open ears, to a single passage chosen from your book—to the not ineloquent dragon-slayer passage which may have an insidious pied-piper sound for young ears and hearts. How now? Isn't this the typical creed of the romantic of 1830, masked by the pessimism of 1850? Even the usual romantic finale is sounded—break, breakdown, return and collapse before an old faith, before *the* old God. How now? Is your pessimists' book not itself a piece of anti-Hellenism and romanticism? Is it not itself something "equally intoxicating and befogging," in any case a narcotic, even a piece of music, *German* music? But listen:

"Let us imagine a coming generation with such intrepidity of vision, with such a heroic penchant for the tremendous; let us imagine the bold stride of these dragon-slayers, the proud audacity with which they turn their back on all the weakling's doctrines of optimism in order to 'live resolutely' in wholeness and fullness: *would it not be necessary* for the tragic man of such a culture, in view of his self-education for seriousness and terror, to desire a new art, the *art of metaphysical comfort,* to desire tragedy as his own proper Helen, and to exclaim with Faust:

> *Should not my longing overleap the distance*
> *And draw the fairest form into existence?*[8]

"Would it not be *necessary?*"—No, thrice no! O you young romantics: it would *not* be necessary! But it is highly probable that it will *end* that way, that *you* will end that way—namely, "comforted," as it is written, in spite of all self-education for seriousness and terror, "comforted metaphysically"—in sum, as romantics end, as *Christians*.

No! You ought to learn the art of *this-worldly* comfort first; you ought to learn to laugh, my young friends, if you are hell-bent on remaining pessimists. Then perhaps, as laughers, you may some day dispatch all metaphysical comforts to the devil—with metaphysics heading the way. Or, to say it in the language of that Dionysian monster who bears the name of Zarathustra:

"Raise up your hearts, my brothers, high, higher! And don't forget your legs! Raise up your legs, too, good dancers; and still better: stand on your heads!

"This crown of the laugher, the rose-wreath crown: I crown myself with this crown; I myself pronounced holy my laughter. I did not find anyone else today strong enough for that.

"Zarathustra, the dancer; Zarathustra, the light one who beckons with his wings, preparing for a flight, beckoning to all birds, ready and heady, blissfully lightheaded;

"Zarathustra, the soothsayer; Zarathustra, the sooth-laugher; not impatient; not unconditional; one who loves leaps and side-leaps: I crown myself with this crown.

"This crown of the laugher, the rose-wreath crown: to you, my brothers, I throw this crown. Laughter I have pronounced holy: you higher men, *learn*—to laugh!"

Thus Spoke Zarathustra, part 4.[9]

Sils-Maria, Oberengadin,
August 1886

Translated by Walter Kaufmann

Preface to Richard Wagner (1871)

To keep at a distance all the possible scruples, excitements, and misunderstandings that the thoughts united in this essay will occasion, in view of the peculiar character of our aesthetic public, and to be able to write these introductory remarks, too, with the same contemplative delight whose reflection—the distillation[10] of good and elevating hours—is evident on every page, I picture the moment when you, my highly respected friend, will receive this essay. Perhaps after an evening walk in the winter snow, you will behold Prometheus unbound on the title page, read my name, and be convinced at once that, whatever this essay should contain, the author certainly has something serious and urgent to say; also that, as he developed these ideas, he was communicating with you as if you were present, and hence could write down only what was in keeping with that presence. You will recall that it was during the same period when your splendid *Festschrift* on Beethoven came into being, amid the terrors and sublimities of the war that had just broken out, that I collected myself for these reflections. Yet anyone would be mistaken if he associated my reflections with the contrast between patriotic excitement and aesthetic wallowing, between courageous seriousness and a cheerful game: if he really read this essay, it would dawn on him, to his surprise, what a seriously German problem is faced here and placed right in the center of German hopes, as a vortex and turning point. But perhaps such readers will find it offensive that an aesthetic problem should be taken so seriously—assuming they are unable to consider art more than a pleasant sideline, a readily dispensable tinkling of bells that accompanies the "seriousness of life," just as if nobody knew what was involved in such a contrast with the "seriousness of life." Let such "serious" readers learn something from the fact that I am convinced that art represents the highest task and the truly metaphysical activity of this life, in the sense of that man to whom, as my sublime predecessor on this path, I wish to dedicate this essay.

Basel, end of the year 1871

Translated by Walter Kaufmann

[The Birth of Tragedy]

1.

We shall have gained much for the science of aesthetics, once we perceive not merely by logical inference, but with the immediate certainty of vision, that the continuous development of art is bound up with the *Apollonian* and *Dionysian* duality—just as procreation depends on the duality of the sexes, involving perpetual strife with only periodically intervening reconciliations. The terms Dionysian and Apollonian we borrow from the Greeks, who disclose to the discerning mind the profound mysteries of their view of art, not, to be sure, in concepts, but in the intensely clear figures of their gods. Through Apollo and Dionysus, the two art deities of the Greeks, we come to recognize that in the Greek world there existed a tremendous opposition, in origin and aims,[11] between the Apollonian art of sculpture and the nonimagistic, Dionysian art of music. These two different tendencies run parallel to each other, for the most part openly at variance; and they continually incite each other to new and more powerful births, which perpetuate an antagonism, only superficially reconciled by the common term "art"; until eventually,[12] by a metaphysical miracle of the Hellenic "will," they appear coupled with each other, and through this coupling ultimately generate an equally Dionysian and Apollonian form of art—Attic tragedy.

In order to grasp these two tendencies, let us first conceive of them as the separate art worlds of *dreams* and *intoxication*. These physiological phenomena present a contrast analogous to that existing between the Apollonian and the Dionysian. It was in dreams, says Lucretius, that the glorious divine figures first appeared to the souls of men; in dreams the great sculptor beheld the splendid bodies of superhuman beings; and the Hellenic poet, if questioned about the mysteries of poetic inspiration, would likewise have suggested dreams and he would have given an explanation like that of Hans Sachs in the *Meistersinger:*

> *The poet's task is this, my friend,*
> *to read his dreams and comprehend.*
> *The truest human fancy seems*
> *to be revealed to us in dreams:*
> *all poems and versification*
> *are but true dreams' interpretation.*

The beautiful illusion[13] of the dream worlds, in the creation of which every man is truly an artist, is the prerequisite of all plastic art, and, as we shall see, of an important part of poetry also. In our dreams we delight in the immediate understanding of figures; all forms speak to us; there is nothing unimportant or superfluous. But even when this dream reality is most intense, we still have, glimmering through it, the sensation that it is *mere appearance:* at least this is my experience, and for its frequency—indeed, normality—I could adduce many proofs, including the sayings of the poets.

Philosophical men even have a presentiment that the reality in which we live and have our being is also mere appearance, and that another, quite different reality lies beneath it. Schopenhauer actually indicates as the criterion of philosophical ability the gift of occasionally being able to view men and things as mere phantoms or dream images. Thus the aesthetically sensitive man stands in the same relation to the reality of dreams as the philosopher does to the reality of existence; he is a close and willing observer, for from these images he derives for himself an interpretation of life, and by reflecting on these processes he trains himself for life.

It is not only the agreeable and friendly images that he experiences in so universally intelligible a way: the serious, the troubled, the sad, the gloomy, the sudden restraints, the tricks of accident, anxious expectation, in short, the whole "divine comedy" of life, including the inferno, also pass before him, not like mere shadows on a wall—for he lives and suffers with these scenes—and yet not without that fleeting sensation of illusion. And perhaps many will, like myself, recall how amid the dangers and terrors of dreams they have occasionally said to themselves in self-encouragement, and not without success: "It is a dream! I will dream on!" I have likewise heard of people who were able to continue one and the same dream for three and even more successive nights—facts which indicate clearly how our innermost being, our common substratum, experiences dreams with profound delight and a joyous necessity.

This joyous necessity of the dream experience has been embodied by the Greeks in their Apollo: Apollo, the god of all plastic energies, is at the same time the soothsaying god. He, who (as the etymology of the name indicates) is the "shining one," the deity of light, is also ruler over the beautiful illusion of the inner world of fantasy. The higher truth, the perfection of these states in contrast to the incompletely intelligible everyday world, this deep consciousness of nature, healing and helping in sleep and dreams, is at the same time the symbolical analogue of the soothsaying faculty and of the arts generally, which make life possible and worth living. But we must also include in our image of Apollo that delicate boundary which the dream image must not overstep lest it have a pathological effect (in which case mere appearance would deceive us as if it were crude reality). We must keep in mind that measured restraint, that freedom from the wilder emotions, that calm of the sculptor god. His eye must be "sunlike," as befits its origin;[14] even when it is angry and betrays ill humor it is still hallowed by beautiful illusion. And so, in one sense, we might apply to Apollo the words of Schopenhauer when he speaks of the man wrapped in the veil of maya[15] (*Die Welt als Wille und Vorstellung*, volume 1, p. 416[16]): "Just as in a stormy sea that, unbounded in all directions, raises and drops mountainous waves, howling, a sailor sits in a boat and trusts in his frail bark: so in the midst of a world of torments the individual human being sits quietly, supported by and trusting in the *principium individuationis.*"[17] In fact, we might say of Apollo that in him the unshaken faith in this *principium* and the calm repose of the man wrapped up in it receive their most sublime expression; and we might call Apollo himself the glorious divine image of the *principium individuationis,* through whose gestures and eyes all the joy and wisdom of "illusion," together with its beauty, speak to us.

In the same work Schopenhauer has depicted for us the tremendous *terror* which seizes man when he is suddenly dumbfounded by the cognitive form of phenomena because the principle of sufficient reason, in some one of its manifestations, seems to suffer an exception. If we add to this terror the blissful ecstasy that wells from the innermost depths of man, indeed of nature, at this collapse of the *principium individuationis,* we steal a glimpse into the nature of the *Dionysian,* which is brought home to us most intimately by the analogy of intoxication.

Either under the influence of the narcotic draught, of which the songs of all primitive men and peoples speak, or with the potent coming of spring that penetrates all nature with joy, these Dionysian emotions awake, and as they grow in intensity, everything subjective vanishes into complete self-forgetfulness. In the German Middle Ages, too, singing and dancing crowds, ever increasing in number, whirled themselves from place to place under this same Dionysian impulse. In these dancers of Saint John and Saint Vitus, we rediscover the Bacchic choruses of the Greeks, with their prehistory in Asia Minor, as far back as Babylon and the orgiastic Sacaea.[18] There are some who, from obtuseness or lack of experience, turn away from such phenomena as from "folk diseases," with contempt or pity born of the consciousness of their own "healthy-mindedness." But of course such poor wretches have no idea how corpselike and ghostly their so-called healthy-mindedness looks when the glowing life of the Dionysian revelers roars past them.

Under the charm of the Dionysian, not only is the union between man and man reestablished, but nature which has become alienated, hostile, or subjugated, celebrates once more her reconciliation with her lost son,[19] man. Freely, earth proffers her gifts, and peacefully the beasts of prey of the rocks and desert approach. The chariot of Dionysus is covered with flowers and garlands; panthers and tigers walk under its yoke. Transform Beethoven's "Hymn to

Joy" into a painting; let your imagination conceive the multitudes bowing to the dust, awestruck—then you will approach the Dionysian. Now the slave is a free man; now all the rigid, hostile barriers that necessity, caprice, or "impudent convention"[20] have fixed between man and man are broken. Now, with the gospel of universal harmony, each one feels himself not only united, reconciled, and fused with his neighbor, but as one with him, as if the veil of maya had been torn aside and were now merely fluttering in tatters before the mysterious primordial unity.

In song and in dance man expresses himself as a member of a higher community; he has forgotten how to walk and speak and is on the way toward flying into the air, dancing. His very gestures express enchantment. Just as the animals now talk, and the earth yields milk and honey, supernatural sounds emanate from him, too: he feels himself a god, he himself now walks about enchanted, in ecstasy, like the gods he saw walking in his dreams. He is no longer an artist, he has become a work of art: in these paroxysms of intoxication the artistic power of all nature reveals itself to the highest gratification of the primordial unity. The noblest clay, the most costly marble, man, is here kneaded and cut, and to the sound of the chisel strokes of the Dionysian world-artist rings out the cry of the Eleusinian mysteries: "Do you prostrate yourselves, millions? Do you sense your Maker, world?"[21]

2.

Thus far we have considered the Apollonian and its opposite, the Dionysian, as artistic energies which burst forth from nature herself, *without the mediation of the human artist*—energies in which nature's art impulses are satisfied in the most immediate and direct way—on the one hand, in the image world of dreams, whose completeness is not dependent upon the intellectual stature or the artistic culture of any single being; on the other hand, as intoxicated reality, which likewise does not heed the single unit, but even seeks to destroy the individual and redeem him by a mystic feeling of oneness. With reference to these immediate art-states of nature, every artist is an "imitator," that is to say, either an Apollonian artist in dreams, or a Dionysian artist in ecstasies, or finally—as for example in Greek tragedy—at once artist in both dreams and ecstasies; so we may perhaps picture him sinking down in his Dionysian intoxication and mystical self-abnegation, alone and apart from the singing revelers, and we may imagine how, through Apollonian dream-inspiration, his own state, i.e., his oneness with the inmost ground of the world, is revealed to him in a *symbolical dream image.*

So much for these general premises and contrasts. Let us now approach the *Greeks* in order to learn how highly these *art impulses of nature* were developed in them. Thus we shall be in a position to understand and appreciate more deeply that relation of the Greek artist to his archetypes which is, according to the Aristotelian expression, "the imitation of nature." In spite of all the dream literature and the numerous dream anecdotes of the Greeks, we can speak of their *dreams* only conjecturally, though with reasonable assurance. If we consider the incredibly precise and unerring plastic power of their eyes, together with their vivid, frank delight in colors, we can hardly refrain from assuming even for their dreams (to the shame of all those born later) a logic of line and contour, colors and groups, a pictorial sequence, reminding us of their finest bas-reliefs, whose perfection would certainly justify us, if a comparison were possible, in designating the dreaming Greeks as Homers and Homer as a dreaming Greek—in a deeper sense than that in which modern man, speaking of his dreams, ventures to compare himself with Shakespeare.

On the other hand, we need not conjecture regarding the immense gap which separates the *Dionysian Greek* from the Dionysian barbarian. From all quarters of the ancient world—to say nothing here of the modern—from Rome to Babylon, we can point to the existence of Dionysian festivals, types which bear, at best, the same relation to the Greek festivals which the bearded satyr, who borrowed his name and attributes from the goat, bears to Dionysus himself. In nearly every case these festivals centered in extravagant sexual licentiousness, whose waves overwhelmed all family life and its venerable traditions; the most savage natural instincts were unleashed, including even that horrible mixture of sensuality and cruelty which has always seemed to me to be the real "witches' brew." For some time, however, the Greeks were apparently perfectly insulated and guarded against the feverish excitements of these festivals, though knowledge of them must have come to Greece on all the routes of land and sea; for the figure of Apollo, rising full of pride, held out the Gorgon's head to this grotesquely uncouth Dionysian power—and really could not have countered any more dangerous force. It is in Doric art that this majestically rejecting attitude of Apollo is immortalized.

The resistance of Apollo to Dionysus became more hazardous, and even impossible, when similar impulses finally burst forth from the deepest roots of the Hellenic nature and made a path for themselves: the Delphic god, by a timely reconciliation, now contented himself with taking the destructive weapons from the hands of his powerful antagonist. This reconciliation is the most important moment in the history of the Greek cult: wherever we turn we note the revolutions resulting from this event. The two antagonists were reconciled; the boundary lines to be observed henceforth by each were sharply defined, and there was to be a periodical exchange of gifts of esteem. At bottom, however, the chasm was not bridged over. But if we observe how, under the pressure of this treaty of peace, the Dionysian power revealed itself, we shall now recognize in the Dionysian orgies of the Greeks, as compared with the Babylonian Sacaea with their reversion of man to the tiger and the ape, the significance of festivals of world redemption and days of transfiguration. It is with them that nature for the first time attains her artistic jubilee; it is with them that the destruction of the *principium individuationis* for the first time becomes an artistic phenomenon.

The horrible "witches' brew" of sensuality and cruelty becomes ineffective; only the curious blending and duality in the emotions of the Dionysian revelers remind us—as medicines remind us of deadly poisons—of the phenomenon that pain begets joy, that ecstasy may wring sounds of agony from us. At the very climax of joy there sounds a cry of horror or a yearning lamentation for an irretrievable loss. In these Greek festivals, nature seems to reveal a sentimental[22] trait; it is as if she were heaving a sigh at her dismemberment into individuals. The song and pantomime of such dually-minded revelers was something new and unheard-of in the Homeric-Greek world; and the Dionysian *music* in particular excited awe and terror. If music, as it would seem, had been known previously as an Apollonian art, it was so, strictly speaking, only as the wave beat of rhythm, whose formative power was developed for the representation of Apollonian states. The music of Apollo was Doric architectonics in tones, but in tones that were merely suggestive, such as those of the cithara. The very element which forms the essence of Dionysian music (and hence of music in general) is carefully excluded as un-Apollonian—namely, the emotional power of the tone, the uniform flow of the melody, and the utterly incomparable world of harmony. In the Dionysian dithyramb man is incited to the greatest exaltation of all his symbolic faculties; something never before experienced struggles for utterance—the annihilation of the veil of maya, oneness as the soul of the species and of nature itself. The essence of nature is now to be expressed symbolically; we need a new world of symbols; and the entire symbolism of the body is called into play, not the mere symbolism of the lips, face, and speech but the whole pantomime of dancing, forcing every member into rhythmic movement. Then the other symbolic powers suddenly press forward, particularly those of music, in rhythmics, dynamics, and harmony. To grasp this collective release of all the symbolic powers, man must have already attained that height of self-abnegation which seeks to express itself symbolically through all these powers—and so the dithyrambic votary of Dionysus is understood only by his peers! With what astonishment must the Apollonian Greek have beheld him! With an astonishment that was all the greater the more it was mingled with the shuddering suspicion that all this was actually not so very alien to him, after all—in fact, that it was only his Apollonian consciousness which, like a veil, hid this Dionysian world from his vision.

3.

To understand this, it becomes necessary to level the artistic structure of the *Apollonian culture,* as it were, stone by stone, until the foundations on which it rests become visible. First of all we see the glorious *Olympian* figures of the gods, standing on the gables of this structure. Their deeds, pictured in brilliant reliefs, adorn its friezes. We must not be misled by the fact that Apollo stands side by side with the others as an individual deity, without any claim to priority of rank. For the same impulse that embodied itself in Apollo gave birth to this entire Olympian world, and in this sense Apollo is its father. What terrific need was it that could produce such an illustrious company of Olympian beings?

Whoever approaches these Olympians with another religion in his heart, searching among them for moral elevation, even for sanctity, for disincarnate spirituality, for compassion and benevolence, will soon be forced to turn his back on them, discouraged and disappointed. For there is nothing here that suggests asceticism, spirituality, or duty. We hear nothing but the accents of an exuberant, triumphant life in which all things, whether good or evil, are deified. And so the spectator may stand quite bewildered before this fantastic excess of life, asking himself by virtue of what magic potion these high-spirited men could have found life so enjoyable that, wherever they turned, their eyes beheld the smile of Helen, the ideal picture of their own existence, "floating in sweet sensuality." But to this spectator, who has already turned his back, we must say: Do not go away, but stay and hear what Greek folk wisdom has to say of this very life, which with such inexplicable gaiety unfolds itself before your eyes.

There is an ancient story that King Midas hunted in the forest a long time for the wise Silenus, the companion of Dionysus, without capturing him. When Silenus at last fell into his hands, the king asked what was the best and most desirable of all things for man. Fixed and immovable, the demigod said not a word, until at last, urged by the king, he gave a shrill laugh and broke out into these words: "Oh, wretched ephemeral race, children of chance and misery, why do you compel me to tell you what it would be most expedient for you not to hear? What is best of all is utterly beyond your reach: not to be born, not to *be*, to be *nothing*. But the second best for you is—to die soon."[23]

How is the world of the Olympian gods related to this folk wisdom? Even as the rapturous vision of the tortured martyr to his suffering.

Now it is as if the Olympian magic mountain had opened before us and revealed its roots to us. The Greek knew and felt the terror and horror of existence. In order to be able to live, he had to interpose between himself and this experience the radiant dream-birth of the Olympians. That immense suspiciousness toward the titanic powers of nature, the Moira[24] enthroned inexorably over all knowledge, the vulture of the great lover of mankind, Prometheus, the terrible fate of the wise Oedipus, the family curse of the Atridae, which drove Orestes to matricide: in short, that entire philosophy of the sylvan god, with its mythical exemplars, which caused the downfall of the melancholy Etruscans—all this was again and again overcome by the Greeks with the aid of the Olympian *middle world* of art; or at any rate it was veiled and withdrawn from sight. It was in order to be able to live that the Greeks had to create these gods from a most profound need. Perhaps we should picture the process to ourselves somewhat as follows: out of the original Titanic divine order of terror, the Olympian divine order of joy gradually evolved through the Apollonian impulse toward beauty, just as roses burst from thorny bushes. How else could this people, so sensitive, so vehement in its desires, so singularly capable of *suffering,* have endured existence, if it had not been revealed to them in their gods, surrounded with a higher glory?

The same impulse which calls art into being, as the complement and consummation of existence, seducing one to a continuation of life, was also the cause of the Olympian world which the Hellenic "will" held up to itself as a transfiguring mirror. Thus do the gods justify the life of man: they themselves live it—the only satisfactory theodicy! Existence under the bright sunshine of such gods is regarded as desirable in itself, and the real pain of Homeric men is caused by parting from it, especially by early parting: so that now, reversing the wisdom of Silenus, we might say of the Greeks that "to die soon is worst of all for them, the next worst—to die at all." Once heard, it will ring out again; do not forget the lament of the short-lived Achilles, mourning the leaflike change and vicissitudes of the race of men and the decline of the heroic age. It is not unworthy of the greatest hero to long for a continuation of life, even though he live as a day laborer.[25] At the Apollonian stage of development, the "will" longs so vehemently for this existence, the Homeric man feels himself so completely at one with it, that lamentation itself becomes a song of praise.

Here we should note that this harmony which is contemplated with such longing by modern man, in fact, this oneness of man with nature (for which Schiller introduced the technical term "naive"), is by no means a simple condition that comes into being naturally and as if inevitably. It is not a condition that, like a terrestrial paradise, *must* necessarily be found at the gate of every culture. This could be believed only by an age which sought to regard Rousseau's Emile also as an artist and imagined that in Homer it had found such an artist Emile, reared at the bosom of nature. Where we encounter the "naive" in art, we should recognize the highest effect of Apollonian culture—which always must first overthrow an empire of Titans and slay monsters, and which must have triumphed over an abysmal and terrifying view of the world and the keenest susceptibility to suffering through recourse to the most forceful and pleasurable illusions. But how rarely is the naive attained—that consummate immersion in the beauty of mere appearance! How unutterably sublime is *Homer* therefore, who, as an individual being, bears the same relation to this Apollonian folk culture as the individual dream artist does to the dream faculty of the people and of nature in general.

The Homeric "naiveté" can be understood only as the complete victory of Apollonian illusion: this is one of those illusions which nature so frequently employs to achieve her own ends. The true goal is veiled by a phantasm: and while we stretch out our hands for the latter, nature attains the former by means of our illusion. In the Greeks the "will" wished to contemplate itself in the transfiguration of genius and the world of art; in order to glorify themselves, its creatures had to feel themselves worthy of glory; they had to behold themselves again in a higher sphere, without this perfect world of contemplation acting as a command or a reproach. This is the sphere of beauty, in which they saw their mirror images, the Olympians. With this mirroring of beauty, the Hellenic will combated its artistically correlative talent for suffering and for the wisdom of suffering—and, as a monument of its victory, we have Homer, the naive artist.

4.

The dream analogy throws some light on the naive artist. Let us imagine the dreamer: in the midst of the illusion of the dream world and without disturbing it, he calls out to himself: "It is a dream, I will dream on." What must we infer? That he experiences a deep inner joy in dream contemplation; on the other hand, to be at all able to dream with this inner joy in contemplation, he must have completely lost sight of the waking reality and its terrible obtrusiveness. Guided by the dream-reading Apollo, we may interpret all these phenomena in roughly this way.

Though it is certain that of the two halves of our existence, the waking and the dreaming states, the former appeals to us as infinitely preferable, more important, excellent, and worthy of being lived—indeed, as that which alone is lived—yet in relation to that mysterious ground of our being of which we are the phenomena, I should, paradoxical as it may seem, maintain the very opposite estimate of the value of dreams. For the more clearly I perceive in nature those omnipotent art impulses, and in them an ardent longing for illusion, for redemption through illusion, the more I feel myself impelled to the metaphysical assumption that the truly existent primal unity, eternally suffering and contradictory, also needs the rapturous vision, the pleasurable illusion, for its continuous redemption. And we, completely wrapped up in this illusion and composed of it, are compelled to consider this illusion as the truly nonexistent—i.e., as a perpetual becoming in time, space, and causality—in other words, as empirical reality. If, for the moment, we do not consider the question of our own "reality," if we conceive of our empirical existence, and of that of the world in general, as a continuously manifested representation of the primal unity, we shall then have to look upon the dream as a *mere appearance of mere appearance,* hence as a still higher appeasement of the primordial desire for mere appearance. And that is why the innermost heart of nature feels that ineffable joy in the naive artist and the naive work of art, which is likewise only "mere appearance of mere appearance."

In a symbolic painting, Raphael, himself one of these immortal "naive" ones, has represented for us this demotion of appearance to the level of mere appearance, the fundamental process of the naive artist and of Apollonian culture. In his *Transfiguration,* the lower half of the picture, with the possessed boy, the despairing bearers, the bewildered, terrified disciples, shows us the reflection of suffering, primal and eternal, the sole ground of the world: the "mere appearance" here is the reflection of eternal contradiction, the father of things. From this mere appearance arises, like ambrosial vapor, a new visionary world of mere appearances, invisible to those wrapped in the first appearance—a radiant floating in purest bliss, a serene contemplation beaming from wide-open eyes. Here we have presented, in the most sublime artistic symbolism, that Apollonian world of beauty and its substratum, the terrible wisdom of Silenus; and intuitively we comprehend their necessary interdependence. Apollo, however, again appears to us as the apotheosis of the *principium individuationis,* in which alone is consummated the perpetually attained goal of the primal unity, its redemption through mere appearance. With his sublime gestures, he shows us how necessary is the entire world of suffering, that by means of it the individual may be impelled to realize the redeeming vision, and then, sunk in contemplation of it, sit quietly in his tossing bark, amid the waves.

If we conceive of it at all as imperative and mandatory, this apotheosis of individuation knows but one law—the individual, i.e., the preservation of the boundaries of the individual, *measure* in the Hellenic sense. Apollo, as ethical deity, exacts measure of his disciples, and, to be able to maintain it, he requires self-knowledge. And so, side by side with the aesthetic necessity for beauty, there occur the demands "know thyself" and "nothing in excess"; consequently, overweening pride and excess are regarded as the truly hostile demons of the non-Apollonian sphere, hence as characteristics of the pre-Apollonian age—that of the Titans; and of the extra-Apollonian world—that of the barbarians. Because of his titanic love for man, Prometheus must be torn to pieces by vultures; because of his excessive wisdom, which could solve the riddle of the Sphinx, Oedipus must be plunged into a bewildering vortex of crime. Thus did the Delphic god interpret the Greek past.

The effects wrought by the *Dionysian* also seemed "titanic" and "barbaric" to the Apollonian Greek; while at the same time he could not conceal from himself that he, too, was inwardly related to these overthrown Titans and heroes. Indeed, he had to recognize even more than this: despite all its beauty and moderation, his entire existence rested on a hidden substratum of suffering and of knowledge, revealed to him by the Dionysian. And behold: Apollo could not live without Dionysus! The "titanic" and the "barbaric" were in the last analysis as necessary as the Apollonian.

And now let us imagine how into this world, built on mere appearance and moderation and artificially dammed up, there penetrated, in tones ever more bewitching and alluring, the ecstatic sound of the Dionysian festival; how in these strains all of nature's *excess* in pleasure, grief, and knowledge became audible, even in piercing shrieks; and let us ask ourselves what the psalmodizing artist of Apollo, with his phantom harp-sound, could mean in the face of this demonic folk song! The muses of the arts of "illusion" paled before an art that, in its intoxication, spoke the truth. The wisdom of Silenus cried "Woe, woe!" to the serene Olympians. The individual, with all his restraint and proportion, succumbed to the self-oblivion of the Dionysian states, forgetting the precepts of Apollo. *Excess* revealed itself as truth. Contradiction, the bliss born of pain, spoke out from the very heart of nature. And so, wherever the Dionysian prevailed, the Apollonian was nullified and destroyed. But, on the other hand, it is equally certain that, wherever the first Dionysian onslaught was successfully withstood, the authority and majesty of the Delphic god exhibited itself as more rigid and menacing than ever. For to me the *Doric* state[26] and Doric art are explicable only as a permanent military encampment of the Apollonian. Only incessant resistance to the titanic-barbaric nature of the Dionysian could account for the long survival of an art so defiantly severe and so encompassed with bulwarks, a training so warlike and rigorous, and a political structure so cruel and relentless.

Up to this point we have simply enlarged upon the observation made at the beginning of this essay: that the Dionysian and the Apollonian, in new births ever following and mutually augmenting one another, controlled the Hellenic genius; that out of the age of "bronze," with its wars of the Titans and its rigorous folk philosophy, the Homeric world developed under the sway of the Apollonian impulse to beauty; that this "naive" splendor was again engulfed by the overwhelming influx of the Dionysian; and that against this new power the Apollonian rose to the austere majesty of Doric art and the Doric view of the world. If amid the strife of these two hostile principles, the older Hellenic history thus falls into four great phases of art, we are now impelled to inquire after the final goal of these developments and processes, lest perchance we should regard the last-attained period, the period of Doric art, as the climax and aim of these artistic impulses. And here the sublime and celebrated art of *Attic tragedy* and the dramatic dithyramb presents itself as the common goal of both these tendencies whose mysterious union, after many and long precursory struggles, found glorious consummation in this child—at once Antigone and Cassandra.

5.

We now approach the real goal of our investigation, which is directed toward knowledge of the Dionysian-Apollonian genius and its art product, or at least toward some intuitive[27] understanding of this mystery of union. Here we shall begin by seeking the first evidence in Greece of that new seed which subsequently developed into tragedy and the dramatic dithyramb. The ancients themselves give us a symbolic answer, when they place the faces of *Homer* and *Archilochus*,[28] as the forefathers and torchbearers of Greek poetry, side by side on gems, sculptures, etc., with a sure feeling that consideration should be given only to these two, equally completely original, from whom a stream of fire flows over the whole of later Greek history. Homer, the aged self-absorbed dreamer, the type of the Apollonian naive artist, now beholds with astonishment the passionate head of the warlike votary of the muses, Archilochus, who was hounded savagely through life. Modern aesthetics, by way of interpretation, could only add that here the first "objective" artist confronts the first "subjective" artist. But this interpretation helps us little, because we know the subjective artist only as the poor artist, and throughout the entire range of art we demand first of all the conquest of the subjective, redemption from the "ego," and the silencing of the individual will and desire; indeed, we find it impossible to believe in any truly artistic production, however insignificant, if it is without objectivity, without pure contemplation devoid of interest.[29] Hence our aesthetics must first solve the problem of how the "lyrist" is possible as an artist—he who, according to the experience of all ages, is continually saying "I" and running through the entire chromatic scale of his passions and desires. Compared with Homer, Archilochus appalls us by his cries of hatred and scorn, by his drunken outbursts of desire. Therefore is not he, who has been called the first subjective artist, essentially the nonartist? But in this case, how to explain the reverence which was shown to him—the poet—in very remarkable utterances by the Delphic oracle itself, the center of "objective" art?

Schiller has thrown some light on the poetic process by a psychological observation, inexplicable but unproblematic to his own mind. He confessed that before the act of creation he did not have before him or within him any series of images in a causal arrangement, but rather a *musical mood*. ("With me the perception has at first no clear and definite object; this is formed later. A certain musical mood comes first, and the poetical idea only follows later.") Let us add to this the most important phenomenon of all ancient lyric poetry: they took for granted *the union,* indeed the *identity,* of the *lyrist with the musician*. Compared with this, our modern lyric poetry seems like the statue of a god without a head. With this in mind we may now, on the basis of our aesthetical metaphysics set forth above, explain the lyrist to ourselves in this manner.

In the first place, as a Dionysian artist he has identified himself with the primal unity, its pain and contradiction. Assuming that music has been correctly termed a repetition and a recast of the world, we may say that he produces the copy of this primal unity as music. Now, however, under the influence of Apollonian dream, this music reveals itself to him again as a *symbolic dream image*. That reflection, without image and concepts of the primordial pain in music, with its redemption in mere appearance, now produces a second mirroring as a specific symbol or example. The artist has already surrendered his subjectivity in the Dionysian process. The image that now shows him his identity with the heart of the world is a dream scene that embodies the primordial contradiction and primordial pain, together with the primordial pleasure, of mere appearance. The "I" of the lyrist therefore sounds from the depths of existence: its "subjectivity," in the sense of modern aestheticians, is a fiction. When Archilochus, the first Greek lyrist, proclaims to the daughters of Lycambes both his mad love and his contempt, it is not his passion alone that dances before us in orgiastic frenzy; but we see Dionysus and the Maenads, we see the drunken reveler Archilochus sunk down in slumber—as Euripides depicts it in the *Bacchae*,[30] the sleep on the high mountain pasture, in the noonday sun. And now Apollo approaches and touches him with the laurel. Then the Dionysian-musical enchantment of the sleeper seems to emit image sparks, lyrical poems, which in their highest development are called tragedies and dramatic dithyrambs.

The plastic artist, like the epic poet who is related to him, is absorbed in the pure contemplation of images. The Dionysian musician is, without any images, himself pure primordial pain and its primordial reechoing. The lyric genius senses a world of images and symbols growing out of his state of mystical self-abnegation and oneness. This world has a coloring, a causality, and a velocity quite different from those of the world of the plastic artist and the epic poet. For the latter lives in these images, and only in them, with joyous satisfaction. He never grows tired of contemplating lovingly even their minutest traits. Even the image of the angry Achilles is only an image to him whose angry expression he enjoys with the dreamer's pleasure in illusion. Thus, by this mirror of illusion, he is protected against becoming one and fused with his figures. In direct contrast to this, the images of the *lyrist* are nothing but *his very* self and, as it were, only different projections of himself, so he, as the moving center of this world, may say "I": of course, this self is not the same as that of the waking, empirically real man, but the only truly existent and eternal self resting at the basis of things, through whose images the lyric genius sees this very basis.

Now let us suppose that among these images he also beholds *himself* as nongenius, i.e., his subject, the whole throng of subjective passions and agitations of the will directed to a definite object which appears real to him. It might seem as if the lyric genius and the allied nongenius were one, as if the former had of its own accord spoken that little word "I." But this mere appearance will no longer be able to lead us astray, as it certainly led astray those who designated the lyrist as the subjective poet. For, as a matter of fact, Archilochus, the passionately inflamed, loving, and hating man, is but a vision of the genius, who by this time is no longer merely Archilochus, but a world-genius expressing his primordial pain symbolically in the symbol of the man Archilochus—while the subjectively willing and desiring man, Archilochus, can never at any time be a poet. It is by no means necessary, however, that the lyrist should see nothing but the phenomenon of the man Archilochus before him as a reflection of eternal being; and tragedy shows how far the visionary world of the lyrist may be removed from this phenomenon which, to be sure, is closest at hand.

Schopenhauer, who did not conceal from himself the difficulty the lyrist presents in the philosophical contemplation of art, thought he had found a way out, on which, however, I cannot follow him. Actually, it was in his profound metaphysics of music that he alone held in his hands the means for a solution. I believe I have removed the difficulty here in his spirit and to his honor. Yet he describes the peculiar nature of song as follows (*Die Welt als Wille und Vorstellung,* volume 1, p. 295):

"It is the subject of the will, *i.e.,* his own volition, which fills the consciousness of the singer, often as a released and satisfied desire (joy), but still oftener as an inhibited desire (grief), always as an affect, a passion, a moved state of mind. Besides this, however, and along with it, by the sight of surrounding nature, the singer becomes conscious of himself as the subject of pure will-less knowing, whose imperturbable blissful peace now appears, in contrast to the stress of desire, which is always restricted and always needy. The feeling of this contrast, this alternation, is really what expresses itself in the song as a whole and what principally constitutes the lyrical state. In it, pure knowing comes to us, as it were, to deliver us from willing and its strain; we follow, but only for moments; willing, the remembrance of our own personal ends, tears us anew from peaceful contemplation; yet ever again the next beautiful environment in which pure will-less knowledge presents itself to us lures us away from willing. Therefore, in the song and the lyrical mood, willing (the personal interest of the ends) and pure perception of the environment are wonderfully mingled; connections between them are sought and imagined; the subjective mood, the affection of the will, imparts its own hue to the perceived environment and vice versa. Genuine song is the expression of the whole of this mingled and divided state of mind."

Who could fail to recognize in this description that lyric poetry is here characterized as an incompletely attained art that arrives at its goal infrequently and only, as it were, by leaps? Indeed, it is described as a semi-art whose *essence* is said to consist in this, that willing and pure contemplation, i.e., the unaesthetic and the aesthetic condition, are wonderfully mingled with each other. We contend, on the contrary, that the whole opposition between the subjective and objective, which Schopenhauer still uses as a measure of value in classifying the arts, is altogether irrelevant in aesthetics, since the subject, the willing individual that furthers his own egoistic ends, can be conceived of only as the antagonist, not as the origin of art. Insofar as the subject is the artist, however, he has already been released from his individual will, and has become, as it were, the medium through which the one truly existent subject celebrates its release in appearance. For to our humiliation *and* exaltation, one thing above all must be clear to us. The entire comedy of art is neither performed for our betterment or education nor are we the true authors of this art world. On the contrary, we may assume that we are merely images and artistic projections for the true author, and that we have our highest dignity in our significance as works of art—for it is only as an *aesthetic phenomenon* that existence and the world are eternally *justified*—while of course our consciousness of our own significance hardly differs from that which the soldiers painted on canvas have of the battle represented on it. Basically, then, all our knowledge of art is completely illusory, because as knowing beings we are not one and identical with that being which, as the sole author and spectator of this comedy of art, creates a perpetual enjoyment for itself. Only insofar as the genius in the act of artistic creation coalesces with this primordial artist of the world, does he know anything of the eternal essence of art; for in this state he is, in a marvelous manner, like the weird image of the fairy tale which can turn its eyes at will and behold itself; he is at once subject and object, at once poet, actor, and spectator.

6.

In connection with Archilochus, scholarly research has discovered that he introduced the *folk song* into literature and on account of this deserved, according to the general estimate of the Greeks, his unique position beside Homer. But what is the folk song in contrast to the wholly Apollonian epos? What else but the *perpetuum vestigium* of a union of the Apollonian and the Dionysian? Its enormous diffusion among all peoples, further reenforced by ever-new births, is testimony to the power of this artistic dual impulse of nature, which leaves its vestiges in the folk song just as the orgiastic movements of a people immortalize themselves in its music. Indeed, it ought also to be historically demonstrable that every period rich in folk songs has been most violently stirred by Dionysian currents, which we must always consider the substratum and prerequisite of the folk song.

First of all, however, we must conceive the folk song as the musical mirror of the world, as the original melody, now seeking for itself a parallel dream phenomenon and expressing it in poetry. *Melody is therefore primary and universal,* and so may admit of several objectifications in several texts. Likewise, in the naive estimation of the people, it is regarded as by far the more important and essential element. Melody generates the poem out of itself, ever again: that is what *the strophic form of the folk song* signifies; a phenomenon which I had always beheld with astonishment, until at last I found this explanation. Anyone who in accordance with this theory examines a collection of folk songs, such as *Des Knaben Wunderhorn,*[31] will find innumerable instances of the way the continuously generating melody scatters image sparks all around, which in their variegation, their abrupt change, their mad precipitation, manifest a power quite unknown to the epic and its steady flow. From the standpoint of the epos, this unequal and irregular image world of lyrical poetry is simply to be condemned: and it certainly has been thus condemned by the solemn epic rhapsodists of the Apollonian festivals in the age of Terpander.[32]

Accordingly, we observe that in the poetry of the folk song, language is strained to its utmost that it may *imitate music;* and with Archilochus begins a new world of poetry, fundamentally opposed to the Homeric. And in saying this we have indicated the only possible relation between poetry and music, between word and tone: the word, the image, the concept here seeks an expression analogous to music and now feels in itself the power of music. In this sense we may discriminate between two main currents in the history of the language of the Greek people, according to whether their language imitated the world of image and phenomena or the world of music. One need only reflect more deeply on the linguistic difference with regard to color, syntactical structure, and vocabulary in Homer and Pindar, in order to understand the significance of this contrast; indeed, it becomes palpably clear that in the period between Homer and Pindar the *orgiastic flute tones of Olympus* must have been sounded, which, even in Aristotle's time, when music was infinitely more developed, transported people to drunken ecstasy, and which, in their primal impact, undoubtedly incited to imitation all the poetic means of expression of contemporaneous man.

I here call attention to a familiar phenomenon of our own times which our aesthetic regards as plainly repulsive. Again and again we have occasion to observe that a Beethoven symphony compels its individual auditors to use figurative speech in describing it, no matter how fantastically variegated and even contradictory may be the composition and makeup of the different worlds of images produced by a piece of music. To exercise its poor wit on such compositions, and to overlook a phenomenon that is certainly worth explaining, are quite in keeping with this aesthetic. Indeed, even when the tone-poet discusses his composition in terms of images, when for instance he designates a certain symphony as the "pastoral" symphony, or a passage in it as the "scene by the brook," or another as the "merry gathering of rustics," these, too, are only symbolical representations born of music—and not the imitated objects of music—representations which can teach us nothing whatsoever concerning the *Dionysian* content of music, and which indeed have no distinctive value of their own beside other images. We have now to transfer this process of a discharge of music in images to some fresh, youthful, linguistically creative people, in order to get some notion of the way in which the strophic folk song originates, and the whole linguistic capacity is excited by this new principle of the imitation of music.

If, therefore, we may regard lyric poetry as the imitative fulguration of music in images and concepts, we should now ask: "As what does music *appear* in the mirror of images and concepts?" *It appears as will,* taking the term in Schopenhauer's sense, i.e., as the opposite of the aesthetic, purely contemplative, and passive frame of mind. Here, however, we must make as sharp a distinction as possible between the concepts of essence and phenomenon; for music, according to its essence, cannot possibly be will, for as such it would, in fact, have to be banished from the realm of art—for the will is the unaesthetic-in-itself; but it *appears* as will. For in order to express its appearance in images, the lyrist needs all the agitations of passion, from the whisper of mere inclination to the roar of madness. Impelled to speak of music in Apollonian symbols, he conceives of all nature, and himself in it, as willing, as desiring, as eternal longing. But insofar as he interprets music by means of images, he himself rests in the calm sea of Apollonian contemplation, though everything around him that he beholds through the medium of music is in urgent and active motion. Indeed, when he beholds himself through this same medium, his own image appears to him as an unsatisfied feeling: his own willing, longing, moaning, rejoicing are to him symbols by which he interprets music. This is the phenomenon of the lyrist: as Apollonian genius he interprets music through the image of the will, while he himself, completely released from the greed of the will, is the pure, undimmed eye of the sun.

Our whole discussion insists that lyric poetry is dependent on the spirit of music just as music itself in its absolute sovereignty does not *need* the image and the concept, but merely *endures* them as accompaniments. The poems of the lyrist can express nothing that did not already exist, in stupendous universality and absoluteness, in the music which compelled him to figurative speech. Language can never adequately render the cosmic symbolism of music, because music stands in symbolic relation to the primordial contradiction and primordial pain in the heart of the primal unity, and therefore symbolizes a sphere which is beyond and prior to all phenomena. Rather, all phenomena, compared with it, are merely symbols: hence *language,* as the organ and symbol of phenomena, can never by any means disclose the innermost heart of music;

language, in its attempt to imitate it, can only be in superficial contact with music; while all the eloquence of lyric poetry cannot bring the deepest significance of the latter one step nearer to us.

7.

We must now avail ourselves of all the principles of art considered so far, in order to find our way through the labyrinth, as we must call it, of *the origin of Greek tragedy.* I do not think I am unreasonable in saying that the problem of this origin has as yet not even been seriously posed, to say nothing of solved, however often the ragged tatters of ancient tradition have been sewn together in various combinations and torn apart again. This tradition tells us quite unequivocally *that tragedy arose from the tragic chorus,* and was originally only chorus and nothing but chorus. Hence we consider it our duty to look into the heart of this tragic chorus as the real protodrama, without resting satisfied with such clichés as that the chorus is the "ideal spectator" or that it represents the people in contrast to the aristocratic region of the scene. This latter explanation has a sublime sound to many a politician—as if the immutable moral law had been embodied by the democratic Athenians in the popular chorus, which always won out over the passionate excesses and extravagances of kings. This theory may be ever so strongly suggested by one of Aristotle's observations; still, it has no influence on the original formation of tragedy, inasmuch as the whole opposition of prince and people—indeed the whole sociopolitical sphere—was excluded from the purely religious origins of tragedy. But even regarding the classical form of the chorus in Aeschylus and Sophocles, which is known to us, we should deem it blasphemy to speak here of intimations of "constitutional popular representation." From this blasphemy, however, others have not shrunk. Ancient constitutions knew of no constitutional representation of the people in *praxi,* and it is to be hoped that they did not even "have intimations" of it in tragedy.

Much more famous than this political interpretation of the chorus is the idea of A. W. Schlegel,[33] who advises us to regard the chorus somehow as the essence and extract of the crowd of spectators—as the "ideal spectator." This view, when compared with the historically-established fact that originally tragedy was only chorus, reveals itself for what it is—a crude, unscholarly, yet brilliant claim that owes its brilliancy only to its concentrated form of expression, to the typically Germanic bias in favor of anything called "ideal," and to our momentary astonishment. For we are certainly astonished the moment we compare our familiar theatrical public with this chorus, and ask ourselves whether it could ever be possible to idealize from such a public something analogous to the Greek tragic chorus. We tacitly deny this, and now wonder as much at the boldness of Schlegel's claim as at the totally different nature of the Greek public. For we had always believed that the right spectator, whoever he might be, must always remain conscious that he was viewing a work of art and not an empirical reality. But the tragic chorus of the Greeks is forced to recognize real beings in the figures on the stage. The chorus of the Oceanides really believes that it sees before it the Titan Prometheus, and it considers itself as real as the god of the scene. But could the highest and purest type of spectator regard Prometheus as bodily present and real, as the Oceanides do? Is it characteristic of the ideal spectator to run onto the stage and free the god from his torments? We had always believed in an aesthetic public and considered the individual spectator the better qualified the more he was capable of viewing a work of art as art, that is, aesthetically. But now Schlegel tells us that the perfect, ideal spectator does not at all allow the world of the drama to act on him aesthetically, but corporally and empirically. Oh, these Greeks! we sigh; they upset all our aesthetics! But once accustomed to this, we repeated Schlegel's saying whenever the chorus came up for discussion.

Now the historical facts, which are quite explicit, speak against Schlegel. The chorus as such, without the stage—the primitive form of tragedy—and the chorus of ideal spectators do not go together. What kind of artistic genre could possibly be extracted from the concept of the spectator, and find its true form in the "spectator as such"? The spectator without the spectacle is an absurd notion. We fear that the birth of tragedy is to be explained neither by any high esteem for the moral intelligence of the masses nor by the concept of the spectator without a spectacle; and we consider the problem too deep to be even touched by such superficial considerations.

An infinitely more valuable insight into the significance of the chorus was displayed by Schiller in the celebrated preface to his *Bride of Messina,* where he regards the chorus as a living wall that tragedy constructs around itself in order to close itself off from the world of reality and to preserve its ideal domain and its poetical freedom.

With this, his chief weapon, Schiller combats the ordinary conception of the natural, the illusion usually demanded in dramatic poetry. Although the stage day is merely artificial, the architecture only symbolical, and the metrical language ideal in character, nevertheless an erroneous view still prevails in the main, as he points out: it is not sufficient that one merely tolerates as poetic license what is actually the essence of all poetry. The introduction of the chorus, says Schiller, is the decisive step by which war is declared openly and honorably against all naturalism in art.

It seems to me that it is this view of the matter for which our would-be superior age uses the disdainful catchword "pseudoidealism." I fear, however, that we, on the other hand, with our present adoration of the natural and the real, have reached the opposite pole of all idealism, namely, the region of waxwork cabinets. There is an art in these, too, as there is in certain novels much in vogue at present; but we really should not be plagued with the claim that such art has overcome the "pseudoidealism" of Goethe and Schiller.

It is indeed an "ideal" domain, as Schiller correctly perceived, in which the Greek satyr chorus, the chorus of primitive tragedy, was wont to dwell. It is a domain raised high above the actual paths of mortals. For this chorus the Greek built up the scaffolding of a fictitious *natural state* and on it placed fictitious *natural beings*. On this foundation tragedy developed and so, of course, it could dispense from the beginning with a painstaking portrayal of reality. Yet it is no arbitrary world placed by whim between heaven and earth; rather, it is a world with the same reality and credibility that Olympus, with its inhabitants, possessed for the believing Hellene. The satyr, as the Dionysian chorist, lives in a religiously acknowledged reality under the sanction of myth and cult. That tragedy should begin with him, that he should be the voice of the Dionysian wisdom of tragedy, is just as strange a phenomenon for us as the general derivation of tragedy from the chorus.

Perhaps we shall have a point of departure for our inquiry if I put forward the proposition that the satyr, the fictitious natural being, bears the same relation to the man of culture that Dionysian music bears to civilization. Concerning the latter, Richard Wagner says that it is nullified[34] by music just as lamplight is nullified by the light of day. Similarly, I believe, the Greek man of culture felt himself nullified in the presence of the satyric chorus; and this is the most immediate effect of the Dionysian tragedy, that the state and society and, quite generally, the gulfs between man and man give way to an overwhelming feeling of unity leading back to the very heart of nature. The metaphysical comfort—with which, I am suggesting even now, every true tragedy leaves us—that life is at the bottom of things, despite all the changes of phenomena, indestructibly powerful and pleasurable—this comfort appears in incarnate clarity in the chorus of satyrs, a chorus of natural beings who live ineradicably, as it were, behind all civilization and remain eternally the same, despite the changes of generations and of the history of nations.

With this chorus the profound Hellene, uniquely susceptible to the subtext and deepest suffering, comforts himself, having looked boldly right into the terrible destructiveness of so-called world history as well as the cruelty of nature, and being in danger of longing for a Buddhistic negation of the will. Art saves him, and through art, life saves him for itself.

For the rapture of the Dionysian state, with its annihilation of the ordinary bounds and limits of existence, contains, while it lasts, a *lethargic* element in which all personal experiences of the past become immersed. This chasm of oblivion separates the worlds of everyday reality and of Dionysian reality. But as soon as this everyday reality reenters consciousness, it is experienced as such, with nausea: an ascetic, will-negating mood is the fruit of these states.

In this sense, the Dionysian man resembles Hamlet: both have once looked truly into the essence of things, they have *gained knowledge,* and nausea inhibits action; for their action could not change anything in the eternal nature of things; they feel it to be ridiculous or humiliating that they should be asked to set right a world that is out of joint. Knowledge kills action; action requires the veils of illusion: that is the doctrine of Hamlet, not that cheap wisdom of Jack the Dreamer who reflects too much and, as it were, from an excess of possibilities does not get around to action. Not reflection, no—true knowledge, an insight into the horrible truth, outweighs any motive for action, both in Hamlet and in the Dionysian man.

Now no comfort avails any more; longing transcends a world after death, even the gods; existence is negated along with its glittering reflection in the gods or in an immortal beyond. Conscious of the truth he has once seen, man now sees everywhere only the horror or absurdity of existence; now he understands what is symbolic in Ophelia's fate; now he understands the wisdom of the sylvan god Silenus: he is nauseated.

Here, when the danger to his will is greatest, *art* approaches as a saving sorceress, expert at healing. She alone knows how to turn these nauseous thoughts about the horror or absurdity of existence into notions with which one can live: these are the *sublime* as the artistic taming of the horrible, and the *comic* as the artistic discharge of the nausea of absurdity. The satyr chorus of the dithyramb is the saving deed of Greek art; faced with the intermediary world of these Dionysian companions, the feelings described here exhausted themselves.

8.

The satyr, like the idyllic shepherd of more recent times, is the offspring of a longing for the primordial and the natural; but how firmly and fearlessly the Greek embraced the man of the woods, and how timorously and mawkishly modern man dallied with the flattering images of a sentimental, flute-playing, tender shepherd! Nature, as yet unchanged by knowledge, with the door barring the way to culture not yet unlocked—that is what the Greek saw in his satyr who nevertheless was not a mere ape. On the contrary, the satyr was the archetype of man, the embodiment of his highest and most intense emotions, the ecstatic reveler enraptured by the proximity of his god, the sympathetic companion in whom the suffering of the god is repeated, one who proclaims wisdom from the very heart of nature, a symbol of the sexual omnipotence of nature which the Greeks used to contemplate with reverent wonder.

The satyr was something sublime and divine: especially to the painfully broken vision of Dionysian man, this is how he had to appear. The contrived shepherd in his dress-ups would have offended him: on the unconcealed and vigorously magnificent characters of nature, his eye rested with sublime satisfaction; here the illusion of culture was expunged from the primordial image of man, here the true human being was disclosed, the bearded satyr jubilating to his god. Confronted with him, the man of culture shriveled into a mendacious caricature.

Schiller is right about these origins of tragic art, too: the chorus is a living wall against the assaults of reality because it—the satyr chorus—represents existence more truthfully, really, and completely than the man of culture does who ordinarily considers himself as the only reality. The sphere of poetry does not lie outside the world as a fantastic impossibility spawned by a poet's brain: it desires to be just the opposite, the unvarnished expression of the truth, and must precisely for that reason discard the mendacious finery of that alleged reality of the man of culture.

The contrast between this real truth of nature and the lie of culture that poses as if it were the only reality is similar to that between the eternal core of things, the thing-in-itself, and the whole world of appearances:[35] just as tragedy, with its metaphysical comfort, points to the eternal life of this core of existence which abides through the perpetual destruction of appearances, the symbolism of the satyr chorus proclaims this primordial relationship between the thing-in-itself and appearance. The idyllic shepherd of modern man is merely a projection of the sum of cultural illusions that are allegedly nature; the Dionysian Greek wants truth and nature in their most forceful form—and sees himself changed, as by magic, into a satyr.

The reveling throng, the votaries of Dionysus jubilate under the spell of such moods and insights whose power transforms them before their own eyes until they imagine that they are beholding themselves as restored geniuses of nature, as satyrs. The later constitution of the chorus in tragedy is the artistic imitation of this natural phenomenon, though, to be sure, at this point the separation of Dionysian spectators and magically enchanted Dionysians became necessary. Only we must always keep in mind that the public at an Attic tragedy found itself in the chorus of the orchestra,[36] and there was at bottom no opposition between public and chorus: everything is merely a great sublime chorus of dancing and singing satyrs or of those who permit themselves to be represented by such satyrs.

Now we are ready to understand Schlegel's formulation in a deeper sense. The chorus is the "ideal spectator"[37] insofar as it is the only beholder, the beholder of the visionary world of the scene.[38] A public of spectators as we know it was unknown to the Greeks: in their theaters the terraced structure of concentric arcs made it possible for everybody to actually *overlook*[39] the whole world of culture around him and to imagine, in absorbed contemplation, that he himself was a chorist.

In the light of this insight, we may call the chorus in its primitive form, in prototragedy, a mirror-image of Dionysian man. This phenomenon is best made clear by imagining an actor who, being truly talented, sees the role he is supposed to play quite palpably before his eyes. The satyr chorus is, first of all, a vision of the Dionysian mass of spectators, just as the world of the stage, in turn, is a vision of this satyr chorus: the force of this vision is strong enough to make the eye insensitive and blind to the impression of "reality," to the men of culture who occupy the rows of seats all around. The form of the Greek theater recalls a lonely valley in the mountains: the architecture of the scene appears like a luminous cloud formation that the Bacchants swarming over the mountains behold from a height—like the splendid frame in which the image of Dionysus is revealed to them.

In the face of our learned views about elementary artistic processes, this artistic protophenomenon, which we bring up here to help explain the tragic chorus, is almost offensive, although nothing could be more certain than the fact that a poet is a poet only insofar as he sees himself surrounded by figures who live and act before him and into whose inmost nature he can see. Owing to a peculiar modern weakness, we are inclined to imagine the aesthetic protophenomenon in a manner much too complicated and abstract.

For a genuine poet, metaphor is not a rhetorical figure but a representative image that he actually beholds in place of a concept. A character is for him not a whole he has composed out of particular traits, picked up here and there, but an obtrusively alive person before his very eyes, distinguished from the otherwise identical vision of a painter only by the fact that it continually goes on living and acting. How is it that Homer's descriptions are so much more vivid than those of any other poet? Because he visualizes so much more vividly. We talk so abstractly about poetry because all of us are usually bad poets. At bottom, the aesthetic phenomenon is simple: let anyone have the ability to behold continually a vivid play and to live constantly surrounded by hosts of spirits, and he will be a poet; let anyone feel the urge to transform himself and to speak out of other bodies and souls, and he will be a dramatist.

The Dionysian excitement is capable of communicating this artistic gift to a multitude, so they can see themselves surrounded by such a host of spirits while knowing themselves to be essentially one with them. This process of the tragic chorus is the *dramatic* protophenomenon: to see oneself transformed before one's own eyes and to begin to act as if one had actually entered into another body, another character. This process stands at the beginning of the development of drama. Here we have something different from the rhapsodist who does not become fused with his images but, like a painter, sees them outside himself as objects of contemplation. Here we have a surrender of individuality and a way of entering into another character. And this phenomenon is encountered epidemically: a whole throng experiences the magic of this transformation.

The dithyramb is thus essentially different from all other choral odes. The virgins who proceed solemnly to the temple of Apollo, laurel branches in their hands, singing a processional hymn, remain what they are and retain their civic names: the dithyrambic chorus is a chorus of transformed characters whose civic past and social status have been totally forgotten: they have become timeless servants of their god who live outside the spheres of society. All the other choral lyric poetry of the Hellenes is merely a tremendous intensification of the Apollonian solo singer, while in the dithyramb we confront a community of unconscious actors who consider themselves and one another transformed.

Such magic transformation is the presupposition of all dramatic art. In this magic transformation the Dionysian reveler sees himself as a satyr, *and as a satyr, in turn, he sees the god,* which means that in his metamorphosis he beholds another vision outside himself, as the Apollonian complement of his own state. With this new vision the drama is complete.

In the light of this insight, we must understand Greek tragedy as the Dionysian chorus which ever anew discharges itself in an Apollonian world of images. Thus the choral parts with which tragedy is interlaced are, as it were, the womb that gave birth to the whole of the so-called dialogue, that is, the entire world of the stage, the actual drama. In several successive discharges this primal ground of tragedy radiates this vision of the drama which is by all means a dream apparition and to that extent epic in nature; but on the other hand, being the objectification of a Dionysian state, it represents not Apollonian redemption through mere appearance but, on the contrary, the shattering of the individual and his fusion with primal being. Thus the drama is the Apollonian embodiment of Dionysian insights and effects, and thereby separated, as by a tremendous chasm, from the epic.

The *chorus* of the Greek tragedy, the symbol of the whole excited Dionysian throng, is thus fully explained by our conception. Accustomed as we are to the function of our modern stage chorus, especially in operas, we could not comprehend why the tragic chorus of the Greeks should be older, more original and important than the "action" proper, as is clearly established by historical evidence. And with this historically proven primacy and originality we could not reconcile the fact that the chorus consisted only of humble beings who served—indeed, initially only of goatlike satyrs. Finally, there remained the riddle of the orchestra in front of the scene. But now we realize that the scene, complete with the action, was basically and originally thought of merely as a *vision;* the chorus is the only "reality" and generates the vision, speaking of it with the entire symbolism of dance, tone, and words. In its vision this chorus beholds its lord and master Dionysus and is therefore eternally the *serving* chorus: it sees how the god suffers and glorifies himself and therefore does not itself *act*. But while its attitude toward the god is wholly one of service, it is nevertheless the highest, namely the Dionysian, expression of *nature* and therefore pronounces in its rapture, as nature does, oracles and wise sayings: *sharing his suffering,* it also shares something of his *wisdom* and proclaims the truth from the heart of the world. That is the origin of the fantastic and seemingly so offensive figure of the wise and rapturous satyr who is at the same time "the simple man" as opposed to the god—the image of nature and its strongest urges, even their symbol, and at the same time the proclaimer of her wisdom and art—musician, poet, dancer, and seer of spirits in *one* person.

Dionysus, the real stage hero and center of the vision, was, according both to this insight and to what has been handed down to us, not actually present at first, in the very oldest period of tragedy; he was merely imagined as present, which means that originally tragedy was only "chorus" and not yet "drama." Later the attempt was made to show the god as real and to represent the visionary figure together with its transfiguring frame as something visible for every eye—and thus "drama" in the narrower sense began. Now the dithyrambic chorus was assigned the task of exciting the mood of the listeners to such a Dionysian degree that, when the tragic hero appeared on the stage, they did not see the awkwardly masked human being, but rather a visionary figure, born, as it were, from their own rapture.

Consider Admetus as he is brooding over the memory of his recently departed wife Alcestis, consuming himself in her spiritual contemplation, when suddenly a similarly formed, similarly walking woman's figure is led toward him, heavily veiled; let us imagine his sudden trembling unrest, his tempestuous comparisons, his instinctive conviction—and we have an analogy with what the spectator felt in his Dionysian excitement when he saw the approach on the stage of the god with whose sufferings he had already fused himself. Involuntarily, he transferred the whole magic image of the god that was trembling before his soul to that masked figure and, as it were, dissolved its reality into the unreality of spirits.

This is the Apollonian state of dreams in which the world of the day becomes veiled, and a new world, clearer, more understandable, more moving than the everyday world and yet more shadowy, originates before our eyes in continual change. Accordingly, we recognize in tragedy a pervasive opposition of styles: the language, color, mobility, and dynamics of speech fall apart into the Dionysian lyrics of the chorus and, on the other hand, the Apollonian dream world, and become two utterly different spheres of expression. The Apollonian appearances in which Dionysus objectifies himself are no longer "an eternal sea, changeful strife, a glowing life,"[40] like the music of the chorus; no longer those forces, merely felt and not condensed into images, in which the enraptured servant of Dionysus senses the nearness of the god: now the clarity and firmness of epic form addresses him from the scene; now Dionysus no longer speaks through forces but as an epic hero, almost in the language of Homer.

9.

Everything that comes to the surface in the Apollonian part of Greek tragedy, in the dialogue, looks simple, transparent, and beautiful. In this sense, the dialogue is an image of the Hellene whose nature is revealed in the dance, since in the dance the greatest strength remains only potential but betrays itself in the suppleness and wealth of movement. Thus the language of Sophocles' heroes amazes us by its Apollonian precision and lucidity, so we immediately have the feeling that we are looking into the innermost ground of their being, with some astonishment that the way to this ground should be so short. But suppose we disregard the character of the hero as it comes to the surface, visibly—after all, it is in the last analysis nothing but a bright image projected on a dark wall, which means appearance through and through; suppose we penetrate into the myth that projects itself in these lucid reflections: then we suddenly experience a phenomenon that is just the opposite of a familiar optical phenomenon. When, after a forceful attempt to gaze on the sun, we turn away blinded, we see dark-colored spots before our eyes, as a cure as it were. Conversely, the bright image projections of the Sophoclean hero—in short, the Apollonian aspect of the mask—are necessary effects of a glance into the inside and terrors of nature; as it were, luminous spots to cure eyes damaged by gruesome night. Only in this sense may we believe that we properly comprehend the serious and important concept of "Greek cheerfulness." The misunderstanding of this concept as cheerfulness in a state of unendangered comfort is, of course, encountered everywhere today.

Sophocles understood the most sorrowful figure of the Greek stage, the unfortunate Oedipus, as the noble human being who, in spite of his wisdom, is destined to error and misery, but who eventually, through his tremendous suffering, spreads a magical power of blessing that remains effective even beyond his decease. The noble human being does not sin, the profound poet wants to tell us: though every law, every natural order, even the moral world may perish through his actions, his actions also produce a higher magical circle of effects which found a new world on the ruins of the old one that has been overthrown. That is what the poet wants to say to us insofar as he is at the same time a religious thinker. As a poet he first shows us a marvelously tied knot of a trial, slowly unraveled by the judge, bit by bit, for his own undoing. The genuinely Hellenic delight at this dialectical solution is so great that it introduces a trait of superior cheerfulness into the whole work, everywhere softening the sharp points of the gruesome presuppositions of this process.

In *Oedipus at Colonus* we encounter the same cheerfulness, but elevated into an infinite transfiguration. The old man, struck by an excess of misery, abandoned solely to *suffer* whatever befalls

him, is confronted by the supraterrestrial cheerfulness that descends from the divine sphere and suggests to us that the hero
attains his highest activity, extending far beyond his life, through
his purely passive posture, while his conscious deeds and desires,
earlier in his life, merely led him into passivity. Thus the intricate
legal knot of the Oedipus fable that no mortal eye could unravel
is gradually disentangled—and the most profound human joy over-
comes us at this divine counterpart of the dialectic.

If this explanation does justice to the poet, one may yet ask
whether it exhausts the contents of the myth—and then it becomes
evident that the poet's whole conception is nothing but precisely
that bright image which healing nature projects before us after a
glance into the abyss. Oedipus, the murderer of his father, the
husband of his mother, the solver of the riddle of the Sphinx! What
does the mysterious triad of these fateful deeds tell us?

There is a tremendously old popular belief, especially in Persia,
that a wise magus can be born only from incest. With the riddle-
solving and mother-marrying Oedipus in mind, we must immediately interpret this to mean that where prophetic and magical powers have broken the spell of present and future, the rigid law of
individuation, and the real magic of nature, some enormously unnatural event—such as incest—must have occurred earlier, as a
cause. How else could one compel nature to surrender her secrets
if not by triumphantly resisting her, that is, by means of something
unnatural? It is this insight that I find expressed in that horrible
triad of Oedipus' destinies: the same man who solves the riddle of
nature—that Sphinx of two species[41]—also must break the most
sacred natural orders by murdering his father and marrying his
mother. Indeed, the myth seems to wish to whisper to us that wisdom, and particularly Dionysian wisdom, is an unnatural abomina-
tion; that he who by means of his knowledge plunges nature into
the abyss of destruction must also suffer the dissolution of nature
in his own person. "The edge of wisdom turns against the wise:
wisdom is a crime against nature": such horrible sentences are
proclaimed to us by the myth; but the Hellenic poet touches the
sublime and terrible Memnon's Column of myth like a sunbeam,
so that it suddenly begins to sound—in Sophoclean melodies![42]

Let me now contrast the glory of activity, which illuminates
Aeschylus' *Prometheus*, with the glory of passivity. What the
thinker Aeschylus had to say to us here, but what as a poet he only

allows us to sense in his symbolic image, the youthful Goethe was able to reveal to us in the audacious words of his Prometheus:

> *Here I sit, forming men*
> *in my own image,*
> *a race to be like me,*
> *to suffer, to weep,*
> *to delight and to rejoice,*
> *and to defy you,*
> *as I do.*

Man, rising to titanic stature, gains culture by his own efforts and forces the gods to enter into an alliance with him because in his very own wisdom he holds their existence and their limitations in his hands. But what is most wonderful in this Prometheus poem, which in its basic idea is the veritable hymn of impiety, is the profoundly Aeschylean demand for *justice*. The immeasurable suffering of the bold "individual" on the one hand and the divine predicament and intimation of a twilight of the gods on the other, the way the power of these two worlds of suffering compels a reconciliation, a metaphysical union—all this recalls in the strongest possible manner the center and main axiom of the Aeschylean view of the world which envisages Moira enthroned above gods and men as eternal justice.

In view of the astonishing audacity with which Aeschylus places the Olympian world on the scales of his justice, we must call to mind that the profound Greek possessed an immovably firm foundation of metaphysical thought in his mysteries, and all his skeptical moods could be vented against the Olympians. The Greek artist in particular had an obscure feeling of mutual dependence when it came to the gods; and precisely in the *Prometheus* of Aeschylus this feeling is symbolized. In himself the titanic artist found the defiant faith that he had the ability to create men and at least destroy Olympian gods, by means of his superior wisdom which, to be sure, he had to atone for with eternal suffering. The splendid "ability" of the great genius for which even eternal suffering is a slight price, the stern pride of the *artist*—that is the content and soul of Aeschylus' poem, while Sophocles in his *Oedipus* sounds as a prelude the *holy man's* song of triumph.

But Aeschylus' interpretation of the myth does not exhaust the astounding depth of its terror. Rather, the artist's delight in what becomes, the cheerfulness of artistic creation that defies all misfortune, is merely a bright image of clouds and sky mirrored in a black lake of sadness. The Prometheus story is an original possession of the entire Aryan community of peoples and evidences their gift for the profoundly tragic. Indeed, it does not seem improbable that this myth has the same characteristic significance for the Aryan character which the myth of the fall has for the Semitic character, and that these two myths are related to each other like brother and sister.[43] The presupposition of the Prometheus myth is to be found in the extravagant value which a naive humanity attached to *fire* as the true palladium of every ascending culture. But that man should freely dispose of fire without receiving it as a present from heaven, either as a lightning bolt or as the warming rays of the sun, struck these reflective primitive men as sacrilege, as a robbery of divine nature. Thus the very first philosophical problem immediately produces a painful and irresolvable contradiction between man and god and moves it before the gate of every culture, like a huge boulder. The best and highest possession mankind can acquire is obtained by sacrilege and must be paid for with consequences that involve the whole flood of sufferings and sorrows with which the offended divinities have to afflict the nobly aspiring race of men. This is a harsh idea which, by the *dignity* it confers on sacrilege, contrasts strangely with the Semitic myth of the fall in which curiosity, mendacious deception, susceptibility to seduction, lust—in short, a series of preeminently feminine affects was considered the origin of evil. What distinguishes the Aryan notion is the sublime view of *active sin* as the characteristically Promethean virtue. With that, the ethical basis for pessimistic tragedy has been found: the justification of human evil, meaning both human guilt and the human suffering it entails.

The misfortune in the nature of things, which the contemplative Aryan is not inclined to interpret away—the contradiction at the heart of the world reveals itself to him as a clash of different worlds, e.g., of a divine and human one, in which each, taken as an individual, has right on its side, but nevertheless has to suffer for its individuation, being merely a single one beside another. In the heroic effort of the individual to attain universality, in the attempt to transcend the curse of individuation and to become the *one* world-being, he suffers in his own person the primordial contradiction that is concealed in things, which means that he commits sacrilege and suffers.

Thus the Aryans understand sacrilege as something masculine,[44] while the Semites understand sin as feminine,[45] just as the original sacrilege is committed by a man, the original sin by a woman. Also, the witches' chorus says:

> *If that is so, we do not mind it:*
> *With a thousand steps the women find it;*
> *But though they rush, we do not care:*
> *With one big jump the men get there.*[46]

Whoever understands this innermost kernel of the Prometheus story—namely, the necessity of sacrilege imposed upon the titanically striving individual—must also immediately feel how unApollonian this pessimistic notion is. For Apollo wants to grant repose to individual beings precisely by drawing boundaries between them, and by again and again calling these to mind as the most sacred laws of the world, with his demands for self-knowledge and measure.

Lest this Apollonian tendency congeal the form to Egyptian rigidity and coldness, lest the effort to prescribe to the individual wave its path and realm might annul the motion of the whole lake, the high tide of the Dionysian destroyed from time to time all those little circles in which the one-sidedly Apollonian "will" had sought to confine the Hellenic spirit. The suddenly swelling Dionysian tide then takes the separate little wave-mountains of individuals on its back, even as Prometheus' brother, the Titan Atlas, does with the earth. This titanic impulse to become, as it were, the Atlas for all individuals, carrying them on a broad back, higher and higher, farther and farther, is what the Promethean and the Dionysian have in common.

In this respect, the Prometheus of Aeschylus is a Dionysian mask, while in the aforementioned profound demand for justice Aeschylus reveals to the thoughtful his paternal descent from Apollo, the god of individuation and of just boundaries. So the dual nature of Aeschylus' Prometheus, his nature which is at the same time Dionysian and Apollonian, might be expressed thus in a conceptual for-

mula: "All that exists is just and unjust and equally justified in
both."

That is your world! A world indeed!—[47]

10.

Indisputable historical evidence tells us that Greek tragedy in its
earliest form had for its sole theme the sufferings of Dionysus, and
that for a long time the only stage hero was Dionysus himself.
But it may be claimed with equal confidence that until Euripides,
Dionysus never ceased to be the tragic hero; that all the celebrated
figures of the Greek stage—Prometheus, Oedipus, etc.—are mere
masks of this original hero, Dionysus. That behind all these masks
there is a deity: that is one essential reason for the typical "ideality"
of these famous figures which has caused so much astonishment.
Somebody, I do not know who, has claimed that all individuals,
taken as individuals, are comic and hence untragic—from which it
would follow that the Greeks simply *could* not suffer individuals
on the tragic stage. In fact, this is what they seem to have felt; and
the Platonic distinction and evaluation of the "idea" and the
"idol," the mere image, is very deeply rooted in the Hellenic
character.

Using Plato's terms, we should have to speak of the tragic figures
of the Hellenic stage somewhat as follows: the one truly real Dionysus appears in a variety of forms, in the mask of a fighting hero,
and entangled, as it were, in the net of the individual will. The god
who appears talks and acts so as to resemble an erring, striving,
suffering individual. That he *appears* at all with such epic precision
and clarity is the work of the dream-interpreter, Apollo, who
through this symbolic appearance interprets to the chorus its Dionysian state. In truth, however, the hero is the suffering Dionysus
of the Mysteries, the god experiencing in himself the agonies of
individuation, of whom wonderful myths tell that as a boy he was
torn to pieces by the Titans and now is worshiped in this state as
Zagreus. Thus it is intimated that this dismemberment, the properly Dionysian *suffering,* is like a transformation into air, water,
earth, and fire, that we are therefore to regard the state of individuation as the origin and primal cause of all suffering, as something objectionable in itself. From the smile of this Dionysus sprang
the Olympian gods, from his tears sprang man. In this existence
as a dismembered god, Dionysus possesses the dual nature of a

cruel, barbarized demon and a mild, gentle ruler. But the hope of the epopts[48] looked toward a rebirth of Dionysus, which we must now intuitively[49] conceive as the end of individuation. It was for this coming third Dionysus that the epopts' roaring hymns of joy resounded. And it is this hope alone that casts a gleam of joy upon the features of a world torn asunder and shattered into individuals; this is symbolized in the myth of Demeter, sunk in eternal sorrow, who *rejoices* again for the first time when told that she may *once more* give birth to Dionysus. This view of things already provides us with all the elements of a profound and pessimistic view of the world, together with the *mystery doctrine of tragedy:* the fundamental knowledge of the oneness of everything existent, the conception of individuation as the primal cause of evil, and of art as the joyous hope that the spell of individuation may be broken in augury of a restored oneness.

We have already suggested that the Homeric epos is the poem of Olympian culture, in which this culture has sung its own song of victory over the terrors of the war of the Titans. Under the predominating influence of tragic poetry, these Homeric myths are now reborn and changed; and this metempsychosis reveals that in the meantime the Olympian culture also has been conquered by a still more profound view of the world. The defiant Titan Prometheus has announced to his Olympian tormentor that someday the greatest danger will menace his rule, unless Zeus should enter into an alliance with him in time. In Aeschylus we recognize how the terrified Zeus, fearful of this end, allies himself with the Titan. Thus the former age of the Titans is once more recovered from Tartarus and brought to the light.

The philosophy of wild and naked nature beholds with the frank, undissembling gaze of truth the myths of the Homeric world as they dance past: they turn pale, they tremble under the piercing glance of this goddess[50]—until the powerful fist of the Dionysian artist forces them into the service of the new deity. Dionysian truth takes over the entire domain of myth as the symbolism of *its* knowledge which it makes known partly in the public cult of tragedy and partly in the secret celebrations of dramatic mysteries, but always in the old mythical garb.

What power was it that freed Prometheus from his vultures and transformed the myth into a vehicle of Dionysian wisdom? It is the Heraclean power of music: having reached its highest manifestation in tragedy, it can invest myths with a new and most profound significance. This we have already characterized as the most powerful function of music. For it is the fate of every myth to creep by degrees into the narrow limits of some alleged historical reality, and to be treated by some later generation as a unique fact with historical claims: and the Greeks were already well on their way toward restamping the whole of their mythical juvenile dream ingeniously and arbitrarily into a historicopragmatical *juvenile history*. For this is the way in which religions are wont to die out: under the stern, intelligent eyes of an orthodox dogmatism, the mythical premises of a religion are systemized as a sum total of historical events; one begins apprehensively to defend the credibility of the myths, while at the same time one opposes any continuation of their natural vitality and growth; the feeling for myth perishes, and its place is taken by the claim of religion to historical foundations. This dying myth was now seized by the newborn genius of Dionysian music; and in these hands it flourished once more with colors such as it had never yet displayed, with a fragrance that awakened a longing anticipation of a metaphysical world. After this final effulgence it collapses, its leaves wither, and soon the mocking Lucians of antiquity catch at the discolored and faded flowers carried away by the four winds. Through tragedy the myth attains its most profound content, its most expressive form; it rises once more like a wounded hero, and its whole excess of strength, together with the philosophic calm of the dying, burns in its eyes with a last powerful gleam.

What did you want, sacrilegious Euripides, when you sought to compel this dying myth to serve you once more? It died under your violent hands—and then you needed a counterfeit, masked myth that, like the ape of Heracles, merely knew how to deck itself out in the ancient pomp. And just as the myth died on you, the genius of music died on you, too. Though with greedy hands you plundered all the gardens of music, you still managed only counterfeit masked music. And because you had abandoned Dionysus, Apollo abandoned you: rouse all the passions from their resting places and conjure them into your circle, sharpen and whet a sophistical dialectic for the speeches of your heroes—your heroes, too, have only copied, masked passions and speak only copied, masked speeches.

11.

Greek tragedy met an end different from that of her older sister arts: thus she died by suicide, in consequence of an irreconcilable conflict; she died tragically, while all the others passed away calmly and beautifully at a ripe old age. If it be consonant with a happy natural state to take leave of life easily, leaving behind a fair posterity, the closing periods of these older arts exhibits such a happy natural state: slowly they sink from sight, and before their dying eyes stand their fairer progeny, who lift up their heads impatiently, with a bold gesture. But when Greek tragedy died, there rose everywhere the deep sense of an immense void. Just as Greek sailors in the time of Tiberius once heard on a lonesome island the soul-shaking cry, "Great Pan is dead," so the Hellenic world was now pierced by the grievous lament: "Tragedy is dead! Poetry itself has perished with her! Away with you, pale, meager epigones! Away to Hades, that you may for once eat your fill of the crumbs of our former masters!"

When a new artistic genre blossomed forth after all, and revered tragedy as its predecessor and mistress, it was noted with horror that she did indeed bear the features of her mother—but those she had exhibited in her long death-struggle. It was *Euripides* who fought this death struggle of tragedy; the later artistic genre is known as *New Attic Comedy*.[51] In it the degenerate form of tragedy lived on as a monument of its exceedingly painful and violent death.

This connection helps to explain the passionate attachment that the poets of the New Comedy felt for Euripides; so that we are no longer surprised at the wish of Philemon, who would have let himself be hanged at once, merely that he might visit Euripides in the lower world—if only he could be certain that the deceased still had possession of his reason. But if we desire, as briefly as possible, and without claiming to say anything exhaustive, to characterize what Euripides has in common with Menander and Philemon, and what appealed to them so strongly as worthy of imitation, it is sufficient to say that Euripides brought the *spectator* onto the stage. He who has perceived the material out of which the Promethean tragic writers prior to Euripides formed their heroes, and how remote from their purpose it was to bring the faithful mask of reality onto the stage, will also be aware of the utterly opposite tendency of Euripides. Through him the everyday man forced his way from the spectators' seats onto the stage; the mirror in which formerly only grand and bold traits were represented now showed the painful fidelity that conscientiously reproduces even the botched outlines of nature.

Odysseus, the typical Hellene of the older art, now sank, in the hands of the new poets, to the figure of the Graeculus, who, as the good-naturedly cunning house-slave, henceforth occupies the center of dramatic interest. What Euripides claims credit for in Aristophanes' *Frogs*,[52] namely, that his nostrums have liberated tragic art from its pompous corpulency, is apparent above all in his tragic heroes. The spectator now actually saw and heard his double on the Euripidean stage, and rejoiced that he could talk so well. But this joy was not all: one could even learn from Euripides how to speak oneself. He prides himself upon this in his contest with Aeschylus: from him the people have learned how to observe, debate, and draw conclusions according to the rules of art and with the cleverest sophistries. Through this revolution in ordinary language, he made the New Comedy possible. For henceforth it was no longer a secret how—and with what maxims—everyday life could be represented on the stage. Civic mediocrity, on which Euripides built all his political hopes, was now given a voice, while heretofore the demigod in tragedy and the drunken satyr, or demiman, in comedy, had determined the character of the language. And so the Aristophanean Euripides prides himself on having portrayed the common, familiar, everyday life and activities of the people, about which all are qualified to pass judgment. If the entire populace now philosophized, managed land and goods, and conducted lawsuits with unheard-of circumspection, he deserved the credit, for this was the result of the wisdom he had inculcated in the people.

It was to a populace thus prepared and enlightened that the New Comedy could address itself: it was Euripides who had taught, as it were, the chorus; only now the chorus of spectators had to be trained. As soon as this chorus was trained to sing in the Euripidean key, there arose that drama which resembles a game of chess—the New Comedy, with its perpetual triumphs of cunning and craftiness. But Euripides—the chorus master—was praised continually: indeed, people would have killed themselves in order to learn still more from him, if they had not known that the tragic poets were quite as dead as tragedy. But with that, the Hellene had given up

his belief in immortality; not only his belief in an ideal past, but also his belief in an ideal future. The words of the well-known epitaph, "frivolous and eccentric when an old man,"[53] also suit aging Hellenism. The passing moment, wit, levity, and caprice are its highest deities; the fifth estate, that of the slaves, now comes to power, at least in sentiment; and if we may still speak at all of "Greek cheerfulness," it is the cheerfulness of the slave who has nothing of consequence to be responsible for, nothing great to strive for, and who does not value anything in the past or future higher than the present.

It was this semblance of "Greek cheerfulness" which so outraged the profound and formidable natures of the first four centuries of Christianity: this womanish flight from seriousness and terror, this craven satisfaction with easy enjoyment, seemed to them not only contemptible, but a specifically anti-Christian sentiment. And it is due to their influence that the conception of Greek antiquity which endured through the centuries clung with almost unconquerable persistency to that pink hue of cheerfulness—as if there had never been a sixth century with its birth of tragedy, its mysteries, its Pythagoras and Heraclitus, as if the works of art of the great period simply did not exist, though these phenomena can hardly be explained as having originated in any such senile and slavish pleasure in existence and cheerfulness, and point to a wholly different conception of the world as the ground of their existence.

The assertion made above, that Euripides brought the spectator onto the stage and thus qualified him to pass judgment on the drama, makes it appear as if the older tragic art had always suffered from bad relations with the spectator; and one might be tempted to extol as an advance over Sophocles the radical tendency of Euripides to produce a proper relation between art and the public. But "public," after all, is a mere word. In no sense is it a homogeneous and constant quantity. Why should the artist be bound to accommodate himself to a power whose strength lies solely in numbers? And if, by virtue of his endowments and aspirations, he should feel himself superior to every one of these spectators, how could he feel greater respect for the collective expression of all these subordinate capacities than for the relatively highest-endowed individual spectator? In truth, if ever a Greek artist throughout a long life treated his public with audacity and self-sufficiency,[54] it was Euripides. When the masses threw themselves at his feet, he openly and with sublime defiance reversed his own tendency, the very tendency with which he had won over the masses. If this genius had had the slightest reverence for the pandemonium of the public, he would have broken down long before the middle of his career, beneath the heavy blows of his failures.

These considerations make it clear that our formula—that Euripides brought the spectator onto the stage in order to make him truly competent to pass judgment—was merely provisional; we must penetrate more deeply to understand his tendency. Conversely, it is well known that Aeschylus and Sophocles during the whole of their lives, and indeed long after, were in complete possession of the people's favor, so there can be no question of a false relation between art and the public in the case of these predecessors of Euripides. What was it, then, which forcibly drove this artist, so richly endowed, so constantly impelled to production, from the path warmed by the sun of the greatest names in poetry and covered by the cloudless heaven of popular favor? What strange consideration for the spectator led him to oppose the spectator? How could he, out of too great a respect for his public—despise his public?

Euripides—and this is the solution of the riddle just propounded—undoubtedly felt himself, as a poet, superior to the masses in general; but to two of his spectators he did not feel superior. He brought the masses onto the stage; but these two spectators he revered as the only competent judges and masters of his art. Complying with their directions and admonitions, he transferred the entire world of sentiments, passions, and experiences, hitherto present at every festival performance as the invisible chorus on the spectators' benches, into the souls of his stage heroes. He yielded to their demands, too, when for these new characters he sought out a new language and a new tone. Only in their voices could he hear any conclusive verdict on his work, and also the encouragement that promised eventual success when, time and again, he found himself condemned by the public judgment.

Of these two spectators, one is—Euripides himself, Euripides *as thinker*, not as poet. It might be said of him, as of Lessing, that his extraordinary fund of *critical* talent, if it did not create, at least constantly stimulated his productive *artistic* impulse. With this gift, with all the brightness and dexterity of his critical thinking, Euripides had sat in the theater and striven to recognize in the masterpieces of his great predecessors, as in paintings that have become dark, feature after feature, line after line. And here he had experienced something which should not surprise anyone initiated into the deeper secrets of Aeschylean tragedy. He observed something incommensurable in every feature and in every line, a certain deceptive distinctness and at the same time an enigmatic depth, indeed an infinitude, in the background. Even the clearest figure always had a comet's tail attached to it which seemed to suggest the uncertain, that which could never be illuminated. A similar twilight shrouded the structure of the drama, especially the significance of the chorus. And how dubious the solution of the ethical problems remained to him! How questionable the treatment of the myths! How unequal the distribution of good and bad fortune! Even in the language of the Old Tragedy there was much he found offensive, or at least enigmatic; especially he found too much pomp for simple affairs, too many tropes and monstrous expressions to suit the plainness of the characters. So he sat in the theater, pondering uneasily, and as a spectator he confessed to himself that he did not understand his great predecessors. But if understanding was for him the real root of all enjoyment and creation, he had to inquire and look around to see whether no one else had the same opinion and also felt this incommensurability. But most people, and among them the finest individuals, had only a suspicious smile for him, and none could explain to him why the great masters were still in the right despite his scruples and objections. And in this state of torment, he found *that other spectator* who did not comprehend tragedy and therefore did not esteem it. Allied with him, he could now venture from his solitude to begin the tremendous struggle against the art of Aeschylus and Sophocles—not with polemical essays, but as a dramatic poet who opposed *his* conception of tragedy to the traditional one.

12.

Before we name this other spectator, let us pause here a moment to recall to our minds our previously described impression of the discordant and incommensurable elements in the nature of Aeschylean tragedy. Let us recall our surprise at the *chorus* and the *tragic hero* of that tragedy, neither of which we could reconcile with our own customs any more than with historical evidence—until we rediscovered this duality itself as the origin and essence of Greek tragedy, as the expression of two interwoven artistic impulses, *the Apollonian and the Dionysian.*

To separate this original and all-powerful Dionysian element from tragedy, and to reconstruct tragedy purely on the basis of an un-Dionysian art, morality, and worldview—this is the tendency of Euripides as it now reveals itself to us in clear illumination.

In the evening of his life, Euripides himself most emphatically propounded to his contemporaries the question of the value and significance of this tendency, using a myth. Is the Dionysian entitled to exist at all? Should it not be forcibly uprooted from Hellenic soil? Certainly, the poet tells us, if it were only possible: but the god Dionysus is too powerful; his most clearheaded adversary—like Pentheus in the *Bacchae*—is unwittingly enchanted by him, and in this enchantment runs to meet his fate. The judgment of the two old men, Cadmus and Tiresias, seems also to be the judgment of the old poet: the reflection of the wisest individuals does not overthrow these old popular traditions, nor the perpetually self-propagating worship of Dionysus; rather it is proper to display at least a diplomatically cautious interest in the presence of such marvelous forces—although the possibility remains that the god may take offense at such lukewarm participation, and eventually transform the diplomat—like Cadmus—into a dragon. This is what we are told by a poet who opposed Dionysus with heroic valor throughout a long life—and who finally ended his career with a glorification of his adversary and with suicide, like a giddy man who, to escape the horrible vertigo he can no longer endure, casts himself from a tower.

This tragedy was a protest against the practicability of his own tendency; but alas, it had already been put into practice! The marvel had happened: when the poet recanted, his tendency had already triumphed. Dionysus had already been scared from the tragic stage, by a demonic power speaking through Euripides. Even Euripides was, in a sense, only a mask: the deity that spoke through him was neither Dionysus nor Apollo, but an altogether newborn demon called *Socrates.*

This is the new opposition: the Dionysian and the Socratic—and the art of Greek tragedy was wrecked on this. Though Euripides may seek to comfort us by his recantation, he does not succeed: the most magnificent temple lies in ruins. What does the lamentation of the destroyer profit us, or his confession that it was the most beautiful of all temples? And even if Euripides has been punished by being changed into a dragon by the art critics of all ages—who could be content with so miserable a compensation?

Let us now approach this *Socratic* tendency with which Euripides combated and vanquished Aeschylean tragedy.

We must now ask ourselves, what could be the aim of the Euripidean design, which, in its most ideal form, would wish to base drama exclusively on the un-Dionysian? What form of drama still remained, if it was not to be born of the womb of music, in the mysterious twilight of the Dionysian? Only *the dramatized epos*—but in this Apollonian domain of art the *tragic* effect is certainly unattainable. The subject matter of the events represented is not decisive; indeed, I suggest that it would have been impossible for Goethe in his projected *Nausikaa* to have rendered tragically effective the suicide of this idyllic being, which was to have completed the fifth act. So extraordinary is the power of the epic-Apollonian that before our eyes it transforms the most terrible things by the joy in mere appearance and in redemption through mere appearance. The poet of the dramatized epos cannot blend completely with his images any more than the epic rhapsodist can. He is still that calm, unmoved contemplation which sees the images *before* its wide-open eyes. The actor in this dramatized epos still remains fundamentally a rhapsodist: the consecration of the inner dream lies on all his actions, so that he is never wholly an actor.

How, then, is the Euripidean play related to this ideal of the Apollonian drama? Just as the younger rhapsodist is related to the solemn rhapsodist of old times. In the Platonic *Ion,* the younger rhapsodist describes his own nature as follows: "When I am saying anything sad, my eyes fill with tears; and when I am saying something awful and terrible, then my hair stands on end with fright and my heart beats quickly." Here we no longer remark anything of the epic absorption in mere appearance, or of the dispassionate coolness of the true actor, who precisely in his highest activity is wholly mere appearance and joy in mere appearance. Euripides is the actor whose heart beats, whose hair stands on end; as Socratic thinker he designs the plan, as passionate actor he executes it. Neither in the designing nor in the execution is he a pure artist. Thus the Euripidean drama is a thing both cool and fiery, equally capable of freezing and burning. It is impossible for it to attain the Apollonian effect of the epos, while, on the other hand, it has alienated itself as much as possible from Dionysian elements. Now, in order to be effective at all, it requires new stimulants, which can no longer lie within the sphere of the only two art-impulses, the Apollonian and the Dionysian. These stimulants are cool, paradoxical *thoughts,* replacing Apollonian contemplation—and fiery *affects,* replacing Dionysian ecstasies; and, it may be added, thoughts and affects copied very realistically and in no sense dipped into the ether of art.

So we see that Euripides did not succeed in basing the drama exclusively on the Apollonian, and his un-Dionysian tendency actually went astray and became naturalistic and inartistic. Now we should be able to come closer to the character of *aesthetic Socratism,* whose supreme law reads roughly as follows, "To be beautiful everything must be intelligible," as the counterpart to the Socratic dictum, "Knowledge is virtue." With this canon in his hands, Euripides measured all the separate elements of the drama—language, characters, dramaturgic structure, and choric music—and corrected them according to this principle.

The poetic deficiency and degeneration, which are so often imputed to Euripides in comparison with Sophocles, are for the most part products of this penetrating critical process, this audacious rationality.

The Euripidean *prologue* may serve as an example of the productivity of this rationalistic method. Nothing could be more uncongenial to the technique of our own stage than the prologue in the drama of Euripides. For a single person to appear at the outset of the play, telling us who he is, what precedes the action, what has happened so far, even what will happen in the course of the play, would be condemned by a modern playwright as a willful, inexcusable abandonment of the effect of suspense. We know everything that is going to happen; who would want to wait until it actually does happen? After all, we do not even have the exciting relation of a prophetic dream to a reality that comes to be later on. But Euripides did not think like that at all. The effect of tragedy never depended on epic suspense, on a fascinating uncertainty as to what is to happen now and afterward, but rather on the great rhetorical-lyrical scenes in which the passion and dialectic of the protagonist swelled to a broad and powerful current. Everything laid the ground for pathos, not for action: and whatever was not directed toward pathos was considered objectionable. But what interferes most with the hearer's pleasurable absorption in such scenes is any missing link, any gap in the texture of the background story. So long as the spectator has to figure out the meaning of this or that person, or the presuppositions of this or that conflict of inclinations and purposes, he cannot become completely absorbed in the activities and sufferings of the chief characters or feel breathless pity and fear.

Aeschylean-Sophoclean tragedy employed the most ingenious devices in the initial scenes to place in the spectator's hands, as if by chance, all the threads necessary for a complete understanding—a trait proving that noble artistry which, as it were, masks the *necessary* formal element and makes it appear accidental. Yet Euripides thought he observed that during these first scenes the spectator was so anxious to solve the problem of the background history that the poetic beauties and the pathos of the exposition were lost on him. So he put the prologue even before the exposition, and placed it in the mouth of a person who could be trusted: often some deity had to guarantee the plot of the tragedy to the public, to remove every doubt as to the reality of the myth—somewhat as Descartes could prove the reality of the empirical world only by appealing to the truthfulness of God and his inability to utter falsehood. Euripides makes use of this same divine truthfulness once more at the close of his drama, in order to reassure the public as to the future of his heroes; this is the task of the notorious *deus ex machina*. Between this epic preview and epic prospect lies the dramatic-lyric present, the "drama" proper.

Thus Euripides as a poet is essentially an echo of his own conscious knowledge; and it is precisely on this account that he occupies such a remarkable position in the history of Greek art. With reference to his critical-productive activity, he must often have felt as if he had to bring to life for drama the beginning of the essay of Anaxagoras: "In the beginning all things were mixed together; then came understanding and created order." Anaxagoras with his "nous"[55] is said to have appeared among philosophers as the first sober person[56] amid a crowd of drunken ones. Euripides may have conceived his relation to the other tragic poets in terms of a similar image. As long as the sole ruler and disposer of the universe, the *nous,* remained excluded from artistic activity, things were all mixed together in a primeval chaos: this was what Euripides must have thought; and so, as the first "sober" one among them, he had to condemn the "drunken" poets. Sophocles said of Aeschylus that he did what was right, though he did it unconsciously. This was surely not how Euripides saw it. He would have agreed only that Aeschylus, *because* he created unconsciously, did what was *wrong*. The divine Plato, too, almost always speaks only ironically of the creative faculty of the poet, insofar as it is not conscious insight, and places it on a par with the gift of the soothsayer and dream-interpreter: the poet is incapable of composing until he has become unconscious and bereft of understanding. Like Plato, Euripides undertook to show to the world the reverse of the "irrational" poet; his aesthetic principle that "to be beautiful everything must be conscious" is, as I have said, the parallel to the Socratic, "to be good everything must be conscious." So we may consider Euripides as the poet of aesthetic Socratism.

Socrates, however, was that *second spectator* who did not comprehend and therefore did not esteem the Old Tragedy; in alliance with him Euripides dared to be the herald of a new art. If it was this of which the older tragedy perished, then aesthetic Socratism was the murderous principle; but insofar as the struggle was directed against the Dionysian element in the older tragedy, we may recognize in Socrates the opponent of Dionysus. He is the new Orpheus who rose against Dionysus, and although he is destined to be torn to pieces by the Maenads of the Athenian court, he still put to flight the powerful god himself—who, as on his flight from Lycurgus the King of Edoni, sought refuge in the depths of the sea: namely, the mystical flood of a secret cult which gradually covered the earth.

13.

That Socrates was closely related to the tendency of Euripides did not escape the notice of contemporaneous antiquity. The most eloquent expression of this felicitous insight was the story current in Athens that Socrates used to help Euripides write his plays. Whenever an occasion arose to enumerate the demagogues of the day,[57] the adherents of the "good old times" would mention both names in the same breath. To the influence of Socrates and Euripides they attributed the fact that the old Marathonian stalwart fitness of body and soul was falling prey more and more to a dubious enlightenment that involved the progressive degeneration of the powers of body and soul. It is in this tone, half indignant, half contemptuous, that Aristophanic comedy used to speak of both of them—to the consternation of modern men, who are quite willing to give up Euripides, but who cannot give sufficient expression to their astonishment that in Aristophanes Socrates should appear as the first and supreme Sophist, as the mirror and epitome of all sophistical tendencies. Their only consolation is to pillory Aristophanes himself as a dissolute, mendacious Alcibiades of poetry. Without here defending the profound instinct of Aristophanes against such attacks, I shall continue to show, by means of the sentiments of the time, the close connection between Socrates and Euripides. With this in view, we must remember particularly how Socrates, as an opponent of tragic art, refrained from attending tragedies and appeared among the spectators only when a new play of Euripides was to be performed. Most famous of all, however, is the close association of the two names by the Delphic oracle, which designated Socrates as the wisest of men and at the same time decided that the second prize in the contest of wisdom belonged to Euripides.

Sophocles was named third in order of rank—he who could boast that, as compared with Aeschylus, he did what was right because he *knew* what was right. Evidently it is precisely the degree of clarity of this *knowledge* which distinguishes these three men in common as the three "knowing ones" of their time.

The most acute word, however, about this new and unprecedented value set on knowledge and insight was spoken by Socrates when he found that he was the only one who acknowledged to himself that he knew *nothing,* whereas in his critical peregrinations through Athens he had called on the greatest statesmen, orators, poets, and artists, and had everywhere discovered the conceit of knowledge. To his astonishment he perceived that all these celebrities were without a proper and sure insight, even with regard to their own professions, and that they practiced them only by instinct. "Only by instinct": with this phrase we touch upon the heart and core of the Socratic tendency. With it Socratism condemns existing art as well as existing ethics. Wherever Socratism turns its searching eyes it sees lack of insight and the power of delusion; and from this lack it infers the essential perversity and reprehensibility of what exists. Basing himself on this point alone, Socrates conceives it to be his duty to correct existence: all alone, with an expression of irreverence and superiority, as the pre-

cursor of an altogether different culture, art, and morality, he
enters a world, to touch whose very hem would give us the greatest happiness.

This is what strikes us as so tremendously problematic whenever
we consider Socrates, and again and again we are tempted to
fathom the meaning and purpose of this most dubious phenomenon of antiquity. Who is it that may dare single-handedly to negate
the Greek genius that, as Homer, Pindar, and Aeschylus, as Phidias,
as Pericles, as Pythia and Dionysus, as the deepest abyss and the
highest height, is sure of our astonished veneration? What demonic
power is this that dares to spill this magic potion into dust? What
demigod is this to whom the chorus of the noblest spirits of mankind must call out:

> *Alas!*
> *You have shattered*
> *The beautiful world*
> *With brazen fist;*
> *It falls, it is scattered.*[58]

We are offered a key to the character of Socrates by the wonderful phenomenon known as "the *daimonion* of Socrates." In exceptional circumstances, when his tremendous intellect wavered, he
found secure support in the utterances of a divine voice that
spoke up at such moments. This voice, whenever it comes, always
dissuades. In this utterly abnormal nature, instinctive wisdom appears only in order to *hinder* conscious knowledge occasionally.
While in all productive men it is instinct that is the creative-
affirmative force, and consciousness acts critically and dissuasively,
in Socrates it is instinct that becomes the critic, and consciousness
that becomes the creator—truly a monstrosity *per defectum!* Specifically, we observe here a monstrous *defectus* of any mystical
disposition, so Socrates might be called the typical *nonmystic,* in
whom, through a hypertrophy, the logical nature is developed as
excessively as instinctive wisdom is in the mystic. But the logical
urge that became manifest in Socrates was absolutely prevented
from turning against itself; in its unbridled flood it displays a natural power such as we encounter to our awed amazement only in the
very greatest instinctive forces. Anyone who, through the Platonic
writings, has experienced even a breath of the divine naiveté and

sureness of the Socratic way of life, will also feel how the enormous driving-wheel of logical Socratism is in motion, as it were, *behind* Socrates, and that it must be viewed through Socrates as through a shadow.

His own sense of this relationship found expression in the dignified seriousness with which he everywhere, even before his judges, insisted on his divine calling. At bottom, it was as impossible to refute him here as to approve of his instinct-disintegrating influence. In view of this indissoluble conflict, when he had at last been brought before the forum of the Greek state, only one kind of punishment was indicated: exile. Being thoroughly enigmatical, unclassifiable, and inexplicable, he might have been asked to leave the city, and posterity would never have been justified in charging the Athenians with an ignominious deed. But that he was sentenced to death, not exile, Socrates himself seems to have brought about with perfect awareness and without any natural awe of death. He went to his death with the calm with which, according to Plato's description, he leaves the Symposium at dawn, the last of the revelers, to begin a new day, while on the benches and on the earth his drowsy table companions remain behind to dream of Socrates, the true eroticist. *The dying Socrates* became the new ideal, never seen before, of noble Greek youths: above all, the typical Hellenic youth, Plato, prostrated himself before this image with all the ardent devotion of his enthusiastic soul.

14.

Let us now imagine the one great Cyclops eye of Socrates fixed on tragedy, an eye in which the fine frenzy of artistic enthusiasm had never glowed. It was denied to this eye to gaze with pleasure into the Dionysian abysses. What, then, did it have to see in the "sublime and greatly lauded" tragic art, as Plato called it? Something rather unreasonable, full of causes apparently without effects, and effects apparently without causes; the whole, moreover, so motley and manifold that it could not but be repugnant to a sober mind, and a dangerous tinder for sensitive and susceptible souls. We know the only kind of poetry he comprehended: the *Aesopian fable;* and this he favored no doubt with the smiling accommodation with which the good honest Gellert[59] sings the praise of poetry in the fable of the bee and the hen:

> *Poems are useful: they can tell*
> *The truth by means of parable*
> *To those who are not very bright.*

But to Socrates, it seemed that tragic art did not even "tell the truth"; moreover, it addressed itself to "those who are not very bright," not to the philosopher: a twofold reason for shunning it. Like Plato, he reckoned it among the flattering arts which portray only the agreeable, not the useful; and therefore he required of his disciples abstinence and strict separation from such unphilosophical attractions—with such success that the youthful tragic poet Plato first burned his poems that he might become a student of Socrates. But where unconquerable propensities struggled against the Socratic maxims, the power of these maxims, together with the impact of his tremendous character, was still great enough to force poetry itself into new and hitherto unknown channels.

An instance of this is Plato, who in condemning tragedy and art in general certainly did not lag behind the naive cynicism of his master; he was nevertheless constrained by sheer artistic necessity to create an art form that was related to those forms of art which he repudiated. Plato's main objection to the older art—that it is the imitation of a phantom and hence belongs to a sphere even lower than the empirical world—could certainly not be directed against the new art; and so we find Plato endeavoring to transcend reality and to represent the idea which underlies this pseudoreality. Thus, by means of a detour, Plato the thinker arrived where he had always been at home as a poet—at the point from which Sophocles and the older art protested solemnly against that objection. If tragedy had absorbed into itself all the earlier types of art, the same might also be said in an eccentric sense of the Platonic dialogue which, a mixture of all extant styles and forms, hovers midway between narrative, lyric, and drama, between prose and poetry, and so has also broken the strict old law of the unity of linguistic form. This tendency was carried still further by the *Cynic* writers, who in the greatest stylistic medley, oscillating between prose and metrical forms, attained also the literary image of the "raving Socrates," whom they represented in real life.

The Platonic dialogue was, as it were, the boat on which the shipwrecked ancient poetry saved herself with all her children: crowded into a narrow space and timidly submitting to the single pilot, Socrates, they now sailed into a new world, which never tired of looking at the fantastic spectacle of this procession. Indeed, Plato has given to all posterity the model of a new art form, the model of the *novel*—which may be described as an infinitely enhanced Aesopian fable, in which poetry holds the same rank in relation to dialectical philosophy as this same philosophy held for many centuries in relation to theology: namely, the rank of *ancilla*.[60] This was the new position into which Plato, under the pressure of the demonic Socrates, forced poetry.

Here *philosophic thought* overgrows art and compels it to cling close to the trunk of dialectic. The *Apollonian* tendency has withdrawn into the cocoon of logical schematism; just as in the case of Euripides we noticed something analogous, as well as a transformation of the *Dionysian* into naturalistic affects. Socrates, the dialectical hero of the Platonic drama, reminds us of the kindred nature of the Euripidean hero who must defend his actions with arguments and counterarguments and, in the process, often risks the loss of our tragic pity; for who could mistake the *optimistic* element in the nature of dialectic, which celebrates a triumph with every syllogism and can breathe only in cool clarity and rationality—the optimistic element which, having once penetrated tragedy, must gradually overgrow its Dionysian regions and impel it necessarily to self-destruction—to the death-leap into the bourgeois drama. Consider the consequences of the Socratic maxims: "Virtue is knowledge; man sins only from ignorance; he who is virtuous is happy." In these three basic forms of optimism lies the death of tragedy. For now the virtuous hero must be a dialectician; now there must be a necessary, visible connection between virtue and knowledge, faith and morality; now the transcendental justice of Aeschylus is degraded to the superficial and insolent principle of "poetic justice" with its customary *deus ex machina*.[61]

As it confronts this new Socratic-optimistic stage world, how does the *chorus* appear now, and indeed the whole musical-Dionysian substratum of tragedy? As something accidental, a dispensable vestige of the origin of tragedy; while we have seen that the chorus can be understood only as the *cause* of tragedy, and of the tragic in general. This perplexity in regard to the chorus already manifests itself in Sophocles—an important indication that even with him the Dionysian basis of tragedy is beginning to crumble. He no longer dares to entrust to the chorus the main share of the effect, but limits its sphere to such an extent that it now appears almost coordinate with the actors, just as if it were elevated from the orchestra into the scene; and thus its character is, of course, completely destroyed, even if Aristotle favors precisely this view of the chorus. This shift in the position of the chorus, which Sophocles at any rate recommended by his practice and, according to tradition, even by a treatise, is the first step toward the *destruction* of the chorus, the phases of which follow one another with alarming rapidity in Euripides, Agathon, and the New Comedy. Optimistic dialectic drives *music* out of tragedy with the scourge of its syllogisms; that is, it destroys the essence of tragedy, which can be interpreted only as a manifestation and projection into images of Dionysian states, as the visible symbolizing of music, as the dreamworld of a Dionysian intoxication.

If we must thus assume an anti-Dionysian tendency operating even prior to Socrates, which merely received in him an unprecedentedly magnificent expression, we must not draw back before the question of what such a phenomenon as that of Socrates indicates; for in view of the Platonic dialogues we are certainly not entitled to regard it as a merely disintegrating, negative force. And though there can be no doubt that the most immediate effect of the Socratic impulse tended to the dissolution of Dionysian tragedy, yet a profound experience in Socrates' own life impels us to ask whether there is *necessarily* only an antipodal relation between Socratism and art, and whether the birth of an "artistic Socrates" is altogether a contradiction in terms.

For with respect to art, that despotic logician occasionally had the feeling of a gap, a void, half a reproach, a possibly neglected duty. As he tells his friends in prison, there often came to him one and the same dream apparition, which always said the same thing to him: "Socrates, practice music." Up to his very last days he comforts himself with the view that his philosophizing is the highest of the muses' arts, and he finds it hard to believe that a deity should remind him of the "common, popular music." Finally, in prison, in order that he may thoroughly unburden his conscience, he does consent to practice this music for which he has but little respect. And in this mood he writes a prelude to Apollo and turns a few Aesopian fables into verse. It was something akin to the demonic warning voice that urged him to these practices; it was his Apollonian insight that, like a barbarian king, he did not understand the noble image of a god and was in danger of sinning against a deity—through his lack of understanding. The voice of the Socratic dream vision is the only sign of any misgivings about the limits of logic. Perhaps—thus he must have asked himself—what is not intelligible to me is not necessarily unintelligent? Perhaps there is a realm of wisdom from which the logician is exiled? Perhaps art is even a necessary correlative of, and supplement for, science?

15.

In the spirit of these last suggestive questions, it must now be said how the influence of Socrates, down to the present moment and even into all future time, has spread over posterity like a shadow that keeps growing in the evening sun, and how it again and again prompts a regeneration of *art*—of art in the metaphysical, broadest and profoundest sense—and how its own infinity also guarantees the infinity of art.

Before this could be recognized, before the innermost dependence of every art on the Greeks, from Homer to Socrates, was demonstrated conclusively, we had to feel about these Greeks as the Athenians felt about Socrates. Nearly every age and stage of culture has at some time or other sought with profound irritation to free itself from the Greeks, because in their presence everything one has achieved oneself, though apparently quite original and sincerely admired, suddenly seemed to lose life and color and shriveled into a poor copy, even a caricature. And so time after time heartfelt anger erupts against this presumptuous little people that made bold for all time to designate everything not native as "barbaric." Who are they, one asks, who, though they display only an ephemeral historical splendor, ridiculously restricted institutions, rather dubious mores, and are marked by ugly vices, yet lay claim to that dignity and preeminence among peoples which characterize genius among the masses? Unfortunately, one was not lucky enough to find the cup of hemlock with which one could simply dispose of such a character; for all the poison that envy, calumny, and rancor created did not suffice to destroy that self-sufficient splendor. And so one feels ashamed and afraid in the presence of the Greeks, unless one prizes truth above all things and dares acknowledge even this truth: that the Greeks, as charioteers, hold in their hands the reins of our own and every other culture, but that almost always chariot and horses are of inferior quality and not up to the glory of their leaders, who consider it sport to run such a team into an abyss which they themselves clear with the leap of Achilles.

In order to vindicate the dignity of such a leader's position for Socrates, too, it is enough to recognize in him a type of existence unheard of before him: the type of the *theoretical man* whose significance and aim it is our next task to try to understand. Like the artist, the theoretical man finds an infinite delight in whatever exists, and this satisfaction protects him against the practical ethics of pessimism with its Lynceus eyes[62] that shine only in the dark. Whenever the truth is uncovered, the artist will always cling with rapt gaze to what still remains covering[63] even after such uncovering; but the theoretical man enjoys and finds satisfaction in the discarded covering and finds the highest object of his pleasure in the process of an ever happy uncovering that succeeds through his own efforts.

There would be no science if it were concerned only with that *one* nude goddess and with nothing else. For in that case her devotees would have to feel like men who wanted to dig a hole straight through the earth, assuming that each of them realized that even if he tried his utmost, his whole life long, he would only be able to dig a very small portion of this enormous depth, and even that would be filled in again before his own eyes by the labors of the next in line, so a third person would seem to do well if he picked a new spot for his drilling efforts. Now suppose someone proved convincingly that the goal of the antipodes cannot be reached in this direct manner: who would still wish to go on working in these old depths, unless he had learned meanwhile to be satisfied with finding precious stones or discovering laws of nature?

Therefore Lessing, the most honest theoretical man, dared to announce that he cared more for the search after truth than for truth itself[64]—and thus revealed the fundamental secret of science, to the astonishment, and indeed the anger, of the scientific community. Beside this isolated insight, born of an excess of honesty if not of exuberance, there is, to be sure, a profound *delusion* that first saw the light of the world in the person of Socrates: the unshakable faith that thought, using the thread of causality, can penetrate the deepest abysses of being, and that thought is capable not only of knowing being but even of *correcting* it. This sublime metaphysical delusion accompanies science as an instinct and leads science again and again to its limits at which it must turn into *art—which is really the aim of this mechanism.*

With the torch of this thought in our hands, let us now look at Socrates: he appears to us as the first who could not only live, guided by this instinct of science, but also—and this is far more— die that way. Hence the image of the *dying Socrates,* as the human being whom knowledge and reasoning have liberated from the fear of death, is the emblem that, above the entrance gate of science, reminds all of its mission—namely, to make existence appear comprehensible and thus justified; and if reasons do not suffice, *myth* has to come to their aid in the end—myth which I have just called the necessary consequence, indeed the purpose, of science.

Once we see clearly how after Socrates, the mystagogue of science, one philosophical school succeeds another, wave upon wave; how the hunger for knowledge reached a never-suspected universality in the widest domain of the educated world, became the real task for every person of higher gifts, and led science onto the high seas from which it has never again been driven altogether; how this universality first spread a common net of thought over the whole globe, actually holding out the prospect of the lawfulness of an entire solar system—once we see all this clearly, along with the amazingly high pyramid of knowledge in our own time, we cannot fail to see in Socrates the one turning point and vortex of so-called world history. For if we imagine that the whole incalculable sum of energy used up for this world tendency had been used *not* in the service of knowledge but for the practical, i.e., egoistic aims of individuals and peoples, then we realize that in that case universal wars of annihilation and continual migrations of peoples would probably have weakened the instinctive lust for life to such an extent that suicide would have become a general custom and individuals might have experienced the final remnant of a sense of duty when, like the inhabitants of the Fiji Islands, they had strangled their parents and friends—a practical pessimism that might even have generated a gruesome ethic of genocide motivated by pity, and which, incidentally, is, and was, present in the world wherever art did not appear in some form—especially as religion and science—as a remedy and a preventive for this breath of pestilence.

By contrast with this practical pessimism, Socrates is the prototype of the theoretical optimist who, with his faith that the nature of things can be fathomed, ascribes to knowledge and insight the power of a panacea, while understanding error as the evil *par excellence*. To fathom the depths and to separate true knowledge from appearance and error, seemed to Socratic man the noblest, even the only truly human vocation. And since Socrates, this mechanism of concepts, judgments, and conclusions has been esteemed as the highest occupation and the most admirable gift of nature, above all other capacities. Even the most sublime ethical deeds, the stirrings of pity, self-sacrifice, heroism, and that calm sea of the soul, so difficult to attain, which the Apollonian Greek called *sophrosune*,[65] were derived from the dialectic of knowledge by Socrates and his like-minded successors down to the present, and accordingly designated as teachable.

Anyone who has ever experienced the pleasure of Socratic insight and felt how, spreading in ever-widening circles, it seeks to embrace the whole world of appearances, will never again find any stimulus toward existence more violent than the craving to complete this conquest and to weave the net impenetrably tight. To one who feels that way, the Platonic Socrates will appear as the teacher of an altogether new form of "Greek cheerfulness" and blissful affirmation of existence that seeks to discharge itself in actions—most often in maieutic and educational influences on noble youths, with a view to eventually producing a genius.

But science, spurred by its powerful delusion, speeds irresistibly toward its limits where its optimism, inherent in the essence of logic, suffers shipwreck. For the periphery of the circle of science has an infinite number of points; and while there is no telling how this circle could ever be surveyed completely, noble and gifted men nevertheless reach, e'er half their time[66] and inevitably, such boundary points on the periphery from which one gazes into what defies illumination. When they see to their horror how logic coils up at these boundaries and finally bites its own tail—suddenly the new form of insight breaks through, *tragic insight* which, merely to be endured, needs art as a protection and remedy.

Our eyes strengthened and refreshed by our contemplation of the Greeks, let us look at the highest spheres of the world that surges around us; then we shall see how the hunger for insatiable and optimistic knowledge[67] that in Socrates appears exemplary has turned into tragic resignation and a need for art—while, to be sure, the same hunger on its lower levels can express itself in hostility to art and must particularly detest Dionysian-tragic art, as was illustrated earlier with the fight of Socratism against Aeschylean tragedy.

Here we knock, deeply moved, at the gates of present and future: will this "turning"[68] lead to ever-new configurations of genius and especially of the *Socrates who practices music?* Will the net of art, even if it is called religion or science, that is spread over existence be woven even more tightly and delicately, or is it destined to be torn to shreds in the restless, barbarous, chaotic whirl that now calls itself "the present"?

Concerned but not disconsolate, we stand aside a little while, contemplative men to whom it has been granted to be witnesses of these tremendous struggles and transitions. Alas, it is the magic of these struggles that those who behold them must also take part and fight.

Translated by Walter Kaufmann

[The following ten sections of *The Birth of Tragedy*, §§ 16–25, are rhapsodic, uneven, and, as often as not, contradictory—not to mention a certain redundance—and do not contribute substantially to the birth of Nietzschean philosophy; therefore, they have been left out. A concise and reliable summary can be found in the volume *Nietzsche on Tragedy* by M. S. Silk and J. P. Stern (Cambridge: Cambridge University Press, 1981), pp. 79–89.]

From *Ecce Homo: How One Becomes What One Is* (1888, published posthumously)

The Birth of Tragedy

1.

To be fair to *The Birth of Tragedy* (1872), one has to forget a few things. Its effect and even fascination were due to what was wrong with it—its practical application to Wagnerism,[69] as if that were a symptom of *ascent*. In this respect, this essay was an event in the life of Wagner: it was only from that moment on that Wagner's name elicited high hopes. People still remind me of this today, sometimes even in the context of *Parsifal*—how I am the one who has it on his conscience that such a high opinion of the *cultural value* of this movement gained prevalence.

Several times I saw this book cited as "The Rebirth of Tragedy out of the Spirit of Music": what people had ears for was only a new formula for the art, the intentions, the task of *Wagner*—and what was really valuable in the essay was ignored. "Greekness and Pessimism" would have been a less ambiguous title—suggesting the first instruction about how the Greeks got over their pessimism, how they *overcame* it.

Precisely their tragedies prove that the Greeks were *not* pessimists: Schopenhauer went wrong at this point, as he went wrong everywhere.

Taken up with some degree of neutrality, *The Birth of Tragedy* looks quite untimely: one would never dream that it was begun amid the thunder of the battle of Wörth. Before the walls of Metz, on cold September nights, while on duty as a medical orderly, I thought through these problems. One might sooner believe that the essay was fifty years older. It is indifferent toward politics—"un-German," to use the language of the present time—it smells offensively Hegelian, and the doleful perfume[70] of Schopenhauer sticks only to a few formulas. An "idea"—the antithesis of the Dionysian and the Apollonian—translated into the realm of metaphysics; history itself as the development of this "idea"; in tragedy, this antithesis is sublated[71] into a unity; and in this perspective, things that had never before faced each other are suddenly juxtaposed, used to illuminate each other, and comprehended—opera, for example, and the revolution.

The two decisive *innovations* of the book are, first, its understanding of the Dionysian phenomenon among the Greeks: for the first time, a psychological analysis of this phenomenon is offered, and it is considered as one root of the whole of Greek art. Secondly, there is the understanding of Socratism: Socrates is recognized for the first time as an instrument of Greek disintegration, as a typical decadent. "Rationality" *against* instinct. "Rationality" at any price as a dangerous force that undermines life.

Profound, hostile silence about Christianity throughout the book. Christianity is neither Apollonian nor Dionysian; it negates all aesthetic values—the only values recognized in *The Birth of Tragedy:* it is nihilistic in the most profound sense, while in the Dionysian symbol the ultimate limit of affirmation is attained. There is one allusion to Christian priests as a "vicious kind of dwarfs" who are "subterranean."

2.

This beginning is exceedingly strange. I had discovered the only equivalent and counterpart in history for my own inmost experience—and thus became the first to comprehend the wonderful phenomenon of the Dionysian. At the same time, my discovery that Socrates was a decadent proved unequivocally how little the sureness of my psychological grasp would be endangered by any moral idiosyncrasy: seeing morality itself as a symptom of decadence is an innovation and a singularity of the first rank in the history of knowledge. How high had I jumped with these two insights above the wretched and shallow chatter about optimism versus pessimism!

I was the first to see the real opposition: the degenerating instinct that turns against life with subterranean vengefulness (Christianity, the philosophy of Schopenhauer, in a certain sense already the philosophy of Plato, and all of idealism as typical forms) versus a formula for the highest affirmation, born of fullness, of overfullness, a yes-saying without reservation, even to suffering, even to guilt, even to everything that is questionable and strange in existence.

This ultimate, most joyous, most wantonly extravagant yes to life represents not only the highest insight but also the *deepest,* that which is most strictly confirmed and born out by truth and science. Nothing in existence may be subtracted, nothing is dispensable— those aspects of existence which Christians and other nihilists repudiate are actually on an infinitely higher level in the order of rank among values than that which the instinct of decadence could approve and call good.[72] To comprehend this requires courage and, as a condition of that, an excess of strength: for precisely as far as courage may venture forward, precisely according to that measure of strength one approaches the truth. Knowledge, saying yes to reality, is just as necessary for the strong as cowardice and the flight from reality—as the "ideal" is for the weak, who are inspired by weakness.

They are not free to know: the decadents *need* the lie—it is one of the conditions of their preservation.

Whoever does not merely comprehend the word "Dionysian" but comprehends *himself* in the word "Dionysian" needs no refutation of Plato or Christianity or Schopenhauer—he *smells the decay.*

3.

How I had thus found the concept of the "tragic" and at long last knowledge of the psychology of tragedy, I have explained most recently in *Twilight of the Idols,* p. 139:[73]

> Saying yes to life even in its strangest and hardest problems; the will to life rejoicing over its own inexhaustibility even in the very sacrifice of its highest types—that is what I called Dionysian, that is what I understood as[74] the bridge to the psychology of the tragic poet. Not in order to get rid of terror and pity, not in order to purge oneself of a dangerous affect by its vehement discharge—Aristotle misunderstood[75] it that way—but in order to be oneself the eternal joy of becoming, beyond all terror and pity—that joy which includes even joy in destroying.

In this sense I have the right to understand myself as the first *tragic philosopher*—that is, the most extreme opposite and antipode of a pessimistic philosopher. Before me this transposition of the Dionysian into a philosophical pathos did not exist: *tragic wisdom* was lacking; I have looked in vain for signs of it even among the *great* Greeks in philosophy, those of the two centuries *before* Socrates. I retained some doubt in the case of *Heraclitus,* in whose proximity I feel altogether warmer and better than anywhere else. The affirmation of passing away *and destroying,* which is the decisive feature of a Dionysian philosophy; saying yes to opposition and war; *becoming,* along with a radical repudiation of the very concept of *being*—all this is clearly more closely related to me than anything else thought to date. The doctrine of the "eternal recurrence," that is, of the unconditional and infinitely repeated circular course of all things—this doctrine of Zarathustra *might* in the end have been taught already by Heraclitus. At least the Stoa has traces of it, and the Stoics inherited almost all of their principal notions from Heraclitus.

4.

A tremendous hope speaks out of this essay. In the end I lack all reason to renounce the hope for a Dionysian future of music. Let us look ahead a century; let us suppose that my attempt to assassinate two millennia of antinature and desecration of man were to succeed. That new party of life which would tackle the greatest of all tasks, the breeding of a higher human race, including the relentless destruction of everything that was degenerating and parasitical, would again make possible that excess of life on earth from which the Dionysian state, too, would have to awaken again. I promise a tragic age: the highest art in saying yes to life, tragedy, will be reborn when humanity has weathered the consciousness of the hardest but most necessary wars *without suffering from it.*

A psychologist might still add that what I heard as a young man listening to Wagnerian music really had nothing to do with Wagner; that when I described Dionysian music I described what *I* had heard—that instinctively I had to transpose and transfigure everything into the new spirit that I carried in me. The proof of that, *as strong as any proof can be,* is my essay on *Wagner in Bayreuth:* in all psychologically decisive passages I alone am discussed—and one need not hesitate to put down my name or the word "Zarathustra" where the text has the word "Wagner." The entire picture of the dithyrambic artist is a picture of the preexistent poet of *Zarathustra*, sketched with profundity and without touching even for a moment the Wagnerian reality. Wagner himself had some notion of that; he did not recognize himself in this essay.

Similarly, "the idea of Bayreuth" was transformed into something that should not puzzle those who know my *Zarathustra:* into the great noon at which the most elect consecrate themselves for the greatest of all tasks. Who knows? The vision of a feast that I shall yet live to see.

The pathos of the first pages is world-historical; the glance spoken of on the seventh page is Zarathustra's distinctive glance; Wagner, Bayreuth, the whole petty German wretchedness are a cloud in which an infinite mirage of the future is reflected. Even psychologically, all decisive traits of my own nature are projected into Wagner's—the close proximity of the brightest and the most calamitous forces, the will to power as no man ever possessed it, the ruthless courage of the intellect, the unlimited power to learn without damage to the will to act. Everything in this essay points to the future: the impending return of the Greek spirit, the necessity of counter-Alexanders who will retie the Gordian knot of Greek culture.

Listen to the world-historical accent with which the concept "tragic attitude" is introduced at the end of section 4: this essay is full of world-historical accents. This is the strangest "objectivity" possible: the absolute certainty about what I am was projected on some accidental reality—the truth about me spoke from some gruesome depth. At the beginning of section 9, the *style* of *Zarathustra* is described with incisive certainty and anticipated; and no more magnificent expression could be found for the *event* of *Zarathustra,* the act of a tremendous purification and consecration of humanity, than was found in section 6.[76]

Translated by Walter Kaufmann

From the so-called
Will to Power

Art in the "Birth of Tragedy" (1888)[77]

1.

The conception of the world that one encounters in the background of this book is singularly gloomy and unpleasant: no type of pessimism known hitherto seems to have attained to this degree of malevolence. The antithesis of a real and an apparent world is lacking here: there is only *one* world, and this is false, cruel, contradictory, seductive, without meaning—a world thus constituted is the real world. *We have need of lies* in order to conquer this reality, this "truth," that is, in order to live. That lies are necessary in order to live is itself part of the terrifying and questionable character of existence.

Metaphysics, morality, religion, science—in this book these things merit consideration only as various forms of lies: with their help one can have *faith* in life. "Life *ought* to inspire confidence": the task thus imposed is tremendous. To solve it, man must be a liar by nature, he must be above all an *artist*. And he *is* one: metaphysics, religion, morality, science—all of them only products of his will to art, to lie, to flight from "truth," to *negation* of "truth." This ability itself, thanks to which he violates reality by means of lies, this artistic ability of man par excellence—he has it in common with everything that is. He himself is, after all, a piece of reality, truth, nature: how should he not also be a piece of *genius in lying!*

That the character of existence is to be misunderstood—profoundest and supreme secret motive behind all that is virtue, science, piety, artistry. Never to see many things, to see many things falsely, to imagine many things: oh, how shrewd one still is in circumstances in which one is farthest from thinking oneself shrewd! Love, enthusiasm, "God"—so many subtleties of ultimate self-deception, so many seductions to life, so much faith in life! In those moments in which man was deceived, in which he duped himself, in which he believes in life: oh, how enraptured he feels! What delight! What a feeling of power! How much artists' triumph in the feeling of power! Man has once again become master of "material"—master of truth! And whenever man rejoices, he is always the same in his rejoicing: he rejoices as an artist, he enjoys himself as power, he enjoys the lie as his form of power.

2.

Art and nothing but art! It is the great means of making life possible, the great seduction to life, the great stimulant of life.

Art as the only superior counterforce to all will to denial of life, as that which is anti-Christian, anti-Buddhist, antinihilist par excellence.

Art as the *redemption of the man of knowledge*—of those who see the terrifying and questionable character of existence, who want to see it, the men of tragic knowledge.

Art as the *redemption of the man of action*—of those who not only see the terrifying and questionable character of existence but live it, want to live it, the tragic-warlike man, the hero.

Art as the *redemption of the sufferer*—as the way to states in which suffering is willed, transfigured, deified, where suffering is a form of great delight.

3.

One will see that in this book pessimism, or to speak more clearly, nihilism, counts as "truth." But truth does not count as the supreme value, even less as the supreme power. The will to appearance, to illusion, to deception, to becoming and change (to objective deception) here counts as more profound, primeval, metaphysical than the will to truth, to reality, to being: the latter is itself merely a form of the will to illusion. In the same way, pleasure counts as being more primeval than pain: pain only as conditioned, as a consequence of the will to pleasure (of the will to become, grow, shape, i.e., *to create:* in creation, however, destruction is included). A highest state of affirmation of existence is conceived from which the highest degree of pain cannot be excluded: the *tragic-Dionysian* state.

4.

In this way, this book is even antipessimistic: that is, in the sense that it teaches something that is stronger than pessimism, "more divine" than truth. Nobody, it seems, would more seriously propose a radical negation of life, a really *active* negation even more than merely *saying* No to life, than the author of this book. Except that he knows—he has experience of it, perhaps he has experience of nothing else!—that art is *worth more* than truth.

In the preface, in which Richard Wagner is invited as to a dialogue, this confession of faith, this artists' gospel, appears: "Art as the real task of life, art as life's *metaphysical* activity."[78]

Translated by Walter Kaufmann

Part II

ON TRUTH

From *Five Prefaces to Five Unwritten Books*

On the Pathos of Truth (1872)

I s fame really only the most succulent morsel of our self-love? It is of course attached only to the rarest of men, as an urgent desire, and moreover only to the rarest moments of such men. These are the moments of sudden brilliance and insight, in which a man stretches out his arm as if to create a world, drawing light from within and streaming it out around himself. It was then that he was pierced by the joyful certainty that what lifted him out and transported him into the farthest distance, the loftiness of this one feeling, must not be kept from posterity; in the eternal necessity for all coming generations of these rarest moments, a man recognizes the necessity of his fame; in its entire future mankind needs him, and just as that moment of brilliance and insight is the summation and essence of his being, so, as the man of this moment, he believes himself to be immortal, while all else he casts away and consigns to temporality as dross, corruption, vanity, animality, or as pleonasm.

We view every disappearance and downfall with dissatisfaction, often with amazement, as if we were experiencing in it something virtually impossible. When a tall tree topples we are displeased, and the collapse of a mountain makes us suffer. Each New Year's Eve causes us to feel the mystery of the contradiction between being and becoming. But that an instant of highest world perfection should disappear, so to speak, without posterity and heirs, like a fleeting gleam of light, is something that insults most grievously the moral individual. Rather, his imperative is: what once was there to propagate more beautifully the concept "man" must also be present for all eternity. That the great moments form a chain, that as a cordillera they bind mankind together through the millennia, that the greatest achievements[1] of a bygone time are also great for me, and that the prescient belief of the desire for fame should be fulfilled—that is the fundamental thought of *culture*.

The terrible struggle of culture is touched off by the demand that greatness should be eternal; for everything else that lives cries "No!" Just as the heavy vapors of this earth, which we are all condemned to breathe, swirl around greatness, so, too, what is conventional, small, mean, filling all the nooks and crannies of the world, throws itself impeding, smothering, choking, obscuring, deluding in the path that greatness must follow to immortality. The path leads through the minds of men! Through the minds of wretched, short-lived beings who, as such, are delivered up to narrow needs, constantly surfacing for the same necessities, for a short while and with effort staving off destruction. They want to live, to live a little—at any price. Who would suspect that among them there could be that arduous relay of the torch through which alone greatness lives on? And yet again and again a few awake who feel so inspired by that greatness—as if the life of man were a glorious thing, as if one should regard as the most beautiful fruit of this bitter plant the knowledge that once someone strode proudly and stoically through this existence, that another did so with profundity, a third with compassion, yet all of them leaving behind a *single* lesson: that this existence is lived most beautifully by him who does not hold it in high esteem. While the common man views his span of being with such doleful earnestness, these others knew how to achieve Olympian laughter or at least sublime scorn during their journey to immortality; they often climbed into their graves with irony—for what did they have that could be buried?

Of those who hunger for fame, believing that their coat of arms can be found hanging on a constellation, the most audacious knights must be sought among the *philosophers*. Their work does not direct them toward an "audience," toward the excitement of the masses and the jubilant acclamations of contemporaries; to travel the road alone is part of their essence. Their gift is the rarest and, in a certain sense, most unnatural in nature; even to those equally gifted it is exclusive and hostile. The wall of their self-sufficiency must be adamant[2] if it is not to be destroyed and broken, for everything is in motion against it, men as well as nature. Their journey to immortality is more troublesome and more difficult than any other, and yet no one can be more confident than the philosopher that his journey will reach its goal, since he has no idea where he should stand, if not on the wide outspread pinions of time in its totality; for disdain of that which belongs to the present moment is an integral part of philosophical contemplation. He has the truth; let the wheel of time roll wherever it wants, it will never be able to escape the truth.

It is important to learn that such men have lived. Even musing on idle possibilities, one could never imagine the pride of, say, Heraclitus, who may serve here as our example. In itself, every striving for knowledge seems indeed unsatisfied and unsatisfying; therefore no one, unless taught by history, would be able to believe in so kingly a self-esteem, so limitless a conviction of being the only successful suitor of truth. Such men live in their own solar system; that is where one must seek them. A Pythagoras, an Empedocles also treated themselves with a superhuman respect, indeed with an almost religious deference; yet the sympathetic bond of their great confidence in the transmigration of souls and the unity of all that lives led them back to other men and thus to the rescue of the latter. But only when stiffening with horror in the wildest of mountain wastes can one hope to sense the feeling of solitude that pierced the hermit of the Ephesian temple of Artemis.[3] No overpowering feeling of sympathetic impulses, no desire to aid and rescue emanates from him: he is like a planet without an atmosphere. His eye turned inward with burning intensity stares outward icy and dead, as if in mere semblance. All around him the waves of delusion and folly crash against the very fortress of his pride; with disgust he turns away from them. Yet even men of deep feeling avoid this tragic mask;[4] perhaps such a being would seem more comprehensible in a secluded shrine amidst statues of the gods alongside of cold, magnificent architecture. Amongst men, as a human being, Heraclitus was unbelievable; and if indeed he was seen observing the play of noisy children, he was in any case contemplating what no mortal had ever contemplated in a like situation—the play of Zeus, the great child of the universe, and the eternal joke of world destruction and world creation. Heraclitus did not need people, not even for achieving knowledge; everything that could be gained by questioning them, everything that wise men before him had in this way worked to gain, was unimportant to him. "I search and study myself," he said in a formula used to describe the study of an oracle: as if he, and no one else, were the true fulfiller and perfecter of the Delphic dictum "Know thyself."

Whatever he descried in this oracle he held for immortal wisdom, eternally worthy of being elucidated, in the same sense that the prophetic pronouncements of the Sibyl are immortal. It is enough for mankind even at its farthest remove: let them but interpret, in the manner of oracle sayings, how he, like the Delphic god, "neither states nor conceals." Although he announces this "without laughter, without finery and scented salves," but rather with a "foaming mouth," it *must* penetrate those thousands of years of the future. For the world will always need the truth, hence it will always need Heraclitus, though he does not need the world. What does *he* care about his fame! "Fame among mortals who are constantly flowing away!" as he exclaims disdainfully. That is something for singers and poets and for those who before him were known as "wise" men—such men are welcome to wolf down the most succulent morsel of their self-love; for him, this fare is too vulgar. His fame has import for other men but not for him; his self-love is the love of truth—and it is precisely this truth which tells him that the immortality of mankind needs him, but he does not need the immortality of the man Heraclitus.

The truth! Fervent delusion of a god! Of what concern is the truth to men!

And what was the Heraclitean "truth"!

And where has it gone? A vanished dream, expunged from mankind's countenance with other dreams! It was not the first one![5]

Regarding what we, with proud metaphor, term "world history" and "truth" and "fame," an unfeeling demon might have nothing more to say than the following: "In some remote corner of the universe, which has been poured out glimmering in countless solar systems, there was once a planet on which clever animals invented the *gaining of knowledge*. That was the most arrogant and mendacious minute of world history, but indeed it was only a minute. After nature had taken breath awhile, the planet froze,[6] and the clever animals had to die. And it was time for this to happen: for although they boasted of having gained much knowledge, in the end they had discovered to their great chagrin that all their knowledge was false. They died, and in dying they cursed the truth. That was the nature of these desperate animals who had invented the gaining of knowledge."

This would be the fate of man if he were but an animal of knowledge; truth would drive him to desperation and annihilation, the truth of being eternally condemned to untruth. But the only belief befitting him is that in an accessible truth, in the illusion which approaches so trustingly. Doesn't man actually live *by means of* being continually deluded? Doesn't nature conceal from him almost everything, indeed precisely that which is closest to him, for example his own body, of which he possesses only a fraudulent "consciousness"? He is locked up in this consciousness and nature has thrown away the key. Woe to the fateful greedy curiosity of the philosopher who longs to peer for a moment through a crack and see out beyond and below the chamber of consciousness: perhaps he will then have a glimpse of how man, in the carelessness of his ignorance, reposes on what is voracious, insatiable, disgusting, ruthless, murderous; hanging, as it were, in dreams on the back of a tiger.

"Leave him hanging," cries *art*. "Wake him," cries the philosopher in the pathos of truth. Yet even while he believes that he is shaking the sleeper, he himself is sinking into an even deeper magical slumber—perhaps he will dream then of "ideas" or of immortality. Art is mightier than the quest for knowledge; while the former desires life, the latter achieves as its final goal only—annihilation.

Translated by Bruce Armstrong

On Truth and Falsity in Their Extramoral Sense (1873)

1.

In some remote corner of the universe, which has been poured out glimmering in countless solar systems, there was once a planet on which clever animals invented the gaining of knowledge. It was the most arrogant and mendacious minute of "world history," but indeed it was only a minute. After nature had taken breath awhile, the planet froze, and the clever animals had to die.—Someone might write a fable after this style, and yet he would not have illustrated sufficiently how wretched, how shadowlike and transitory, how purposeless and random the human intellect appears in nature. There were eternities during which it did not exist, and when it has passed away, nothing will have happened. For this intellect has no further mission transcending the life of man. No, it is purely human and none but its owner and procreator regards it with such pathos as to suppose that the world revolves around it. If, however, we and the gnat could understand each other we should learn that even the gnat swims through the air with the same pathos, and feels within itself the flying center of the world. Nothing in nature is so reprehensible or so insignificant that it will not, at the smallest puff of that force cognition, immediately swell up like a balloon; and just as a mere porter wants to have his admirer, so the very proudest man, the philosopher, imagines he sees from all sides the eyes of the universe telescopically directed upon his actions and thoughts.

It is remarkable that this is accomplished by the intellect, which, after all, has been given to the most unfortunate, the most delicate, the most transient beings only as an expedient, in order to detain them for a moment in existence, from which without that extra gift they would have every cause to flee as swiftly as Lessing's son.[7] That arrogance connected with cognition and sensation, spreading blinding fogs before the eyes and over the sense of men, deludes itself therefore as to the value of existence, owing to the fact that it bears within itself the most flattering evaluation of cognition. Its most general effect is deception; but even its most particular effects have something of deception in their nature.

The intellect, as a means for the preservation of the individual, develops its chief power in dissimulation; for it is by dissimulation that the feebler and less robust individuals preserve themselves, since it has been denied them to fight the battle of existence with horns or the sharp teeth of beasts of prey. In man this art of dissimulation reaches its acme of perfection: in him deception, flattery, falsehood and fraud, slander, display, pretentiousness, disguise, cloaking convention, and playacting in front of others and in front of himself, in short, the continual fluttering to and fro around the *one* flame—vanity: all these things are so much the rule, and the law, that few things are more incomprehensible than the way in which an honest and pure impulse to truth could have arisen among men. They are deeply immersed in illusions and dream fancies; their eyes glance only over the surface of things and see "forms"; their sensation nowhere leads to truth, but contents itself with receiving stimuli and, so to speak, with playing a blindly groping game on the back of things. In addition to that, at night man allows his dreams to lie to him throughout his life, without his moral sense ever trying to prevent them; whereas men are said to exist who by the exercise of a strong will have overcome the habit of snoring. What indeed *does* man know about himself! Is he able even once to see himself complete, placed as it were in an illuminated glass case? Does not nature keep secret from him most things, even about his body, e.g., the convolutions of the intestines, the quick flow of the blood currents, the intricate vibrations of the fibers, so as to banish and lock him up in proud, fraudulent knowledge? Nature threw away the key; and woe to the fateful curiosity which might be able for a moment to look out and down through a crevice in the chamber of consciousness, and discover that man, in the careless indifference of his ignorance, is resting on what is ruthless, voracious, insatiable, and murderous, and, as it were, hanging in dreams on the back of a tiger. Whence indeed, with this state of affairs, arises the impulse to truth?

As far as the individual tries to preserve himself against other individuals, in the natural state of things he uses the intellect in most cases only for dissimulation; since, however, man both from necessity and boredom wants to exist socially and in herds, he must make peace and at least endeavor to cause the most extreme *bellum omnium contra omnes*[8] to disappear from his world. This peace treaty brings with it a something which looks like the first step towards the attainment of that enigmatical bent for truth. For that which henceforth is to be "truth" is now fixed; that is to say, a uniformly valid and binding designation of things is invented, and the legislature of language also gives the first laws of truth: since here, for the first time, originates the contrast between truth and falsity. The liar uses the valid designations, the words, in order to make the unreal appear as real; e.g., he says, "I am rich," whereas the right designation for his state would be "poor." He abuses the fixed conventions by convenient substitution or even inversion of terms. If he does this in a selfish and moreover harmful fashion, society will no longer trust him but will even exclude him. In this way men avoid not so much being defrauded, but being injured by fraud. At bottom, at this juncture, too, they hate not deception, but the evil, hostile consequences of certain species of deception. And it is in a similarly limited sense only that man desires truth: he covets the agreeable, life-preserving consequences of truth; he is indifferent toward pure, ineffective knowledge; he is even inimical toward truths that possibly might prove harmful or destroying. And moreover, what, after all, are those conventions of language? Are they possibly products of knowledge, of the love of truth; do the designations and the things coincide? Is language the adequate expression of all realities?

Only by means of forgetfulness can man ever arrive at imagining that he possesses "truth" in that degree just indicated. If he does not mean to content himself with truth in the shape of tautology, that is, with empty husks, he will always obtain illusions instead of truth. What is a word? The expression of a nerve stimulus in sounds. But to infer a cause outside us from the nerve stimulus is already the result of a wrong and unjustifiable application of the proposition of causality. Indeed, if truth alone had been decisive with the genesis of language, if only the point of view of certainty had determined designations, could we dare to say: the stone is hard, as if "hard" was known to us otherwise and not merely as an entirely subjective stimulus! We divide things according to genders; we designate the tree as masculine,[9] the plant as feminine:[10] what arbitrary metaphors! How far flown beyond the canon of certainty! We speak of a "serpent"; the designation fits nothing but the sinuosity, and could therefore also appertain to the worm. What arbitrary demarcations! what one-sided preferences given sometimes to this, sometimes to that quality of a thing! The different languages placed side by side show that with words, truth or adequate expression matters little: for otherwise there would not be so many languages. The "thing-in-itself" (it is just this which would be the pure ineffective truth) is also quite incomprehensible to the creator of language and not worth making any great endeavor to obtain. He designates only the relations of things to men, and for their expression he calls to his help the most daring metaphors. A nerve stimulus, first transformed into an image! First metaphor! The image again copied into a sound! Second metaphor! And each time he leaps completely out of one sphere right into the midst of an entirely different one. One can imagine a man who is completely deaf and has never had a sensation of tone and of music; just as this man will possibly marvel at Chladni's sound figures in the sand, will discover their cause in the vibrations of the string, and will then proclaim that now he knows what man calls "tone": even so does it happen to us all with language. When we talk about trees, colors, snow, and flowers, we believe we know something about the things themselves, and yet we only possess metaphors of the things, and these metaphors do not in the least correspond to the original essentials. Just as the sound shows itself as a sandfigure, in the same way the enigmatic x of the thing-in-itself is first perceived as nerve stimulus, then as image, and finally as sound. At any rate, then, the genesis of language did not proceed along logical lines, and the whole material in which and with which the man of truth, the investigator, the philosopher works and builds originates, if not from some never-never land, at any rate not from the essence of things.

Let us especially think about the formation of ideas. Every word immediately becomes an idea when, rather than serving as a sort of reminder of that unique, entirely individualized first experience to which it owes its origin, it instead simultaneously must fit innumerable, more or less similar (which really means never equal and, therefore, altogether unequal) cases. Every idea originates through equating the unequal. As certainly as no one leaf is exactly similar to any other, so certain is it that the idea "leaf" has been formed through an arbitrary omission of these individual differences, through a forgetting of the differentiating qualities, and this idea now awakens the notion that in nature there is, besides the leaves, a something called *the* leaf, perhaps a primal form according to which all leaves were woven, drawn, accurately measured, colored, crinkled, painted, but by unskilled hands, so that no copy had turned out correct and trustworthy as a true copy of the primal form. We call a man "honest"; we ask, why has he acted so honestly today? Our customary answer runs, "On account of his honesty." *The* honesty! That means again: the leaf is the cause of the leaves. We really and truly do not know anything at all about an essential quality that might be called *the* honesty, but we do know about numerous individualized, and therefore unequal, actions which we equate by omission of the unequal, and now designate as honest actions; finally out of them we formulate a *qualitas occulta*[11] with the name "honesty." The disregarding of the individual and real furnishes us with the idea, as it likewise also gives us the form; whereas nature knows of no forms and ideas, and therefore knows no species but only an x, to us inaccessible and indefinable. For our antithesis of individual and species is anthropomorphic, too, and does not come from the essence of things, although, on the other hand, we do not dare to say that it does not correspond to it; for that would be a dogmatic assertion and, as such, just as undemonstrable as its contrary.

What therefore is truth? A mobile army of metaphors, metonymies, anthropomorphisms: in short a sum of human relations which became poetically and rhetorically intensified, metamorphosed, adorned, and after long usage seem to a nation fixed, canonic and binding; truths are illusions of which one has forgotten that they *are* illusions; worn-out metaphors which have become powerless to affect the senses; coins with their images effaced and now no longer of account as coins but merely as metal.

Still, we do not yet know whence the impulse to truth comes, for up to now we have heard only about the obligation which society imposes in order to exist: to be truthful, that is, to use the usual metaphors; therefore, expressed morally: we have heard only about the obligation to lie according to a fixed convention, to lie gregariously in a style binding for all. Now man of course forgets that matters are going thus with him, he therefore lies in that fashion pointed out unconsciously and according to habits of centuries' standing—and by *this very unconsciousness,* by this very forgetting, he arrives at a feeling of truth. Through this feeling of being obliged to designate one thing as "red," another as "cold," a third one as "mute," awakes a moral emotion relating to truth. Out of the antithesis, "liar," whom nobody trusts, whom all exclude, man demonstrates to himself the venerableness, reliability, usefulness of truth. Now as a *"rational"* being he submits his actions to the sway of abstractions; he no longer suffers himself to be carried away by sudden impressions, concrete sensations; he first generalizes all these impressions into paler, cooler ideas, in order to attach to them the ship of his life and actions. Everything which makes man stand out in bold relief against the animal depends on this faculty of transforming the concrete metaphors into an abstract schema, and therefore resolving a perception into an idea. For within the realm of those schemata something becomes possible that never could succeed under the first perceptual impressions: to build up a pyramidal order with castes and grades, to create a new world of laws, privileges, suborders, delimitations, which now stands opposite the other perceptual world of first impressions and assumes the appearance of being the more fixed, general, known, human of the two and therefore the regulating and imperative one. Whereas every metaphor of perception is individual and without its equal and therefore knows how to escape all attempts to classify it, the great edifice of ideas shows the rigid regularity of a Roman columbarium, and in logic breathes forth the sternness and coolness which we find in mathematics. He who has been breathed upon by this coolness will scarcely believe that the idea, too, bony and hexahedral, and permutable as a die, remains, however, only as the *residuum of a metaphor,* and that the illusion of the artistic metamorphosis of a nerve stimulus into images is, if not the mother, then the grandmother of every idea. Now in this aleatory game of ideas, "truth" means to use every die as it is marked, to count its points carefully, to form exact classifications, and never to violate the order of castes and the sequences of rank. Just as the Romans and Etruscans cut up the sky by means of strong mathematical lines and as if into a *templum,* forced a god into the space marked off in this fashion, so every nation has above its head such a sky of ideas divided up mathematically, and it understands the demand for truth to mean that every conceptual god is to be looked for only in *his* own sphere. One may here well admire man, who succeeded in piling up an infinitely complex dome of ideas on a movable foundation and, as it were, on running water, as a powerful genius of architecture. Of course, in order to obtain hold on such a foundation, it must be like an edifice of cobwebs so light as to be carried away by the waves: so firm as not to be blown asunder by every wind. In this way man as an architectural genius rises high above the bee; she builds with wax, which she brings together out of nature; he with the much more delicate material of ideas, which he must first manufacture within himself. He is very much to be admired here—but not on account of his impulse for truth, his bent for pure cognition of things. If somebody hides a thing behind a bush, seeks it again and finds it in the selfsame place, then there is not much to boast of, respecting this seeking and finding; thus, however, matters stand with the seeking and finding of "truth" within the realm of reason. If I make the definition of the mammal and then declare after inspecting a camel, "Behold a mammal," then no doubt a truth is brought to light thereby, but it is of very limited value, I mean it is anthropomorphic through and through, and does not contain one single point which is "true-in-itself," real and universally valid, apart from man. The seeker after such truths seeks at the bottom only the metamorphosis of the world in man; he strives for an understanding of the world as a humanlike thing, and by his battling, gains at best the feeling of an assimilation. Similarly, as the astrologer contemplated the stars in the service of man and in connection with man's happiness and unhappiness, such a seeker contemplates the whole world as related to man, as the infinitely protracted echo of an original sound: man; as the multiplied copy of the one archetype: man. His procedure is to apply man as the measure of all things, whereby he starts from the error of believing that he has these things immediately before him as pure objects. He therefore forgets that the original metaphors of perception *are* metaphors, and takes them for the things themselves.

Only by forgetting that primitive world of metaphors, only by the hardening and stiffening of an original mass of images pouring forth as a fiery liquid out of the primal faculty of human fantasy, only by the invincible faith, that *this* sun, *this* window, *this* table is a truth in itself: in short only by the fact that man forgets himself as subject, and what is more, as an *artistically creating* subject: only by all this does he live with some repose, safety, and consequence. If he were able to get out of the prison walls of this faith, even for an instant only, his "self-consciousness" would be destroyed at once. Already it costs him some trouble to admit to himself that the insect and the bird perceive a world different from his own, and that the question, which of the two world perceptions is more accurate, is quite a senseless one, since to decide this question it would be necessary to apply the standard of *right perception,* i.e., to apply a standard which *does not exist.* On the whole it seems to me that the "right perception"—which would mean the adequate expression of an object in the subject—is a nonentity full of contradictions: for between two utterly different spheres, as between subject and object, there is no causality, no accuracy, no expression, but, at the utmost, an *aesthetic* relation—I mean an allusive transposition, a stammering translation into quite a distinct foreign language, for which purpose, however, there is needed at any rate an intermediate sphere, an intermediate force, freely composing and freely inventing. The word "phenomenon" contains many seductions, and on that account I avoid it as much as possible, for it is not true that the essence of things appears in the empiric world. A painter who had no hands and wanted to express the picture distinctly present to his mind by the agency of song, would still reveal much more with this switching from one medium than the empirical world reveals about the essence of things. The very relation of a nerve stimulus to the produced image is in itself no necessary one; but if the same image has been reproduced millions of times and has been the inheritance of many successive generations of man, and in the end appears each time to all mankind as the result of the same cause, then it attains finally for man the same importance as if it were *the* unique, necessary image and as if that relation between the original nerve stimulus and the image produced were a close relation of causality: just as a dream eternally repeated would be perceived and judged as though real. But the hardening and stiffening of a metaphor does not at all guarantee the necessity and exclusive justification of that metaphor.

Surely every human being who is at home with such contemplations has felt a deep distrust against any idealism of that kind, as often as he has distinctly convinced himself of the eternal rigidity, omnipresence and infallibility of nature's laws: he has arrived at the conclusion that as far as we can penetrate the heights of the telescopic and the depths of the microscopic world, everything is quite secure, complete, infinite, determined, and continuous. Science will eternally be able to dig in these shafts with success, and all things found are sure to have to harmonize and not to contradict one another. How little does this resemble a product of fantasy, for if it were one it would necessarily betray somewhere its nature of appearance and unreality. Against this it may be objected in the first place that if each of us had for himself a different sensibility, if we ourselves were only able to perceive sometimes as a bird, sometimes as a worm, sometimes as a plant, or if one of us saw the same stimulus as red, another as blue, if a third person ever perceived it as a tone, then nobody would talk of such an orderliness of nature, but would conceive of her only as an extremely subjective structure. Secondly, what is, for us in general, a law of nature? It is not known in itself but only in its effects, which is to say, in its relations to other laws of nature, which again are known to us only as sums of relations. Therefore all these relations always refer merely to each other and are absolutely incomprehensible to us in their essence; only that which we add: time, space, i.e., relations of sequence and numbers, are really known to us in them. Everything wonderful, however, that we marvel at in the laws of nature, everything that demands an explanation and might seduce us into distrusting idealism, lies really and solely in the mathematical rigor and inviolability of the conceptions of time and space. These, however, we produce within ourselves and throw them forth with that necessity with which the spider spins; since we are compelled to conceive all things under these forms only, then it is no longer wonderful that in all things we actually conceive none but these forms: for they all must bear within themselves the laws of number, and this very idea of number is the most marvelous in all things. All obedience to law which impresses us so forcibly in the orbits of stars and in chemical processes coincides at bottom with those qualities which we ourselves attach to those things, so that it is we who thereby make the impression upon ourselves. Whence it clearly follows that the artistic formation of metaphors with which every sensation in us begins, already presupposes those forms, and is therefore only consummated within them; only out of the persistency of these primal forms can the possibility be explained how afterwards out of the metaphors themselves a structure of ideas could again be compiled. For the latter is an imitation of the relations of time, space, and number in the realm of metaphors.

2.

As we saw, it is *language* which has worked originally at the construction of ideas; in later times it is *science*. Just as the bee simultaneously works on the cells and fills them with honey, thus science works irresistibly at the great columbarium of ideas, the cemetery of perceptions, builds ever newer and higher stories; supports, purifies, renews the old cells, and endeavors above all to fill that gigantic framework and to arrange within it the whole of the empirical world, i.e., the anthropomorphic world. And as the man of action binds his life to reason and its ideas in order to avoid being swept away and losing himself, so the seeker after truth builds his hut close to the towering edifice of science in order to aid in its construction and to find protection behind its existing bulwarks. And he needs protection. For there are awful powers which continually press upon him, and which confront the "truth" of science with "truths" fashioned in quite another way, bearing crests[10] of the most heterogeneous character.

That impulse towards the formation of metaphors, that fundamental impulse of man which we cannot reason away for one moment—for thereby we should reason away man himself—is in truth not defeated nor even subdued by the fact that out of its evaporated products, the ideas, a regular and rigid new world has been built as a fortress to dominate it. This impulse seeks for itself a new realm of action and another riverbed, and finds it in *myth* and more generally in *art*. This impulse constantly confuses the rubrics and cells of the ideas by producing new transpositions, metaphors, metonymies; it constantly shows its passionate longing to make the existing world of waking man as motley and irregular, as illogically incoherent, as attractive and eternally new as the world of dreams. For indeed, waking man per se is only clear about his being awake through the rigid and orderly fabric of ideas, and it is for this very reason that he sometimes comes to believe that he is dreaming when that fabric of ideas is for a moment torn by art. Pascal is quite right when he asserts that, if the same dream came to us every night, we should be just as much occupied by it as by the things which we see every day; to quote his words, "If an artisan were certain that he would dream every night for fully twelve hours that he was a king, I believe that he would be just as happy as a king who dreams every night for twelve hours that he is an artisan." The wide-awake day of a mythically aroused people, let us say of the earlier Greeks, is in fact through the continually working wonder, which the *mythos* presupposes, more akin to the dream than to the day of the thinker sobered by science. If every tree may at some time talk as a nymph, or a god, under the disguise of a bull, carry away virgins; if the goddess Athene herself be suddenly seen while, with a beautiful team, she drives, accompanied by Pisistratus, through the markets of Athens—and every honest Athenian did believe this—at any moment, as in a dream, everything is possible; and all nature swarms around man as if she were nothing but the masquerade of the gods, who found it a huge joke to deceive man by assuming all possible forms.

Man himself, however, has an invincible tendency to let himself be deceived, and he is like one enchanted with happiness when the rhapsodist narrates to him epic romances in such a way that they appear real, or when the actor on the stage makes the king appear more kingly than reality shows him. Intellect, that master of dissimulation, is free and dismissed from its service as slave, so long as it is able to deceive without *injuring,* and then it celebrates its Saturnalia. Never is it richer, prouder, more luxuriant, more skillful and daring; with a creator's delight it throws metaphors into confusion, shifts the boundary stones of the abstractions, so that, for instance, it designates the stream as the mobile way which carries man to that place whither he would otherwise go. Now it has thrown off its shoulders the emblem of servitude. Hitherto with gloomy officiousness it endeavored to point out the way to a poor individual coveting existence, and it fared forth for plunder and booty like a servant for his master, but now it itself has become a master and may wipe from its countenance the expression of indigence. Whatever it now does, compared with its former doings, bears within itself dissimulation, just as its former doings bore the character of distortion. It copies human life, but takes it for a good thing and seems to rest quite satisfied with it. That enormous framework of ideas, by clinging to which needy man saves himself through life, is to the freed intellect only a scaffolding and a toy for its most daring feats, and when it smashes it to pieces, throws it into confusion, and then reassembles it, ironically, pairing the strangest, separating the nearest items, it manifests that it has no use for those makeshifts of exigency, and that it is now no longer led by ideas but by intuitions. From these intuitions no regular road leads into the land of the spectral schemata, the abstractions; for them the word is not made; when man sees them he is dumb, or speaks in forbidden metaphors and in unheard-of combinations of ideas, in order to correspond creatively with the impression of the powerful present intuition at least by destroying and jeering at the old barriers of ideas.

There are ages when the rational and the intuitive man stand side by side, the one full of fear of the intuition, the other full of scorn for the abstraction; the latter just as irrational as the former is inartistic. Both desire to rule over life; the one by knowing how to meet the most important needs with foresight, prudence, regularity; the other as an "over-joyous hero" by ignoring those needs and regarding that life only as real which simulates appearance and beauty. Wherever intuitive man, as, for instance, in the earlier history of Greece, brandishes his weapons more powerfully and victoriously than his opponent, there, under favorable conditions, a culture can develop and art can establish her rule over life. That dissembling, that denying of neediness, that splendor of metaphorical notions and especially that directness of dissimulation accompany all utterances of such a life. Neither the house of man, nor his way of walking, nor his clothing, nor his earthen jug suggests that necessity invented them, it seems as if they all were intended as the expressions of a sublime happiness, an Olympian cloudlessness, and as it were a playing at seriousness. Whereas the man guided by ideas and abstractions only wards off misfortune by means of them, without even enforcing for himself happiness out of the abstractions; whereas he strives after the greatest possible freedom from pains, the intuitive man dwelling in the midst of culture has from his intuitions a harvest: besides the warding off of evil, he attains a continuous inpouring of illumination, enlivenment, and redemption. Of course, when he *does* suffer, he suffers more: and he even suffers more frequently since he cannot learn from experience, but again and again falls into the same ditch into which he has fallen before. In suffering he is just as irrational as in happiness; he cries aloud and finds no consolation. How different matters are in the same misfortune with the Stoic, taught by experience and ruling himself by ideas! He who otherwise only looks for uprightness, truth, freedom from deceptions, and shelter from ensnaring and sudden attack, in his misfortune performs the masterpiece of dissimulation, just as the other did in his happiness; he shows no twitching mobile human face but, as it were, a mask with dignified, harmonious features; he does not cry out and does not even alter his voice; when a heavy thundercloud bursts upon him, he wraps himself up in his cloak, and with slow and measured step walks away from beneath it.

Translated by Maximilian A. Mügge

Part III

APHORISMS, ESSAYS, NOTES

From *Untimely Meditations* and Related Writings

On the Use and Disadvantage of History for Life (1874)

(Selection)

1.

[Youth] knows the remedies and medicines for the historical disease, for an excess of history. What are they called?

It is no marvel that they bear the names of poisons—the antidotes to history are the *unhistorical* and the *suprahistorical*. . . .

By the word "unhistorical" I mean the art and power of being able to *forget* and enclose oneself within a limited *horizon;* I call those forces "suprahistorical" which turn the eyes from the process of becoming to that which gives existence an eternal and immutable character, to *art* and *religion*. *Science*—for it is science that would speak of poisons—sees in this power, in these forces, hostile forces and powers: for it considers only that view of things to be true and right, and therefore scientific, which sees everything as a result of the process of becoming, as historical, and nothing as immutably existent and eternal. Thus it lives in a deep antagonism towards the eternalizing forces of art and religion; at the same time it hates the act of forgetting that is the death of knowledge, and tries to remove all limitation of horizon and cast men into an infinite boundless sea, whose waves are bright with the clear knowledge—of becoming.

If they could only live therein! Just as towns collapse in an earthquake and become desolate, just as man dwells only fleetingly and with trembling on volcanic ground; so life falls in on itself and becomes weak and spiritless if the *earthquake of ideas*[1] set off by science takes from man the foundation of his peace and security, the belief in what is stable and eternal. Should life dominate knowledge and science, or knowledge life? Which of the two is the higher, and decisive power? There is no room for doubt: life is the higher, and the dominating power, for the knowledge that annihilated life would have annihilated itself as well. Knowledge presupposes life and has the same interest in maintaining it that every creature has in its own preservation. Thus, science must be watched over and controlled by something higher; a *hygienics of life* places itself near science, and one of its maxims runs thus: the unhistorical and the suprahistorical are the natural antidotes against life becoming overgrown by history; they are the cures for the historical disease. It is likely that we who are sick with history will also be sickened by its antidotes. But this is no proof that the treatment we have chosen is wrong. . . .

Translated by Adrian Collins

Schopenhauer as Educator (1874)
(Selection)
6.

. . . Science has the same relationship to wisdom as virtuousness has to holiness: it is cold and dry, it is loveless and knows no deep feelings of dissatisfaction and yearning. It is as useful to itself as it is harmful to its servants, insofar as it transmits its own character into the latter, thereby ossifying their humanity. As long as we essentially mean by culture the furthering of science, culture passes by the great suffering man with pitiless indifference because scholarship sees everywhere only problems of knowledge, and because suffering is really, within its world, something unseemly and incomprehensible, that is, at most, another problem to be solved.

Translated by J. W. Hillesheim
and Malcolm R. Simpson

The Battle between Science and Wisdom
(1875; fragmentary)
(Selections)

Socrates, I have to admit, stands so close to me that I am almost always fighting a battle against him.

. . . Socrates *knocked the whole thing down* the instant it achieved its *closest* proximity to truth; that is particularly *ironic.* . . .

Socrates is *the revenge for Thersites:*[2] wonderful Achilles killed the ugly plebeian Thersites, enraged by his words at the death of Penthesilea;[3] the ugly plebeian Socrates killed the *authority*[4] of the wonderful myth in Greece.

Early Greek philosophy is the philosophy of *nothing but statesmen.* How miserably things stand with our statesmen! That is, by the way, the most important difference between the pre-Socratics and the post-Socratics.

Among them there was not "the dreadful pretension to happiness" that one encounters beginning with Socrates. Everything does not revolve around the condition of their souls; for one cannot think about this condition without danger. Later, the *gnothi seauton*[5] of Apollo was misunderstood. . . .

Repeatedly with the Greeks the older form is *superior,* for example in the *dithyramb* and in the *tragedy.* The danger of the Greeks lay in all varieties of *virtuosity;* with Socrates the virtuosos of life begin, Socrates, the new dithyramb, the new tragedy, *the invention of the rhetorician!*

The rhetorician is a Greek invention! of *the later period.* They invented "form in itself" (and also the philosopher for it).

How should Plato's battle against rhetoric be viewed? He *envies* its influence.

Early Greece *revealed its powers in a series of philosophers.* With Socrates this revelation *breaks off:* he attempts to *create himself all by himself* and to reject all tradition. . . .

These earlier philosophers can be presented as having felt Greek air and habits as *ban* and *bars:* in other words, self-liberators (the battle of Heraclitus against Homer and Hesiod, Pythagoras against secularization, all of them against myth, especially Democritus). They lack something in their nature compared to the Greek artist and presumably also the statesman.

I conceive of them as *forerunners of a reformation* of the Greeks: but not as forerunners of Socrates. Rather, their reformation did not come to pass, with Pythagoras it remained sectarian. A group of occurrences all carrying this spirit of reformation—the *development* of *tragedy*. The *reformer manqué* is *Empedocles:* when he failed, there remained only Socrates. . . .

Fragmentary; translated by Bruce Armstrong

Richard Wagner in Bayreuth (1876)
(Selections)

4.

. . . The gaze with which the mysterious eye of tragedy affixes us is no enervating and paralyzing magic. Nevertheless, it does demand calm as long as it is directed at us; for art is not there for the actual battle, but rather for the moments of calm before and during the battle, for those minutes when both, looking back and anticipating what is coming, we understand its symbolism and, with a feeling of mild fatigue, are approached by a refreshing dream. Day is dawning and the battle is about to begin, the sacred shadows vanish, and art is once more far away from us; but its comfort from that early hour remains with man. Wherever he turns, the individual realizes only too clearly his own shortcomings, his partial and total inadequacy; how could he fight courageously if previously he had not been consecrated to something transcending the individual! The worst torments of the individual—the lack of a communality of knowledge among men, the uncertainty of ultimate insight, and the inequality of men's abilities—all this makes him needful of art. We cannot be happy so long as everything about us suffers and causes suffering for itself; we cannot be moral so long as the course of human events is determined by violence, treachery, and injustice; we cannot even be wise, so long as the whole of mankind does not compete for wisdom, and does not lead the individual into life and knowledge in the wisest possible manner. How, then, would it be possible to endure this feeling of threefold insufficiency if one were not able to recognize something sublime and important in one's struggles, strivings, and defeats, if one did not learn from tragedy how to delight in the rhythm of the great passion and its sacrifice? Art is certainly no teacher or educator of practical conduct: the artist is never in this sense an educator or adviser; the things after which the tragic heroes strive are not necessarily those intrinsically worth striving after. As in a dream so in art, the valuation of things is altered while we are under its spell. What we, during that time, regard as so worthy of effort, and what makes us sympathize with the tragic hero when he prefers death to renouncing the object of his desire, can seldom retain the same value and energy when transferred to everyday life: this is why art is the activity of man at rest. The battles it shows us are simplifications of life's battles; its problems are abbreviations of the infinitely complicated calculations of man's actions and volitions. But from this very fact—that it creates the *illusion* of a simpler world, a more rapid solution of the riddle of life—art derives its greatness and indispensability. No one who suffers from life can do without this illusion, just as no one can do without sleep. The more difficult the insight into the laws of life becomes, the more fervently we yearn for the illusion of simplification, if only for an instant; and the greater becomes the tension between mankind's general knowledge of things and the individual's moral and intellectual capacity. Art exists *to prevent the bow from snapping*.

The individual must be consecrated to something transcending the personal—that is the aim of tragedy: he must forget the terrible anxiety which death and time tend to create in him; for at any moment of his life, at any fraction of time in the whole of his span of years, something sacred may cross his path which will amply compensate him for all his strife and travail. This means *having a tragic outlook*. And if all mankind must perish some day—and who could question this!—it has been given its highest aim for all time to come, namely that of growing together into such unity and oneness that it can, *as a totality*, confront its impending doom with a tragic outlook; this highest task contains the entire ennobling of man; its final repudiation by humanity would be the saddest blow which the soul of the philanthropist could receive. That is how I feel in the matter! There is but *one* hope and *one* guarantee for the future of man, and that is *that his tragic outlook may not die out.* If he ever completely lost it, an agonized cry, the like of which has never been heard, would have to resound all over the world; on the other hand, there is no pleasure more blissful than that of knowing what we know—how tragic thought has once again been born into this world. For this joy is thoroughly transpersonal and general: it is the wild rejoicing of humanity over the guaranteed coherence and continuance of all that is human.

9.

... Wagner's *poetic* ability is shown by his thinking in visible and tangible events, and not in ideas; that is to say, he thinks mythically, as the people have always done. Myth is not founded on thought, as the children of an artificial culture would have us believe; but it is in itself a way of thinking: it conveys an idea of the world, but through the medium of a chain of events, of action and of suffering. *The Ring of the Nibelung* is a huge system of thought without the conceptual form of the latter. A philosopher could perhaps provide its exact equivalent, something which would be entirely devoid of image and action, in which case we would be in possession of the same thing rendered in two disparate modes—the one for the people, and the other for the exact opposite of the people; that is to say, theoretical man. But Wagner makes no appeal to the latter, for theoretical man can know as little of poetry or myth as the deaf man can know of music; both of them being conscious only of movements which seem meaningless to them. It is impossible to appreciate either one of these disparate modes from the standpoint of the other: as long as the poet's spell is upon one, one thinks with him just as though one were merely a feeling, seeing, and hearing creature; the conclusions thus reached are the connections of the events one perceives, and are therefore not logical but actual causalities.

Translated by Anthony M. Ludovici

From *Human, All-Too-Human: A Book for Free Spirits* (1878)

Of First and Last Things

(Selections)

1.

Chemistry of ideas and sensations. Philosophical problems adopt in almost all matters the same form of question as they did two thousand years ago: How can something spring from its opposite (for instance, reason out of unreason, the sentient out of the dead, logic out of unlogic, disinterested contemplation out of desirous volition, life for others out of egoism, truth out of error)? Metaphysical philosophy has helped itself over those difficulties hitherto by denying the origin of one thing in another, and assuming a miraculous origin for more highly valued things, immediately out of the kernel and essence of the "thing in itself." Historical philosophy, on the contrary, which is no longer to be thought of as separate from physical science, the youngest of all philosophical methods, has ascertained in single cases (and presumably this will happen in everything) that there are no opposites except in the usual exaggeration of the popular or metaphysical point of view; and that an error of reason lies at the bottom of the opposition: according to this explanation, strictly understood, there is neither an unegotistical action nor an entirely disinterested point of view; they are both only sublimations in which the fundamental element appears almost evaporated, and is only to be discovered by the closest observation. All that we require, and which can only be given us by the present advance of the single sciences, is a *chemistry* of the moral, religious, aesthetic ideas and sentiments, as well as of those impulses which we experience in ourselves both in the great and in the small phases of cultural and societal intercourse, and even in solitude; but what if this chemistry should result in the fact that also in this case the most beautiful colors have been obtained from base, even despised materials? Would many be inclined to pursue such examinations? Humanity likes to put all questions as to origin and beginning out of its mind; must one not be almost dehumanized to feel a contrary tendency in one's self?

2.

Original fault of philosophers. All philosophers have the common fault that they start from man in his present state and hope to attain their end by an analysis of him. Unconsciously they look upon "man" as an *aeterna veritas,* as a thing unchangeable in all commotion, as a sure measure of things. But everything that the philosopher says about man is really nothing more than testimony about the man of a *very limited* space of time. A lack of the historical sense is the original fault of all philosophers; many, indeed, unconsciously mistake the very latest variety of man, such as has arisen under the influence of certain religions, certain political events, for the permanent form from which one must set out. They do not want to learn that man has developed, that his faculty of knowledge has developed also; whilst for some of them the entire world is spun out of this faculty of knowledge. Now everything *essential* in human development happened in prehistoric times, long before those four thousand years which we know something of; man may not have changed much during this time. But the philosopher sees "instincts" in the present man and takes it for granted that these belong to the unalterable facts of mankind, and, consequently, can furnish a key to the understanding of the world; the entire teleology is so constructed that man of the last four thousand years is spoken of as an *eternal* being, toward which all things in the world have from the beginning a natural direction. But everything results from a process of becoming; there are *no eternal facts,* as there are likewise no absolute truths. Therefore, *historical philosophizing* is henceforth necessary, and with it the virtue of modesty.

6.

The scientific spirit partially but not wholly powerful. The *smallest* subdivisions of science taken separately are dealt with purely objectively—the general, great sciences, on the contrary, regarded as a whole, call up the question—certainly a very nonobjective one— "For what purpose? To what end?" It is this utilitarian considera- tion which causes them to be dealt with less impersonally when taken as a whole than when considered in their various parts. In philosophy, above all, as the apex of the entire pyramid of science, the question as to the utility of knowledge is involuntarily brought forward, and every philosophy has the unconscious intention of ascribing to it the *greatest* usefulness. For this reason there is so much high-flying metaphysics in all philosophies and such a shyness of the apparently unimportant solutions of physics; for the impor- tance of knowledge for life *must* appear as great as possible. Here is the antagonism between the separate provinces of science and philosophy. The latter desires, what art does, to give the greatest possible depth and meaning to life and actions; in the former one seeks knowledge and nothing further, whatever may emerge thereby. So far there has been no philosopher in whose hands phi- losophy has not grown into an apology for knowledge; on this point, at least, every one is an optimist: that the greatest usefulness must be ascribed to knowledge. They are all tyrannized over by logic, and logic is, in its essence, optimism.

7.

The disrupter of science. Philosophy separated from science when it asked the question, "Which is the knowledge of the world and of life which enables man to live most happily?" This happened in the Socratic schools; the veins of scientific investigation were bound up by the point of view of *happiness*—and still are.

26.

Reaction as progress. Now and again there appear rugged, power- ful, impetuous, but nevertheless backward-lagging minds which conjure up once more a past phase of mankind; they serve to prove that the new tendencies against which they are working are not yet sufficiently strong, that they still lack something, otherwise they would show better opposition to those conjurers. Thus, for exam- ple, Luther's Reformation bears witness to the fact that in his cen- tury all the impulses of freedom of the intellect were still uncertain, faint, and youthful; science could not yet lift up its head. Indeed the whole Renaissance seems like an early spring which is almost snowed under again. But in our own century as well, Schopenhauer's metaphysics showed that even now the scientific spirit is not yet strong enough; thus the whole medieval Christian view of the world and concept of man could celebrate its resurrection in Schopenhauer's doctrine, in spite of the long achieved destruction of all Christian dogmas. There is much science in his doctrine, but it does not dominate it: it is rather the old well-known "need for the metaphysical" that does so. It is certainly one of the greatest and quite invaluable advantages which we gain from Schopenhauer, that he occasionally forces our feeling back into older, mightier modes of contemplating the world and man, to which no other path would so easily lead us. The gain to history and justice is very great—I do not think that anyone would so easily succeed now in doing justice to Christianity and its Asiatic relations without Schopenhauer's assistance, which is specially impossible from the basis of Christianity as it still exists. Only after this great *success of justice,* only after we have corrected so essential a point of the historical mode of contemplation that the Age of Enlightenment brought with it, may we again bear onward the banner of enlightenment, the banner with the three names, Petrarch, Erasmus, Voltaire. We have turned reaction into progress.

28.

Ill-famed words. Away with those wearisomely hackneyed terms optimism and pessimism! For the occasion for using them becomes less and less from day to day; only the chatterboxes still find them so absolutely necessary. For why in all the world should anyone wish to be an optimist unless he had a God to defend who *must* have created the best of worlds if he himself be goodness and perfection—what thinker, however, still needs the hypothesis of a God? But every occasion for a pessimistic confession of faith is also lacking when one has no interest in offending the advocates of God, the theologians, or the theologizing philosophers, and in energetically defending the opposite view, that evil reigns, that pain is greater than pleasure, that the world is a bungled piece of work, the manifestation of an ill will to life. But who still bothers about the theologians now—except the theologians? Apart from all theology and combating, it is quite clear that the world is not good and not bad (to say nothing of its being the best or the worst), and that the terms "good" and "evil" have significance only with respect to man, and indeed, perhaps, they are not justified even here in the way they are usually employed; in any case we must get rid of both the calumniating and the glorifying conception of the world.

33.

Error about life necessary for life. Every belief in the value and worthiness of life is based on fallacious thinking; it is only possible through the fact that sympathy for the general life and suffering of mankind is very weakly developed in the individual. Even the rarer people who think beyond themselves do not contemplate this general life, but only limited parts of it. If one understands how to direct one's attention chiefly to the exceptions—I mean to the highly gifted and the uncorrupted souls—if one regards the production of these as the aim of the whole world development and rejoices in their operation, then one may believe in the value of life, because one thereby *overlooks* the other men—one consequently thinks fallaciously. So, too, when one directs one's attention to all mankind, but only considers *one* species of impulses in them, the less egoistical ones, and excuses them with regard to the other instincts, one may then again entertain hopes regarding mankind in general and thereby believe in the value of life, consequently in this case also through fallaciousness of thought. Let one, however, behave in this or that manner: with such behavior one is an *exception* amongst men. Now, most people bear life without any considerable grumbling, and consequently *believe* in the value of existence, but precisely because each one is solely willing and affirming himself, and does not step out of himself like those exceptions; everything extrapersonal is imperceptible to them, or at most seems only a faint shadow. Therefore on this alone is based the value of life for the ordinary everyday man: that he regards himself as more important than the world. The great lack of imagination from which he suffers is the reason why he cannot enter into the feelings of other beings, and therefore sympathizes as little as possible with their fate and suffering. He, on the other hand, who really *could* sympathize therewith, would have to despair of the value of life; were he to succeed in comprehending and feeling in himself the general consciousness of mankind, he would collapse, cursing existence; for mankind as a whole has *no* goals, consequently man, in considering his whole course, cannot find in it his comfort and support, but finds his despair. If, in all that he does, he considers the final aimlessness of man, his own activity assumes in his eyes the character of wastefulness. But to feel oneself wasted—as humanity, not just as an individual—as we see the single blossom of nature wasted, is a feeling above all other feelings. But who is capable of it? Assuredly only a poet, and poets always know how to console themselves.

34.

For tranquillity. But does not our philosophy thus become a tragedy? Does not truth become hostile to life, to that which is better? A question seems to weigh upon our tongue and yet hesitate to make itself heard: whether one *can* consciously remain in untruthfulness? Or, supposing one were *obliged* to do this, would not death be preferable? For there is no longer any "must"; morality, in so far as it had any "must" or "shalt," has been destroyed by our mode of contemplation, just as religion has been destroyed. Knowledge can only allow pleasure and pain, benefit and injury to subsist as motives; but how will these motives agree with the sense of truth? They also contain errors (for, as already said, inclination and aversion, and their very incorrect determinations, practically regulate our pleasure and pain). The whole of human life is deeply immersed in untruthfulness; the individual cannot draw it up out of this well, without thereby taking a deep dislike to his whole past, without finding his present motives—those of honor, for instance—inconsistent, and without opposing scorn and disdain to the passions which impel us toward the future and happiness in the future. Is it true that there remains but one sole way of thinking which brings with it despair as a personal experience, as a theoretical result, a philosophy of destruction? I believe that the decision with regard to the aftereffects of the knowledge will be given through the *temperament* of a man; I could imagine another aftereffect, just as well as the one described, which is possible in certain natures, by means of which a life would arise much simpler, freer from emotions than is the present one, so that though at first, indeed, the old motives of passionate desire might still have strength from old hereditary habit, they would gradually become weaker under the influence of purifying knowledge. One would live at last amongst men, and with one's self as with *Nature,* without praise, reproach, or agitation, feasting one's eyes, as if it were a play, upon much of which one was formerly afraid. One would be free from the emphasis, and would no longer feel the goading, of the thought that one is not only nature or more than nature. Certainly, as already remarked, a good temperament would be necessary for this, an even, mild, and basically joyous soul, a disposition which would not need to be on its guard against malicious tricks and sudden outbreaks, and would not convey in its utterances anything of a grumbling or harsh nature—those well-known vexatious qualities of old dogs and men who have long been chained up. On the contrary, a man from whom the ordinary fetters of life have fallen to such an extent that he continues to live only for the sake of ever better knowledge must be able to renounce without envy and regret much, indeed almost everything that is precious to other men; he must regard as the *all-sufficing* and the most desirable condition the free, fearless soaring over men, customs, laws, and the traditional valuations of things. The joy of this condition he gladly communicates, and he *has* perhaps nothing else to communicate—which constitutes, to be sure, yet another privation and renunciation. If, nevertheless, more is demanded from him, he will point with a friendly shake of his head to his brother, the free man of action, and will perhaps not conceal a little derision, for as regards this "freedom" it is a very peculiar case.

Translated by Helen Zimmern

Concerning the History of Moral Sentiments
(Selections)

38.

Useful in what way? Let it remain undecided whether psychological observation is advantageous or disadvantageous to man; but it is certain that it is necessary, because science cannot do without it. Science, however, has no consideration for ultimate purposes, any more than nature has, but just as the latter occasionally achieves things of the greatest suitableness without intending to do so, so also true science, as the *imitator of nature in ideas,* will occasionally and in many ways further the usefulness and welfare of man and attain that which is suitable—*but also without intending to do so* . . .

102.

"Man always acts rightly." We do not accuse nature of being immoral because it sends a thunderstorm and makes us wet—why do

we call those who injure us immoral? Because in the latter case we take for granted a free will functioning voluntarily; in the former we see necessity. But this distinction is an error. Thus we do not call even intentional injury immoral in all circumstances; for instance, we kill a fly unhesitatingly and intentionally, only because its buzzing annoys us; we punish a criminal intentionally and hurt him in order to protect ourselves and society. In the first case it is the individual who, in order to preserve himself, or even to avoid a mere nuisance, does intentional injury; in the second case it is the state. All morals allow intentional injury in the case of *necessity,* that is, when it is a matter of *self-preservation.* But these two points of view suffice to explain all evil actions committed by men against men: we are desirous of obtaining pleasure or avoiding pain; in any case it is always a question of self-preservation. Socrates and Plato are right: whatever man does, he always does the right thing, that is, he does that which seems to him good (useful) according to the degree of his intellect, the particular standard of his reasonableness.

Translated by Helen Zimmern

The Religious Life
(Selections)
108.

The double fight against evil. When misfortune[6] overtakes us we can surmount it either by eliminating its cause or by altering the effect it has on our sensibilities; in other words, through redefining it as something positive, the usefulness of which will only be evident later. Religion and art (also metaphysical philosophy) work to alter the sensibilities, partly by changing our judgment of experience (for instance, with the help of the phrase "whom the Lord loveth He chasteneth"), partly through the awakening of a pleasure in pain, in emotion generally (whence the tragic art takes its starting point). The more a man is inclined to redefine and arrange meanings, the less he will grasp the causes of evil and eliminate them; the momentary mitigation and narcotization commonly utilized for, say, toothache suffices him even in more serious sufferings. The more the dominion of religions and all arts of narcosis lessens, the more strictly men attend to the actual elimination of evil; which is certainly bad for writers of tragedy, for the material for tragedy is growing scarcer because the domain of pitiless, inexorable fate is growing ever narrower—but worse still for the priests, for they have hitherto lived on the narcotization of human evils.

126.

The art and power of false interpretation. All the visions, terrors, torpors, and ecstasies of the saint are well-known forms of disease, which are only, by reason of deep-rooted religious and psychological errors, differently *interpreted* by him, namely not as diseases. Thus, perhaps, the *daimonion* of Socrates was only a malady of the ear, which he, in accordance with his ruling moral code of thought, *expounded* differently from what would be the case now. It is the same thing with the madness and ravings of the prophets and soothsayers; it is always the degree of knowledge, fantasy, effort, morality in the head and heart of the *interpreters* which has *made* so much of it. For the greatest achievements of the people who are called geniuses and saints, it is necessary that they should secure interpreters by force who *misunderstand* them for the good of mankind.

Translated by Helen Zimmern

From the Soul of Artists and Authors
(Selections)

165.

Genius and insignificance. It is precisely the original artists, those who create out of themselves, who in certain circumstances can bring forth complete emptiness and staleness, while the more dependent natures, the so-called talented ones, are full of memories of all kinds of good things, and even in a state of weakness produce something tolerable. But if the original ones are abandoned by themselves, memory renders them no assistance; they become empty.

212.

Old doubts about the effect of art. Should pity and fear really be discharged through tragedy, as Aristotle would have it, so that the hearers return home colder and quieter? Should ghost stories really make us less fearful and superstitious? In the case of certain physical processes, in the satisfaction of love, for instance, it is true that with the fulfillment of a need there follows an alleviation and temporary decrease in the impulse. But fear and pity are not in this sense the needs of particular organs which require to be relieved. And in time every instinct is even *strengthened* by practice in its satisfaction, in spite of that periodical alleviation. It might be possible that in each single case pity and fear would be soothed and relieved by tragedy; nevertheless, they might, on the whole, be increased by tragic influences, and Plato would be right in saying that tragedy makes us altogether more timid and lachrymose. The tragic poet himself would then of necessity acquire a gloomy and fearful view of the world, and a yielding, irritable, tearful soul; it would also agree with Plato's view if the tragic poets, and likewise the entire part of the community that derived particular pleasure from them, degenerated into ever greater licentiousness and intemperance. But what right, indeed, has our age to give an answer to that great question of Plato's as to the moral influence of art? If we even had art—where have we an influence, *any kind* of an art influence?

222.

What remains of art. It is true that art has a much greater value in the case of certain metaphysical presuppositions, for instance when the belief obtains that the character is unchangeable and that the essence of the world manifests itself continually in all character and action; thus the artist's work becomes the symbol of the *eternally constant*, while according to our views the artist can only endow his image with temporary value, because man on the whole has developed and is mutable, and even the individual man has nothing fixed and constant. The same holds true of another metaphysical presupposition: assuming that our visible world were only an appearance, as metaphysicians declare, then art would come very near to the real world, for there would then be far too much similarity between the world of appearance and the artist's world of images; and the remaining difference would place the meaning of art higher even than the meaning of nature, because art would represent identical forms, the types and models of nature. But those presuppositions are false; and what position does art retain after this acknowledgment? Above all, for millennia it has taught us to look upon life in every shape with interest and pleasure and to carry our feelings so far that at last we exclaim, "However it may be, life is good." This lesson of art, to take pleasure in existence and to regard human life as a piece of nature, without excessive empathy, as an object of regular development—this lesson has grown into us; it reappears as an all-powerful need of knowledge. We could renounce art, but we would not therewith forfeit the ability it has taught us—just as we have given up religion, but not the emotional intensification and exaltation acquired through religion. As the plastic arts and music are the standards of that wealth of feeling really acquired and obtained through religion, so also, after a disappearance of art, the intensity and multiplicity of the joys of life which it had implanted in us would still demand satisfaction. The scientific man is the further development of the artistic man.

223.

The afterglow of art. Just as in old age we remember our youth and celebrate festivals of memory, so in a short time mankind will stand towards art: its relation will be that of a touching memory of the joys of youth. Never, perhaps, in former ages was art grasped so seriously and thoughtfully as now when it appears to be surrounded by the magic of death. We call to mind that Greek city in southern Italy, which once a year still celebrated its Greek feasts, amidst tears and mourning, since foreign barbarism was triumphing ever more over the customs its people brought with them into the land; and never has Hellenism been so much appreciated, nowhere has this golden nectar been drunk with so great delight, as amongst these fast disappearing Hellenes. The artist will soon come to be regarded as a splendid relic, and to him, as to a wonderful stranger on whose power and beauty depended the happiness of former ages, there will be paid such honor as we seldom grant to ourselves. The best in us is perhaps inherited from former times and their sentiments, to which it is hardly possible for us now to return by direct ways; the sun has already disappeared, but the heavens of our life are still glowing and illumined by it, although we can behold it no longer.

Translated by Helen Zimmern

Signs of Higher and Lower Culture
(Selections)

244.

In the neighborhood of insanity. The sum of sensations, knowledge, and experiences, that is, the whole burden of culture, has become so great that an overstraining of nerves and powers of thought is a common danger, indeed the cultivated classes of European countries are throughout neurotic, and almost every one of their great families is on the verge of insanity in one of their members. True, health is now sought in every possible way; but above all a diminution of that tension of feeling, of that oppressive burden of culture, is necessary, which, even though it might be bought at a heavy sacrifice, would at least give us room for the great hope of a *new Renaissance*. To Christianity, to the philosophers, poets, and musicians we owe an abundance of deeply emotional sensations; in order that these may not get beyond our control we must invoke the spirit of science, which on the whole makes us somewhat colder and more sceptical, and in particular cools the faith in final and absolute truths; it is chiefly through Christianity that this faith has grown so wild.

251.

The future of science. To him who works and seeks in it, science gives much pleasure—to him who *learns* its facts, very little. But as all important truths of science must gradually become commonplace and everyday matters, even this small amount of pleasure ceases, just as we have long ceased to take pleasure in learning the admirable multiplication table. Now if science goes on giving less pleasure in itself, and always takes away more pleasure in throwing suspicion on the consolations of metaphysics, religion and art, that greatest of all sources of pleasure, to which mankind owes almost its whole humanity, becomes impoverished. Therefore a higher culture must give man a double brain, two brain chambers, so to speak, one to perceive science and the other to perceive nonscience, which can lie side by side, without confusion, divisible, exclusive; this is a necessity of health. In one part lies the source of strength, in the other lies the regulator; heat must be generated by illusions, one-sidednesses, passions; and the malicious and dangerous consequences of overheating must be averted by the help of scientific cognition. If this necessity of the higher culture is not satisfied, the further course of human development can almost certainly be foretold: the interest in what is true ceases as it provides less pleasure; illusion, error, and fancy reconquer step by step the territory they once dominated, because they are united to pleasure; the ruin of science, the relapse into barbarism, is the next result; mankind must begin to weave its fabric afresh after having, like Penelope, destroyed it during the night. But who will assure us that it will always find the necessary strength for this?

261.

. . . *Oh! Greek history passes so quickly!* Since then life has never been lived so extravagantly and in so boundless a manner. I cannot persuade myself that the history of the Greeks followed that *natural* course for which it is so celebrated. They were much too variously gifted to be *gradual* in the orderly manner of the tortoise when running a race with Achilles, and that is called natural development. The Greeks went rapidly forward, but equally rapidly downwards; the movement of the whole machine is so intensified that a single stone thrown amid its wheels would make it fly apart. Such a stone, for instance, was Socrates; the hitherto so wonderfully regular, although certainly too rapid, development of the philosophical science was destroyed in one night. It is no idle question whether Plato, had he remained free from the Socratic charm, would not have discovered a still higher type of the philosophic man, which type is forever lost to us. We look into the ages before him as into a sculptor's workshop of such types. The fifth and sixth centuries B.C. seemed to promise something more and higher even than they produced; but they stopped short at promising and announcing. And yet there is hardly a greater loss than the loss of a type, of a new, hitherto undiscovered highest *possibility of the philosophic life.* Even of the older types the greater number are badly transmitted; it seems to me that all philosophers, from Thales to Democritus, are remarkably difficult to recognize, but whoever succeeds in re-creating these figures walks amongst specimens of the mightiest and purest type. This ability is certainly rare; it was even absent in those later Greeks who occupied themselves with the knowledge of the older philosophy; Aristotle, especially, hardly seems to have had eyes in his head when he stands before these earlier ones. And thus it appears as if these splendid philosophers had lived in vain, or as if they had only been intended to pave the way for the quarrelsome and talkative followers of the Socratic schools. As I have said, here is a gap, a break in development; some great misfortune must have happened, and the only statue which might have revealed the meaning and purpose of that great artistic training was either broken or unsuccessful; what actually happened has remained forever a secret of the workshop. . . .

272.

Phases of individual culture.[7] The strength and weakness of intellectual productiveness depend far less on inherited talents than on the accompanying amount of *energy*. Most educated young people of thirty begin to decline at this early solstice of their lives and are afterwards uninterested in new intellectual changes. Therefore, for the salvation of a constantly increasing culture, a new generation is immediately necessary, which will not do very much either, for in order to acquire for himself the father's culture, the son must exhaust almost all the inherited energy which the father himself possessed at that stage of life when his son was born; with what little is left over he gets further on (for as here the road is being traversed for the second time progress is a little quicker; in order to learn that which the father knew, the son does not consume quite so much strength). Men of great energy, like Goethe, for instance, get through almost more than four generations in succession would be capable of; but then they advance too quickly, so that the rest of mankind only catches up with them in the next century, and even then perhaps not completely, because the coherence of culture and the continuity of development have been weakened by the frequent interruptions. Men catch up more quickly with the ordinary phases of intellectual culture which has been acquired in the course of history. Nowadays they begin to acquire culture as religiously inclined children, and perhaps about their tenth year these sentiments attain to their highest point, and are then changed into weakened forms (pantheism), while they draw near to science; they entirely pass by God, immortality, and such things, but are overcome by the witchcraft of a metaphysical philosophy. Eventually they find even this unworthy of belief; art, on the contrary, seems to vouchsafe more and more, so that for a time metaphysics barely continues to exist either as a transition to art or as an artistically transfiguring temperament. But the scientific sense grows more imperious and conducts men to natural sciences and history, and particularly to the severest methods of knowledge, while art is allotted an increasingly milder and less exacting importance. All this usually happens within the first thirty years of a man's life. It is the recapitulation of an assignment for which humanity had labored perhaps thirty thousand years.

276.

Microcosm and macrocosm of culture. The best discoveries about culture man makes within himself when he finds two heterogeneous powers ruling therein. Supposing someone were living as much in love for the plastic arts or for music as he was carried away by the spirit of science, and that he were to regard it as impossible for him to end this contradiction by the destruction of one and complete liberation of the other power, there would therefore remain nothing for him to do but to erect around himself such a large edifice of culture that those two powers might both dwell within it, although at different ends, while between them there dwelt reconciling, intermediary powers, with predominant strength to quell, in case of need, the rising conflict. But such an edifice of culture in the single individual will bear a great resemblance to the culture of entire periods, and will afford continuous analogical teaching concerning it. For wherever the great architecture of culture manifested itself, it was its mission to compel opposing powers to agree, by means of an overwhelming accumulation of other less irreconcilable powers, without thereby oppressing and fettering them.

278.

The simile of the dance. It must now be regarded as a decisive sign of great culture if someone possesses sufficient strength and flexibility to be as pure and rigorous in the pursuit of knowledge as, in other moments, to be capable of giving poetry, religion, and metaphysics a hundred paces' start and then feeling their force and beauty. Such a position amid two such different demands is very difficult, for science urges the absolute supremacy of its methods, and if this insistence is not yielded to, there arises the other danger of a weak wavering between different impulses. Meanwhile, to provide a glimpse in simile at least, on a solution of this difficulty, it may be remembered that *dancing* is not the same as a dull reeling to and fro between different impulses. Culture at its highest level will resemble a bold dance—wherefore, as has been said, there is need of much strength and suppleness.

Translated by Helen Zimmern

Man in Society
(Selection)
361.

The experience of Socrates. If one has become a master in one thing, one has generally remained, precisely thereby, a complete dabbler in most other things; but one forms the very reverse opinion, as was already experienced by Socrates. This is the annoyance which makes association with masters disagreeable.

Translated by Helen Zimmern

Man Alone by Himself
(Selection)
635.

On the whole, scientific methods are at least as important results of investigation as any other results, for the scientific spirit is based upon a knowledge of method, and if the methods were lost, all the results of science could not prevent the renewed prevalence of superstition and absurdity. Clever people may *learn* as much as they like of the results of science, but one still notices in their conversation, and especially in the hypotheses they make, that they lack the scientific spirit; they do not possess that instinctive distrust of the deviations of thinking which, in consequence of long training, has taken root in the soul of every scientific man. It is enough for them to find any kind of hypothesis on a subject, they are then all on fire for it, and imagine the matter is thereby settled. To have an opinion is with them equivalent to immediately becoming fanatical for it, and finally taking it to heart as a conviction. In the case of an unexplained matter, they become heated for the first idea that comes into their head which has any resemblance to an explanation—a course from which the worst results constantly follow, especially in the field of politics. On that account everybody should nowadays have become thoroughly acquainted with at least *one* science, for then he would at least know what is meant by method, and how necessary is the utmost circumspection. To women in particular, this advice is to be given at present: as to those who are irretrievably the victims of all hypotheses, especially when these have the appearance of being witty, attractive, enlivening, and invigorating. Indeed, on close inspection one sees that by far the greater number of educated people still desire convictions from a thinker, and nothing but convictions, and that only a small minority want *certainty.* The former want to be forcibly carried away in order thereby to obtain an increase of strength; the latter few have the detached interest which disregards personal advantages, the increase of strength. The former class, who greatly predominate, are always reckoned upon when the thinker comports himself and labels himself as a *genius,* and thus views himself as a higher being to whom authority belongs. In so far as genius of this kind upholds the ardor of convictions, and arouses distrust of the cautious and modest spirit of science, it is an enemy of truth, however much it may think itself the wooer thereof.

Translated by Helen Zimmern

From
Human, All-Too-Human II

Mixed Opinions and Maxims (1879)
(Selections)

90.

The good and the good conscience. You hold that all good things have at all times had a good conscience? Science, which is certainly a very good thing, has come into the world without such a conscience and quite free from all pathos; instead it has come clandestinely, by roundabout ways, walking with shrouded or masked face like a criminal, and always with the *feeling* at least of being a smuggler. Good conscience has bad conscience for its stepping stone,[8] not for its opposite. For all that is good has at one time been new and consequently strange, antimoral, *immoral,* and has gnawed like a worm at the heart of the fortunate discoverer.

98.

Theatricality and honesty of unbelievers. There is no book that contains in such abundance or expresses so faithfully all that man occasionally finds salutary—ecstatic inward happiness, ready for sacrifice or death in the belief in and contemplation of *his* truth—as the book that tells of Christ. From that book a clever man may learn all the means whereby a book can be made into a world book, a *vade-mecum* for all,[9] and especially that master means of representing everything as discovered, nothing as future and uncertain. All influential books try to leave the same impression, as if the widest intellectual horizon[10] were circumscribed here and as if about the sun that shines here every planet visible at present or in the future must revolve.—Must not then all *purely scientific* books be poor in influence on the same grounds as such books are rich in influence? Is not the book fated to live humbly and among humble folk, only to be crucified in the end and never resurrected? In relation to what the religious proclaim regarding their "knowledge" and their "holy" spirit, are not all upright men of science "poor in spirit"? Can any religion demand more self-denial and draw the selfish out of themselves more inexorably than science?— This and similar things we may say, in any case with a certain theatricality, when we have to defend ourselves against believers, for it is hardly possible to conduct a defense without a certain amount of theatricality. But between ourselves our language must be more honest, and we employ a freedom that those believers are not even allowed, in their own interests, to understand. Away, then, with the monastic cowl of self-denial, with the appearance of humility! Much more and much better—so rings our truth! If science were not linked with the *pleasure* of knowledge, the *utility* of the thing known, what should we care for science? If a little faith, love, and hope did not lead our souls to knowledge, what would attract us to science? And if in science the ego means nothing, still the inventive, happy ego, every upright and industrious ego, means a great deal in the republic of the men of science. The homage of those who pay homage, the joy of those whom we wish well or honor, in some cases glory and a moderate degree of personal immortality, is the attainable reward for every suppression of personality: to say nothing here of lesser possibilities and rewards, although it is precisely on their account that the majority have sworn, and always continue to swear, fidelity to the laws of the republic and of science. If we had not remained in some degree *unscientific*, what would science matter to us? Taking everything together and speaking in plain language: "To a purely knowing being knowledge would be indifferent."—Not the quality but the quantity of faith and devoutness distinguishes us from the pious, the believers. We are content with less. But should one of them cry out to us: "Be content and show yourselves contented!" we could easily answer: "As a matter of fact, we do not belong to the most discontented class. But you, if your faith makes you happy, show yourselves to be happy. Your faces have always done more harm to your faith than our arguments! If that glad message of your Bible were written in your faces, you would not need to demand belief in the authority of that book in such stiff-necked fashion. Your words, your actions ought continually to make the Bible superfluous—through you a new Bible ought continually to come into being! As it is, your apology for Christianity is rooted in your unchristianity, and with your defense you write your own condemnation. If you, however, should wish to emerge from your dissatisfaction with Christianity, you should ponder over the experience of two thousand years, which, clothed in the modest form of a question, may be voiced as follows: If Christ really intended to redeem the world, may he not be said to have failed?"

99.

The poet as guide to the future. All the surplus poetical force that still exists in modern humanity, but is not spent in forming our lives, should (without any deduction) be devoted to a definite goal—not to depicting the present nor to reviving and summarizing the past, but to pointing the way to the future. Nor should this be done with the assumption that the poet, like an imaginative political economist, had to anticipate a more favorable national and social state of things and picture their realization. Rather will he, just as the earlier poets did with the images of the gods, aim at perfecting the fair image of man. He will divine those cases where, in the midst of our modern world and reality (which will not be shirked or repudiated in the usual poetic fashion), a great, noble soul is still possible, where it may be embodied in harmonious, equable conditions, where it may become permanent, visible, and representative of a type, and so, by the stimulus to imitation and envy, help to create the future. The poems of such a poet would be distinguished by appearing secluded and protected from the heated atmosphere of the passions. The irremediable failure, the shattering of the entire human instrument, the scornful laughter and gnashing of teeth, and all tragedy and comedy in the usual old sense, would appear by the side of this new art as a wearisome and archaic simplification[11] of the image of man. Strength, kindness, gentleness, purity, and an unsought, innate moderation in the personalities and their action: a leveled ground, giving rest and pleasure to the foot: a shining heaven mirrored in faces and events: science and art welded into a new unity: the mind living together with its sister, the soul, without arrogance or jealousy, and enticing from contrasts the grace of seriousness, not the impatience of discord—all this would be the general environment, the golden background on which the delicate *differences* of the embodied ideals would make the real picture, that of ever growing human majesty. Many roads to this poetry of the future start from *Goethe,* but the quest needs good pathfinders and above all a far greater strength than is possessed by modern poets, who unscrupulously represent the half-animal and the immaturity and anomalousness that are mistaken by them for power and naturalness.

100.

The muse as Penthesilea.[12] "Better to rot than to be a woman who does not *excite.*" When once the muse thinks thus, the end of her art is again at hand. But it can be a tragic and also a comic finale.

205.

Brisk air. The best and healthiest element in science, as amid the mountains, is the keen air that plays about it.—Intellectual weaklings[13] (such as artists) dread and abuse science on account of this atmosphere.

221.

Exceptional Greeks. In Greece, deep, thorough, serious minds were the exception. The national instinct tended rather to regard the serious and thorough as a kind of distortion. To borrow forms from a foreign source, not to create but to transform into the fairest shapes[14]—that is Greek. To imitate, not for utility but for artistic illusion, again and again to gain the mastery over forced seriousness, to arrange, beautify, simplify—that is the continual task from Homer to the Sophists of the third and fourth centuries of our era, who are all outward show, pompous speech, declamatory gestures, and address themselves to shallow souls that care only for appearance, sound, and effect. And now let us estimate the greatness of those exceptional Greeks, who created *science!* Whoever tells of them tells the most heroic story of the human mind!

Translated by Paul V. Cohen

The Wanderer and His Shadow (1880)
(Selections)

6.

Earthly infirmities and their main cause. If we look about us, we are always coming across men who have eaten eggs all their lives without observing that the oblong-shaped taste the best; who do not know that a thunderstorm is beneficial to the digestion; that perfumes are most fragrant in cold, clean air; that our sense of taste varies in different parts of our mouths; that every meal at which we talk well or listen well does harm to the digestion. If we are not satisfied with these examples of defective powers of observation, we shall concede all the more readily that the *everyday matters* are very imperfectly seen and rarely observed by the majority. Is this a matter of indifference?—Let us remember, after all, that from this defect are derived *nearly all the bodily and spiritual infirmities* of the individual. Ignorance of what is good and bad for us, in the arrangement of our mode of life, the division of our day, the selection of our friends and the time we devote to them, in business and leisure, commanding and obeying, our feeling for nature and for art, our eating, sleeping, and meditation; ignorance and lack of keen perceptions *in the smallest and most ordinary details*—this it is that makes the world "a vale of tears" for so many. Let us not say that here as everywhere the fault lies with human *unreason*. Of reason there is enough and to spare, but it is *wrongly directed* and *artificially diverted* from these little intimate things. Priests and teachers, and the sublime thirst for power of all idealists, coarser and subtler, work to convince even the child that something else is of paramount importance: the salvation of the soul, service of the state, the advancement of science, or status and property—all as ways of serving the whole of mankind; whereas the needs of the individual, his requirements great and small during the twenty-four hours of the day, are said to be quite paltry or indifferent.—Even Socrates attacked with all his might this arrogant neglect of the human for the benefit of humanity, and loved to indicate by a quotation from Homer the true extent and quintessence of all anxiety and reflection: "All that really matters," he said, "is the good and evil I find at home."

16.

Where indifference is necessary. Nothing would be more perverse than to wait for the truths that science will finally establish concerning the first and last things, and until then to think (and especially to believe) in the *traditional* way, as one is so often advised to do. The impulse that bids us seek nothing but *certainties* in this domain is a belated *religious offshoot*, nothing better—a hidden and only apparently skeptical variety of the "metaphysical need," the underlying idea being that for a long time there will be no likelihood of these ultimate certainties being obtained, and that until then the "believer" is right not to trouble himself about the whole subject. We have no *need* of these certainties about the farthermost horizons in order to live a full and vigorous human life, any more than the ant needs them in order to be a good ant. Rather, we must ascertain the origin of that odious significance that we have attached to these things for so long. For this we require the *history* of ethical and religious sentiments, since it is only under the influence of such sentiments that these most acute problems of knowledge have become so weighty and terrifying. Into the outermost regions to which the mental eye can penetrate (without ever penetrating *into* them), we have smuggled such concepts as guilt and punishment (everlasting punishment, too!). The darker those regions, the more careless we have been. For ages men have let their imaginations run riot where nothing could be established with certainty, and have induced posterity to accept these fantasies as something serious and true, with this abominable lie as their final trump card: that faith is worth more than knowledge. What we need now in regard to these ultimate things is not knowledge rather than faith, but *indifference toward faith and pretended knowledge* in these matters! Everything must lie nearer to us than what has hitherto been preached to us as the most important thing. I mean the questions: "What end does man serve?" "What is his fate after death?" "How does he make his peace with God?" and all the rest of those oddities. The problems of the dogmatic philosophers, be they idealists, materialists, or realists, concern us as little as do these religious questions. They all have the same object in view—to force us to a decision in matters where neither faith nor knowledge is needed. It is better even for the most ardent lover of knowledge that the territory open to investigation and to reason should be encircled by a belt of fog-laden, treacherous marshland, a zone impenetrable, indeterminable, always in flux. It is just by the comparison with the realm of darkness on the edge of the world of knowledge that this bright and near, indeed nearest, region rises in value.—We must once more become *good friends of the everyday matters,* and not, as hitherto, despise them and look beyond them at clouds and specters of the night. In forests and caverns, in marshy tracts and under overcast skies, on such levels of culture man has lived for millennia, and in poverty. There he has learnt to *despise* the present, his everyday surroundings, his life, and himself, and we, the inhabitants of the brighter fields of nature and the mind, still inherit in our blood some taint of this contempt for that which is nearest.

72.

Divine missionaries. Socrates, too, feels himself to be a divine missionary, but I am not sure what admixture of Attic irony and fondness for jesting is present even here, whereby this odious, arrogant conception is toned down. He talks of the fact without unction—his images of the gadfly and the horse are simple and not sacerdotal. The real religious task which he has set himself—to *test* God in a hundred ways and see whether he spoke the truth—betrays a bold and free attitude, in which the missionary walked by the side of his God. This testing of God is one of the most subtle compromises between piety and freethinking that has ever been devised.—Nowadays we do not even need this compromise any longer.

86.

Socrates. If all goes well, the time will come when, in order to advance themselves on the path of morality and reason, men will rather take up the *Memorabilia* of Socrates than the Bible, and when Montaigne and Horace will be used as pioneers and guides for the understanding of Socrates, the simplest and most enduring of mediating sages. Leading back to him are the roads of the most different philosophic modes of life, which are in truth the modes of the different temperaments, crystallized by reason and habit and all ultimately directed towards the delight in life and in the self. The apparent conclusion is that the most peculiar thing about Socrates was his share in all the temperaments. Socrates excels the founder of Christianity by virtue of his gay style of seriousness and by that *wisdom of sheer roguish pranks* which constitutes the best state of soul in a man. Moreover, he had a superior intelligence.

313.

The monotone of the sage. Cows sometimes have a look of wondering which stops short on the path to questioning. In the eye of the higher intelligence, on the other hand, the *nil admirari*[14a] is spread out like the monotony of a cloudless sky.

315.

A hint to enthusiasts. He who loves to be carried away, and would like to be carried on high, must beware lest he become too *heavy.* For instance, he must not learn much, and especially not let himself be *crammed* with science. Science makes men ponderous—take care, you enthusiasts!

Translated by Paul V. Cohen

From *Dawn: Thoughts about Morality as a Prejudice* (1881)

(Selections)

6.

The sleight of hand[15] *and its counterpart.* That which is astounding in science is diametrically opposed to that which is in the art of sleight of hand. For the latter would wish to make us believe that we see a very simple causality, where, in reality, an exceedingly complex causality is in operation. Science, on the other hand, forces us to give up our belief in the simple causality exactly where everything looks so easily comprehensible and we are fooled by mere appearances. The "simplest" things are *very complicated*—we can never be sufficiently astonished at them!

41.

Determining the value of the vita contemplativa. Let us not forget, as men leading a contemplative life, what kind of evils and misfortunes have overtaken the men of the *vita activa* as a result of the various aftereffects of contemplation—in short, what sort of account the *vita activa,* for its part, has to offer *us,* if we exhibit too much boastfulness before it with respect to our beneficial deeds. *First:* the so-called *religious* natures, who predominate among the lovers of contemplation and consequently represent their commonest type, have at all times acted in such a manner as to render life difficult for practical men, and tried to make them disgusted with it, if possible: to darken the sky, to obliterate the sun, to cast suspicion upon joy, to depreciate hope, to paralyze the active hand—all this they knew how to do, just as, for miserable times

and feelings, they had their consolations, alms, blessings, and bene-
dictions. *Second:* the artists, somewhat less numerous than the religious element, but nevertheless a type of man frequently devoted to
the *vita contemplativa;* as individuals, they are usually intolerable,
capricious, jealous, violent, quarrelsome: this must be subtracted
from the joyous and exalting effects of their works. *Third:* the
philosophers, a species in which religious and artistic powers exist
side by side in such a way, however, that there is also room for a
third thing: a keen enjoyment of rigorous proofs. The philosophers
have been the authors of evil in the same sense as the religious men
and artists; on top of this, they have bored many men with their
penchant for dialectics. Their number, though, has always been
very small. *Fourth:* the thinkers and scientific workers. They have
seldom striven for effects; instead, they have quietly dug their mole
tunnels. Thus they have caused little irritation or unpleasantness
and even, unwittingly, have made life easier for the men of the *vita
activa* by serving as objects of mockery and derision. Lastly, science
ended by becoming of much advantage to all; and if, *on account
of this utility,* many of the men who were destined for the *vita
activa* are now slowly making their way along the road to science
in the sweat of their brow, and not without brainracking and male-
dictions, this is not the fault of the crowd of thinkers and scientific
workers: it is "self-wrought pain."

144.

Closing our ears to lamentation. When we allow ourselves to be
made gloomy by the lamentation and suffering of other mortals,
when we allow our own sky to be darkened by clouds: who must
bear the consequences of such gloom? No doubt those other mortals, in addition to all their other burdens! If we want to be the
echo of their lamentation, we can neither *help* nor *comfort* them;
nor can we do so if we were continually keeping our ears open to
listen to them—unless we could learn the art of the Olympians
and henceforth be *edified* by the misfortunes of mankind, instead
of feeling unhappy about them. But this is somewhat too Olympian
for us although, in our enjoyment of tragedy, we have already taken
a step towards this ideal divine cannibalism.

270.

Apparent toleration. Those are good, benevolent, and rational
words on and in favor of science, but, wait! I see *behind* your

toleration of science. In your heart of hearts you think, in spite of all you say, that *it is not necessary for you,* that it shows magnanimity on your part to tolerate and even to advocate it, more especially as science on its part does not exhibit this magnanimity in regard to your opinions! Do you know that you have no right whatever to exercise this toleration? that this condescending gesture of yours is an even coarser disparagement of science than any of that open scorn which a presumptuous priest or artist might allow himself to indulge in towards science? What is lacking in you is a strong sense for everything that is true and actual; it is not agonizing, not a torture for you to find that science is in contradiction to your own sentiment; you are unacquainted with that intense desire for knowledge ruling over you like a law; you do not feel a duty in the need to be present with your own eyes *wherever* knowledge is being gained, and hold fast to *whatever* knowledge has been gained. You *do not know* that which you are treating with such toleration! and it is only because you do not know it that you can succeed in adopting such a gracious attitude towards it. You, precisely you, would look upon science with hatred and fanaticism if it for once cast its shining and illuminating glance upon you! What does it matter to us, then, if you do exhibit toleration—towards a *phantom*! and not even towards us! And what do we matter!

327.

A fable. The Don Juan of knowledge—no philosopher or poet has yet succeeded in discovering him. He is wanting in love for the things he recognizes, but he possesses wit and an itching lust and enjoys the hunt for knowledge and the intrigues in connection with it—even up to the highest and most distant stars of knowledge—until at last there is nothing left for him to pursue but the absolutely painful element of knowledge, like the drunkard who ends by drinking absinthe and aquafortis. That is why last of all he feels a longing for hell, for this is the final knowledge which *seduces* him. Perhaps even this would disappoint him, as all things do which one knows! and then he would have to stand still for all eternity, nailed fast to this disappointment, transformed into the Stony Guest, yearning for a last supper of knowledge which will never more fall to his share! For the whole world of things has not another mouthful left to offer to this hungry one.

328.

What idealistic theories disclose. We are most certain to find idealistic theories among unscrupulously practical men; for such men stand in need of the luster of these theories for the sake of their reputation. They adopt them instinctively and they do not feel at all hypocritical in doing so—no more than Englishmen feel hypocritical with their Christianity and their Sabbath-keeping. On the other hand, contemplative natures who have to keep themselves on their guard against all kinds of fantasies and who dread to be reputed as enthusiasts, are only to be satisfied with hard realistic theories: they take possession of them under the same instinctive compulsion without thereby losing their honesty.

433.

Seeing with new eyes. Presuming that by the term "beauty in art" is always implied the imitation of the one who *is happy*—and this I consider to be true—depending on how an age or a people or a great autonomous individuality conceives of him: what then is disclosed by the so-called *realism* of our modern artists in regard to the happiness of our epoch? It is undoubtedly *its* type of beauty which we now most easily grasp and enjoy. As a consequence, we are induced to believe that this happiness which is now peculiar *to us* is based on realism, on the sharpest possible senses, and on the true conception of the actual—that is to say, not upon reality, but upon knowledge *of reality.* The results of science have already gained so much in depth and extent that the artists of our century have involuntarily become the glorifiers of scientific "blessings" per se.

547.

The tyrants of the intellect. The progress of science is at the present time no longer hindered by the purely accidental fact that man lives for about seventy years, which was the case far too long. In former times people wished to cover the entire range of knowledge within this period, and all the methods of knowledge were valued according to this general desire. Minor questions and individual experiments were looked upon as contemptible: people wanted to take the shortest path under the impression that, since everything in this world seemed to be arranged with a view to man's needs, even the attainability of knowledge was regulated in view of the limits of human life.

To solve everything at a single stroke, with one word—this was the secret desire; and the task was represented in the symbol of the Gordian knot or the egg of Columbus. No one doubted that it was possible to reach the goal of knowledge after the manner of Alexander or Columbus, and to settle all questions with *one* answer. "There is an enigma to be solved," seemed to be the aim of life in the eyes of the philosopher: it was necessary in the first place to find out what this enigma was, and to condense the problem of the world into the simplest enigmatic formula possible. The boundless ambition and delight of being the "unraveler of the world" charmed the dreams of many a thinker: nothing seemed to him worth troubling about but the means of bringing everything to a satisfactory conclusion for him. Philosophy thus became a kind of supreme struggle for the tyrannical sway over the intellect, and no one doubted that such a tyrannical domination was reserved for some very happy, subtle, ingenious, bold, and powerful person—a single individual!—and many (the last was Schopenhauer) fancied themselves to be this privileged person.

From this it follows that, on the whole, science has up to the present remained in a rather backward state owing to the *moral narrow-mindedness* of its disciples, and that henceforth it will have to be pursued on a nobler and *more generous* basis. "What do I matter?" is written over the door of the thinker of the future.

Translated by J. M. Kennedy

From *The Gay Science* (1882/87)

Books I–III

(Selections)

7.

Something for the industrious. Anyone who now wishes to make a study of moral matters opens up for himself an immense field for work. All kinds of passions have to be thought through and pursued individually through different ages, peoples, and great and small individuals; all their reason and all their evaluations and perspectives on things have to be brought into the light. So far, all that has given color to existence still lacks a history. Where could you find a history of love, of avarice, of envy, of conscience, of pious respect for tradition, or of cruelty? Even a comparative history of law or at least of punishment is so far lacking completely. Has anyone made a study of different ways of dividing up the day or of the consequences of a regular schedule of work, festivals, and rest? What is known of the moral effects of different foods? Is there any philosophy of nutrition? (The constant revival of noisy agitation for and against vegetarianism proves that there is no such philosophy!) Has anyone collected men's experiences of living together—in monasteries, for example? Has the dialectic of marriage and friendship ever been explicated? Have the manners of scholars, of businessmen, artists, or artisans been studied and thought about? There is so much in them to think about.

Whatever men have so far viewed as the conditions of their existence—and all the reason, passion, and superstition involved in such a view—has this been researched exhaustively? The most industrious people will find that it involves too much work simply to observe how differently men's instincts have grown, and might yet grow, depending on different moral climates. It would require whole generations, and generations of scholars who would collaborate systematically, to exhaust the points of view and the material. The same applies to the demonstration of the reasons for the differences between moral climates ("why is it that the sun of one fundamental moral judgment and main standard of value shines here and another one there?"). And it would be yet another job to establish the erroneousness of all these reasons and the whole nature of moral judgments to date.

If all these jobs were done, the thorniest question of all would emerge into the foreground: whether science can furnish goals of action after it has proved that it can take such goals away and annihilate them; and then experimentation would be in order that would allow every kind of heroism to find satisfaction—centuries of experimentation that might eclipse all the great projects and sacrifices of history to date. So far, science has not yet built its cyclopic buildings; but the time for that, too, will come.

11.

Consciousness. Consciousness is the last and latest development of the organic and hence also what is most unfinished and least strong. Consciousness gives rise to countless errors that lead an animal or man to perish sooner than necessary, "exceeding destiny," as Homer puts it. If the conserving association of the instincts were not so very much more powerful, and if it did not serve on the whole as a regulator, humanity would have to perish of its misjudgments and its fantasies with open eyes, of its lack of thoroughness and its credulity—in short, of its consciousness; rather, without the former, humanity would long have disappeared.

Before a function is fully developed and mature it constitutes a danger for the organism, and it's a good thing if during this time it is subjected to some tyranny! Thus consciousness is tyrannized—not least by our pride in it. One thinks that it constitutes the *very core* of man; what is abiding, eternal, ultimate, and most fundamental in him. One takes consciousness for a given quantity. One denies its growth and its intermittences. One takes it for the "unity of the organism."

This ridiculous overestimation and misunderstanding of consciousness has the very useful consequence that it prevents an all too fast development of consciousness. Believing that they possess consciousness, men have not exerted themselves very much to acquire it; and things haven't changed much in this respect. To this day the task of *incorporating* knowledge and making it instinctive is only beginning to dawn on the human eye and is not yet clearly discernible; it is a task that is seen only by those who have comprehended that so far we have incorporated only our errors and that all our consciousness relates to errors.

12.

On the aim of science. What? The aim of science should be to give men as much pleasure and as little displeasure as possible? But what if pleasure and displeasure were so tied together that whoever *wanted* to have as much as possible of one *must* also have as much as possible of the other—that whoever wanted to learn to "jubilate up to the heavens" would also have to be prepared for "depression unto death"?[16] And that is how things may well be. At least the Stoics believed that this was how things were, and they were consistent when they also desired as little pleasure as possible, in order to get as little displeasure as possible out of life. (When they kept saying "the virtuous man is the happiest man," this was both the school's eye-catching sign for the great mass and a casuistic subtlety for the subtle.)

To this day you have the choice: either *as little displeasure as possible*, painlessness in brief—and in the last analysis socialists and politicians of all parties have no right to promise their people more than that—or *as much displeasure as possible* as the price for the growth of an abundance of subtle pleasures and joys that have rarely been relished yet. If you decide for the former and desire to diminish and lower the level of human pain, you also have to diminish and lower the level of their *capacity for joy.* Actually, *science* can promote either goal. So far it may still be better known for its power of depriving man of his joys and making him colder, more like a statue, more stoic. But it might yet be found to be the *great dispenser of pain.* And then its counterforce might be found at the same time: its immense capacity for making new galaxies of joy flare up.

37.

Owing to three errors. During the last centuries science has been promoted, partly because it was by means of science that one hoped to understand God's goodness and wisdom best—this was the main motive of the great Englishmen (like Newton); partly because one believed in the absolute utility of knowledge, and especially in the most intimate association of morality, knowledge, and happiness—this was the main motive of the great Frenchmen (like Voltaire); partly because one thought that in science one possessed and loved something unselfish, harmless, self-sufficient, and truly innocent, in which man's evil impulses had no part whatever—the main motive of Spinoza who felt divine when attaining knowledge—in sum, owing to three errors.

46.

Our amazement. There is a profound and fundamental happiness for us in the fact that scientific discoveries stand up under examination and furnish the basis, again and again, for further discoveries. After all, this could be otherwise. Indeed, we are so convinced of the uncertainty and fantasies of our judgments and of the eternal change of all human laws and concepts that we are really amazed how *well* the results of science stand up. Formerly, nothing was known of this mutability of everything human; the *mores* of morality[17] sustained the faith that all of man's inner life was attached to iron necessity with eternal clamps. Perhaps people then experienced a similarly voluptuous amazement when they listened to fairy tales. The miraculous gave a great deal of pleasure to those who at times grew tired of the rule and of eternity. To lose firm ground for once! To float! To err! To be mad! That was part of the paradise and the debauchery of bygone ages, while our bliss is like that of a man who has suffered shipwreck, climbed ashore, and now stands with both feet on the firm old earth—amazed that it does not waver.

80.

Art and nature. The Greeks (or at least the Athenians) liked to hear people speak well. Nothing distinguishes them so thoroughly from non-Greeks as does this truly greedy craving. Even of passion on the stage they demanded that it should speak well, and they endured the unnaturalness of dramatic verse with rapture. In nature, passion is so poor in words, so silent and embarrassed; or when it finds words, so confused and irrational and ashamed of itself. Thanks to the Greeks, all of us have now become accustomed to this unnatural stage convention, just as we tolerate, and tolerate gladly, thanks to the Italians, that other unnatural convention: passion that *sings*.

We have developed a need that we cannot satisfy in reality: to hear people in the most difficult situations speak well and at length; we are delighted when the tragic hero still finds words, reasons, eloquent gestures, and altogether intellectual brightness, where life approaches abysses and men in reality usually lose their heads and certainly linguistic felicity. This kind of *deviation from nature* is perhaps the most agreeable repast for human pride: for its sake man loves art as the expression of a lofty, heroic unnaturalness and convention. We rightly reproach a dramatic poet if he does not transmute everything into reason and words but always retains in his hands a residue of *silence*—just as we are dissatisfied with the operatic composer who cannot find melodies for the highest emotions but only an emotion-filled "natural" stammering and screaming. At this point nature is *supposed to be* contradicted. Here the vulgar attraction of illusion is *supposed* to give way to a higher attraction.

The Greeks went far, very far in this respect—alarmingly far. Just as they made the stage as narrow as possible and denied themselves any effects by means of deep backgrounds; just as they made facial expressions and easy movements impossible for the actor and transformed him into a solemn, stiff, masked bogey—they also deprived passion itself of any deep background and dictated to it a law of beautiful speeches. Indeed, they did everything to counteract the elementary effect of images that might arouse fear and pity—for *they did not want fear and pity*. Giving all honor—and the highest honors—to Aristotle, he certainly did not hit the nail, much less on the head, when he discussed the ultimate end of Greek tragedy.[18] Just look at the Greek tragic poets to see what it was that most excited their industry, their inventiveness, their competition: certainly not the attempt to overwhelm the spectator with sentiments. The Athenian went to the theater *in order to hear beautiful speeches*. And beautiful speeches were what concerned Sophocles: pardon this heresy!

It is very different with *serious opera*. All of its masters take pains to prevent anyone from understanding their characters. Occasionally picking up a word must help the inattentive listener, but on the whole the situation must explain itself, and the speeches do not matter! That is what all of them think, and hence they have their fun with the words. Perhaps they merely lacked the courage to express fully their ultimate lack of regard for words. With just a little more impertinence, Rossini would have had everybody sing nothing but la-la-la-la—and that would have made good, rational sense. Confronted with the characters in an opera, we are not supposed to take their word for it, but the sound! That is the difference, that is the beautiful *unnaturalness* for whose sake one goes to the opera. Even the *recitativo secco* really is not meant to be heard as words and text: this kind of half-music is only supposed, first, to give the musical ear a little rest (rest from the *melody* as the most sublime but therefore also most strenuous enjoyment of this art) and then very soon also something else: namely, a growing impatience, a growing irritation, a new desire for *whole* music, for melodies.

How are things with Richard Wagner's art, when we consider it in this perspective? Different perhaps? Often it has seemed to me as if one had to memorize the words *and* the music of his creations before the performance; otherwise, it seemed to me, one *heard* neither the words nor even the music.

107.

Our ultimate gratitude to art. If we had not welcomed the arts and invented this kind of cult of the untrue, then the realization of general untruth and mendaciousness that now comes to us through science—the realization that delusion and error are conditions of human knowledge and sensation—would be utterly unbearable. *Honesty* would lead to nausea and suicide. But now there is a counterforce against our honesty that helps us to avoid such consequences: art as the *good* will to appearance. We do not always keep our eyes from rounding off something and, as it were, finishing the poem: and then it is no longer eternal imperfection that we carry across the river of becoming—then we have the sense of carrying a *goddess*, and feel proud and childlike as we perform this service. As an aesthetic phenomenon existence is still *bearable* for us, and art furnishes us with eyes and hands and above all the good conscience to be *able* to turn ourselves into such a phenomenon. At times we need a rest from ourselves by looking upon, by looking *down* upon, ourselves and, from an artistic distance, laughing *over* ourselves or weeping *over* ourselves. We must discover the *hero* no less than the *fool* in our passion for knowledge; we must occasionally find pleasure in our folly, or we cannot continue to find pleasure in our wisdom. Precisely because we are at bottom grave and serious human beings—really, more weights than human beings—nothing does us as much good as a *fool's cap:* we need it in relation to ourselves—we need all exuberant, floating, dancing, mocking, childish, and blissful art lest we lose the *freedom above things* that our ideal demands of us. It would mean a *relapse* for us, with our irritable honesty, to get involved entirely in morality and, for the sake of the overly severe demands that we make on ourselves in these matters, to become virtuous monsters and scarecrows. We should be *able* also to stand *above* morality—and not only to *stand* with the anxious stiffness of a man who is afraid of slipping and falling any moment, but also to *float* above it and *play.* How then could we possibly dispense with art—and with the fool?—And as long as you are in any way *ashamed* before yourselves, you do not yet belong with us.

123.

Knowledge as more than a mere means. Without this new passion—I mean the passion to know—science would still be promoted; after all, science has grown and matured without it until now. The good faith in science, the prejudice in its favor that dominates the modern state (and formerly dominated even the church) is actually based on the fact that this unconditional urge and passion has manifested itself so rarely, and that science is considered *not* a passion but a mere condition or an "ethos." Often mere *amour-plaisir*[19] of knowledge (curiosity) is felt to be quite sufficient, or *amour-vanité,*[20] being accustomed to it with the ulterior motive of honors and sustenance; for many people it is actually quite enough that they have too much leisure and do not know what to do with it except to read, collect, arrange, observe, and recount—their "scientific impulse" is their boredom.

Pope Leo X once sang the praises of science (in his brief to Beroaldo[21]): he called it the most beautiful ornament and the greatest pride of our life and a noble occupation in times of happiness as well as unhappiness; and finally he said: "without it all human endeavors would lack any firm foothold—and even with it things are changeable and insecure enough." But this tolerably skeptical pope keeps silent, like all other ecclesiastical eulogists of science, abut his ultimate judgment. From his words one might infer, although this is strange enough for such a friend of the arts, that he places science above art; but in the end it is nothing but good manners when he does not speak at this point of what he places high above all of the sciences, too: "revealed truth" and the "eternal salvation of the soul." Compared to that, what are ornaments, pride, entertainment, and the security of life to him? "Science is something second-class, not anything ultimate, unconditional, not an object of passion"—this judgment Leo retained in his soul: the truly Christian judgment about science.

In antiquity the dignity and recognition of science were diminished by the fact that even her most zealous disciples placed the striving for *virtue* first, and one felt that knowledge had received the highest praise when one celebrated it as the best means to virtue. It is something new in history that knowledge wants to be more than a mere means.

125.

The madman. Have you not heard of that madman who lit a lantern in the bright morning hours, ran to the market place, and cried incessantly: "I seek God! I seek God!" As many of those who did not believe in God were standing around just then, he provoked much laughter. Has he got lost? asked one. Did he lose his way like a child? asked another. Or is he hiding? Is he afraid of us? Has he gone on a voyage? emigrated?—Thus they yelled and laughed.

The madman jumped into their midst and pierced them with his eyes. "Whither is God?" he cried; "I will tell you. *We have killed him*—you and I. All of us are his murderers. But how did we do this? How could we drink up the sea? Who gave us the sponge to wipe away the entire horizon? What were we doing when we unchained this earth from its sun? Whither is it moving now? Whither are we moving? Away from all suns? Are we not plunging continually? Backward, sideward, forward, in all directions? Is there still any up or down? Are we not straying as through an infinite nothing? Do we not feel the breath of empty space? Has it not become colder? Is not night continually closing in on us? Do we not need to light lanterns in the morning? Do we hear nothing as yet of the noise of the gravediggers who are burying God? Do we smell nothing as yet of the divine decomposition? Gods, too, decompose. God is dead! God remains dead! And we have killed him!

"How shall we comfort ourselves, the murderers of all murderers? What was holiest and mightiest of all that the world has yet owned has bled to death under our knives: who will wipe this blood off us? What water is there for us to clean ourselves? What festivals of atonement, what sacred games shall we have to invent? Is not the greatness of this deed too great for us? Must we ourselves not become gods simply to appear worthy of it? There has never been a greater deed; and whoever is born after us—for the sake of this deed he will belong to a higher history than all history hitherto."

Here the madman fell silent and looked again at his listeners; and they, too, were silent and stared at him in astonishment. At last he threw his lantern on the ground, and it broke into pieces and went out. "I have come too early," he said then. "My time is not yet. This tremendous event is still on its way, still traveling; it has not yet reached the ears of men. Lightning and thunder require time; the light of the stars requires time; deeds, though done, still require time to be seen and heard. This deed is still more distant from them than the most distant stars—*and yet they have done it themselves.*"

It has been related further that on the same day the madman forced his way into several churches and there struck up his *requiem aeternam deo.*[21a] Led out and called to account, he is said always to have replied nothing but: "What, after all, are these churches now if they are not the tombs and sepulchers of God?"

153.

Homo poeta. "I myself, having made this tragedy of tragedies all by myself, insofar as it is finished—I, having first tied the knot of morality into existence before I drew it so tight that only a god could untie it (which is what Horace demands)—I myself have now slain all gods in the fourth act, for the sake of morality. Now, what is to become of the fifth act? From where am I to take the tragic solution?—Should I begin to think about a comic solution?"[22]

Translated by Walter Kaufmann

Sanctus Januarius

(Selections)

276.

For the new year. I still live, I still think: I still have to live, for I still have to think. *Sum, ergo cogito: cogito, ergo sum!*[23] Today everybody permits himself the expression of his wish and his dearest thought; hence I, too, shall say what it is that I wish from myself today, and what was the first thought to run across my heart this year—what thought shall be for me the reason, warranty, and sweetness of my life henceforth! I want to learn more and more to see as beautiful what is necessary in things; then I shall be one of those who make things beautiful. *Amor fati:*[24] let that be my love henceforth! I do not want to wage war against what is ugly. I do not want to accuse; I do not even want to accuse those who accuse. *Looking away* shall be my only negation. And all in all and on the whole: some day I wish to be only a yes-sayer.

293.

Our air. We know very well how science strikes those who merely glance at it in passing, as if they were walking by, as women do and unfortunately also many artists: the severity of its service, its inexorability in small as in great matters, and the speed of weighing and judging matters and condemning makes them feel dizzy and afraid. Above all they are terrified to see how the most difficult is demanded and the best is done without praise and decorations. Indeed, what one hears is, as among soldiers, mostly reproaches and harsh rebukes; for doing things well is considered the rule, and failure is the exception; but the rule always tends to keep quiet. This "severity of science" has the same effect as the forms and good manners of the best society: it is frightening for the uninitiated. But those who are used to it would never wish to live anywhere else than in this bright, transparent, vigorous, electrified air—in this *virile* air. Anywhere else things are not clean and airy enough for them; they suspect that elsewhere their best art would not really profit others nor give real delight to themselves; that among misunderstandings half of their lives would slip through their fingers; that they would be required to exercise a great deal of caution, conceal things, exercise self-control—so many ways of losing a lot of strength for no good reason. But in this severe and clear element they have their full strength; here they can fly. Why, then, go down into those muddy waters where one has to swim and wade and get one's wings dirty?

No, it is too hard for us to live there. Is it our fault that we were born for the air, clean air, we rivals of the beams of light, and that we wish we could ride on ethereal dust specks like these beams—not away from the sun but *toward the sun!* That, however, we cannot do. Let us therefore do what alone we can do: bring light to the earth, be "the light of the earth"! And to that end we have our wings and our speed and severity; for this are we virile and even terrible like fire. Let those be terrified by us who do not know how to gain warmth and light from us!

328.

To harm stupidity. Surely, the faith preached so stubbornly and with so much conviction, that egoism is reprehensible, has on the whole harmed egoism (while *benefiting,* as I shall repeat a hundred times, *the herd instincts!*)—above all, by depriving egoism of its good conscience and bidding us to find in it the true source of all unhappiness. "Your selfishness is the misfortune of your life"—that was preached for thousands of years and harmed, as I have said, selfishness and deprived it of much spirit, much cheerfulness, much ingenuity, much beauty; it made selfishness stupid and ugly and poisoned it.

The ancient philosophers taught that the main source of misfortune was something very different. Beginning with Socrates, these thinkers never wearied of preaching: "Your thoughtlessness and stupidity, the way you simply live according to the rule, your submission to your neighbor's opinion is the reason why you so rarely achieve happiness; we thinkers, as thinkers, are the happiest of all."

Let us not decide here whether this sermon against stupidity had better reasons on its side than did the sermon against selfishness. What is certain, however, is that it deprived stupidity of its good conscience; these philosophers *harmed* stupidity!

340.

The dying Socrates. I admire the courage and wisdom of Socrates in everything he did, said—and did not say. This mocking and enamored monster and pied piper of Athens, who made the most overweening youths tremble and sob, was not only the wisest chatterer of all time: he was equally great in silence. I wish he had remained taciturn also at the last moment of his life; in that case he might belong to a still higher order of spirits. Whether it was death or the poison or piety or malice—something loosened his tongue at that moment and he said: "O Crito, I owe Asclepius a rooster." This ridiculous and terrible "last word" means for those who have ears: "O Crito, *life is a disease*." Is it possible that a man like him who had lived cheerfully and like a soldier in the sight of everyone, should have been a pessimist? He had merely kept a cheerful mien while concealing all his life long his ultimate judgment, his inmost feeling. Socrates, Socrates *suffered life!* And then he still revenged himself—with this veiled, gruesome, pious, and blasphemous saying. Did a Socrates need such revenge? Did his overrich virtue lack an ounce of magnanimity? —Alas, my friends, we must overcome even the Greeks![25]

341.

The greatest weight.[26] What, if some day or night a demon were to steal after you into your loneliest loneliness and say to you: "This life as you now live it and have lived it, you will have to live once more and innumerable times more; and there will be nothing new in it, but every pain and every joy and every thought and sigh and everything unutterably small or great in your life will have to return to you, all in the same succession and sequence—even this spider and this moonlight between the trees, and even this moment and I myself. The eternal hourglass of existence is turned upside down again and again, and you with it, speck of dust!"

Would you not throw yourself down and gnash your teeth and curse the demon who spoke thus? Or have you once experienced a tremendous moment when you would have answered him: "You are a god and never have I heard anything more divine." If this thought gained possession of you, it would change you as you are or perhaps crush you. The question in each and every thing, "Do you desire this once more and innumerable times more?" would lie upon your actions as the greatest weight. Or how well-disposed would you have to become to yourself and to life *to crave nothing more fervently* than this ultimate eternal confirmation and seal?

342.

Incipit tragoedia.[27] When Zarathustra was thirty years old, he left his home and Lake Urmi[28] and went into the mountains. There he enjoyed his spirit and his solitude, and for ten years did not tire of that. But at last his heart changed—and one morning he rose with the dawn, stepped before the sun, and spoke to it thus: "You great star, what would your happiness be if you did not have those for whom you shine? For ten years you have climbed up to my cave. You would have become weary of your light and of the journey had it not been for me and my eagle and my serpent; but we waited for you every morning, took your overflow from you, and blessed you for it. Behold, I am sick of my wisdom, like a bee that has gathered too much honey; I need hands outstretched to receive it; I want to give away and distribute until the wise among men enjoy their folly once again and the poor their riches. For that I must descend to the depths, as you do in the evening when you go behind the sea and still bring light to the underworld, you overrich star. Like you I must *go under*,[29] as men put it, to whom I wish to descend. Bless me then, you calm eye that can look without envy even upon an all too great happiness. Bless the cup that wants to overflow in order that the water may flow from it golden and carry the reflection of your rapture everywhere. Behold, this cup wants to become empty again, and Zarathustra wants to become man again."—Thus Zarathustra began to go under.

Translated by Walter Kaufmann

We Fearless Ones

(Selections)

344.

How we, too, are still pious. In science convictions have no rights of citizenship, as one says with good reason. Only when they decide to descend to the modesty of hypotheses, of a provisional experimental point of view, of a regulative fiction, may they be granted admission and even a certain value in the realm of knowledge—though always with the restriction that they remain under police supervision, under the police of mistrust.—But does this not mean, if you consider it more precisely, that a conviction may obtain admission to science only when it *ceases* to be a conviction? Would it not be the first step in the discipline of the scientific spirit that one would not permit oneself any more convictions?

Probably this is so; only we still have to ask: *To make it possible for this discipline to begin,* must there not be some prior conviction—even one that is so commanding and unconditional that it sacrifices all other convictions to itself? We see that science also rests on a faith; there simply is no science "without presuppositions." The question whether *truth* is needed must not only have been affirmed in advance, but affirmed to such a degree that the principle, the faith, the conviction finds expression: "*Nothing* is needed *more* than truth, and in relation to it everything else has only second-rate value."

This unconditional will to truth—what is it? Is it the will *not to allow oneself to be deceived?* Is it the will *not to deceive?* For the will to truth could be interpreted in the second way, too—if only the special case "I do not want to deceive myself" is subsumed under the generalization "I do not want to deceive." But why not deceive? But why not allow oneself to be deceived?

Note that the reasons for the former principle belong to an altogether different realm from those for the second. One does not want to allow oneself to be deceived because one assumes that it is harmful, dangerous, calamitous to be deceived. In this sense, science would be a long-range prudence, a caution, a utility; but one could object in all fairness: How is that? Is wanting not to allow oneself to be deceived really less harmful, less dangerous, less calamitous? What do you know in advance of the character of existence to be able to decide whether the greater advantage is on the side of the unconditionally mistrustful or of the unconditionally trusting? But if both should be required, much trust *as well as* much mistrust, from where would science then be permitted to take its unconditional faith or conviction on which it rests, that truth is more important than any other thing, including every other conviction? Precisely this conviction could never have come into being if both truth and untruth constantly proved to be useful, which is the case. Thus the faith in science, which after all exists undeniably, cannot owe its origin to such a calculus of utility; it must have originated *in spite of* the fact that the disutility and dangerousness of "the will to truth," of "truth at any price" is proved to it constantly. "At any price": how well we understand these words once we have offered and slaughtered one faith after another on this altar!

Consequently, "will to truth" does *not* mean "I will not allow myself to be deceived" but—there is no alternative—"I will not deceive, not even myself"; *and with that we stand on moral ground.* For you only have to ask yourself carefully, "Why do you not want to deceive?" especially if it should seem—and it does seem!—as if life aimed at semblance, by which I mean error, deception, simulation, delusion, self-delusion, and when the great sweep of life has actually always shown itself to be on the side of the most unscrupulous *polytropoi.*[30] Charitably interpreted, such a resolve might perhaps be a quixotism, a minor slightly mad enthusiasm; but it might also be something more serious: namely, a principle that is hostile to life and destructive.—"Will to truth"—that might be a concealed will to death.

Thus the question "Why science?" leads back to the moral problem: *Why have morality at all* when life, nature, and history are "not moral"? No doubt, those who are truthful in that audacious and ultimate sense that is presupposed by the faith in science *thus affirm another world* than the world of life, nature, and history; and insofar as they affirm this "other world"—look, must they not by the same token negate its counterpart, this world, *our* world?—But you will have gathered what I am driving at: namely, that it is still a *metaphysical faith* upon which our faith in science rests—that even we seekers after knowledge today, we godless antimetaphysicians, still take our fire, too, from the flame lit by a faith that is thousands of years old, that Christian faith which was also the faith of Plato: that God is the truth, that truth is divine.—But what if this should become more and more incredible, if nothing should prove to be divine anymore unless it were error, blindness, the lie—if God himself should prove to be our most enduring lie?

370.

What is romanticism? It may perhaps be recalled, at least among my friends, that initially I approached the modern world with a few crude errors and overestimations and, in any case, *hopefully.* Who knows on the basis of what personal experiences I understood the philosophical pessimism of the nineteenth century as if it were a symptom of a superior force of thought, of more audacious courage, and of more triumphant *fullness* of life than had characterized the eighteenth century, the age of Hume, Kant, Condillac, and the sensualists. Thus tragic insight appeared to me as the distinctive *luxury* of our culture, as its most precious, noblest, and most dangerous squandering, but, in view of its overrichness, as a *permissible* luxury. In the same way, I reinterpreted German music for myself as if it signified a Dionysian power of the German soul: I believed that I heard in it the earthquake through which some primeval force that had been dammed up for ages finally liberated itself—indifferent whether everything else that one calls culture might begin to tremble. You see, what I failed to recognize at that time both in philosophical pessimism and in German music was what is really their distinctive character—their *romanticism*.

What is romanticism? Every art, every philosophy may be viewed as a remedy and an aid in the service of growing and struggling life; they always presuppose suffering and sufferers. But there are two kinds of sufferers: first, those who suffer from the *overfullness of life*—they want a Dionysian art and likewise a tragic view of life, a tragic insight—and then those wo suffer from the *impoverishment of life* and seek rest, stillness, calm seas, redemption from themselves through art and knowledge, or intoxication, convulsions, anaesthesia, and madness. All romanticism in art and insight corresponds to the dual needs of the latter type, and that included (and includes) Schopenhauer as well as Richard Wagner, to name the two most famous and pronounced romantics whom I *misunderstood* at that time—*not*, incidentally, to their disadvantage, as one need not hesitate in all fairness to admit. He that is richest in the fullness of life, the Dionysian god and man, cannot only afford the sight of the terrible and questionable but even the terrible deed and any luxury of destruction, decomposition, and negation. In his case, what is evil, absurd, and ugly seems, as it were, permissible, owing to an excess of procreating, fertilizing energies that can still turn any desert into lush farmland. Conversely, those who suffer most and are poorest in life would need above all mildness, peacefulness, and goodness in thought as well as deed—if possible, also a god who would be truly a god for the sick, a healer and savior;[31] also logic, the conceptual understandability of existence—for logic calms and gives confidence—in short, a certain warm narrowness that keeps away fear and encloses one in optimistic horizons.

Thus I gradually learned to understand Epicurus, the opposite of a Dionysian pessimist; also the "Christian" who is actually only a kind of Epicurean—both are essentially romantics—and my eye grew ever sharper for that most difficult and captious form of *back-*

ward inference in which the most mistakes are made: the backward inference from the work to the maker, from the deed to the doer, from the ideal to those who *need it,* from every way of thinking and valuing to the commanding *need* behind it.

Regarding all aesthetic values, I now avail myself of this main distinction: I ask in every instance, "is it hunger or superabundance that has here become creative?" At first glance, another distinction may seem preferable—it is far more obvious—namely, the question whether the desire to fix, to eternalize, the desire for *being* prompted creation, or the desire for destruction, for change, for novelty, for future, for *becoming.* But both of these kinds of desire are seen to be ambiguous when one considers them more closely; they can be interpreted in accordance with the first scheme that is, as it seems to me, preferable. The desire for *destruction,* change, and becoming can be an expression of an overflowing energy that is pregnant with future (my term for this is, as is known, "Dionysian"); but it can also be the hatred felt by the ill-constituted, deprived, and disadvantaged,[32] who destroy, *must* destroy, because what exists, indeed all existence, all being, outrages and provokes them. To understand this feeling, consider our anarchists closely.

The will to *eternalize* also requires a dual interpretation. It can be prompted, first, by gratitude and love; art with this origin will always be an art of apotheoses, perhaps dithyrambic like Rubens, or blissfully mocking like Hafiz, or bright and gracious like Goethe, spreading a Homeric light and glory over all things. But it can also be the tyrannic will of one who suffers deeply, who struggles, is tormented, and would like to turn what is most personal, singular, and narrow, the real idiosyncrasy of his suffering, into a binding law and compulsion—one who, as it were, revenges himself on all things by forcing his own image, the image of his torture, on them, branding them with it. This last version is *romantic pessimism* in its most expressive form, whether it be Schopenhauer's philosophy of will or Wagner's music—romantic pessimism, the last *great* event in the fate of our culture.

(That there still *could* be an altogether different kind of pessimism, a classical type—this premonition and vision belongs to me as inseparable from me, as *my proprium* and *ipsissimum;*[33] only the word "classical" offends my ears, it is far too trite and has become round and indistinct. I call this pessimism of the future— for it comes! I see it coming!—*Dionysian* pessimism.)

372.

Why we are not idealists. Formerly philosophers were afraid of the senses. Have we perhaps unlearned this fear too much? Today all of us are believers in the senses,[34] we philosophers of the present and the future, *not* in theory but in praxis, in practice.

They, however, thought that the senses might lure them away from their own world, from the cold realm of "ideas," to some dangerous southern island where they feared that their philosopher's virtues might melt away like snow in the sun. Having "wax in one's ears" was then almost a condition of philosophizing; a real philosopher no longer listened to life insofar as life is music; he *denied* the music of life—it is an ancient philosopher's superstition that all music is sirens' music.[35]

We today are inclined to make the opposite judgment (which actually could be equally wrong): namely, that *ideas* are worse seductresses than our senses, for all their cold and anemic appearance, and not even in spite of this appearance: they have always lived on the "blood" of the philosopher; they always consumed his senses and even, if you will believe us, his "heart." These old philosophers were heartless; philosophizing was always a kind of vampirism. Looking at these figures, even Spinoza, don't you have a sense of something profoundly enigmatic and uncanny? Don't you notice the spectacle that unrolls before you, how they *become ever paler*—how desensualization is interpreted more and more ideally? Don't you sense a long concealed vampire in the background who begins with the senses and in the end is left with, and leaves, mere bones, mere clatter? I mean categories, formulas, *words* (for, forgive me, what was left of Spinoza, *amor intellectualis dei,*[36] is mere clatter and no more than that: What is *amor,* what *deus,* if there is not a drop of blood in them?).

In sum: All philosophical idealism to date was something like a disease, unless it was, as it was in Plato's case, the caution of an overrich and dangerous health, the fear of *overpowerful* senses, the prudence of a prudent Socratic.—Perhaps we moderns are merely not healthy enough *to be in need of* Plato's idealism? And we are not afraid of the senses because—

373.

"Science" as a prejudice. It follows from the laws of the order of rank that scholars, insofar as they belong to the spiritual middle

class, can never catch sight of the really great problems and question marks; moreover, their courage and their eyes simply do not reach that far—and above all, their needs which led them to become scholars in the first place, their inmost assumptions and desires that things might be such and such, their fears and hopes, all come to rest and are satisfied too soon. Take, for example, that pedantic Englishman Herbert Spencer. What makes him "enthuse" in his way and then leads him to draw a line of hope, a horizon of desirability—that eventual reconciliation of "egoism and altruism" about which he raves—almost nauseates the likes of us; a human race that adopted such Spencerian perspectives as its ultimate perspectives would seem to us worthy of contempt, of annihilation! But the mere fact that he had to experience as his highest hope something that to others appears and may appear only as a disgusting possibility poses a question mark that Spencer would have been incapable of foreseeing.

It is no different with the faith with which so many materialistic natural scientists rest content nowadays, the faith in a world that is supposed to have its equivalent and its measure in human thought and human valuations—a "world of truth" that can be mastered completely and forever with the aid of our square little reason. What? Do we really want to permit existence to be degraded for us like this—reduced to a mere exercise for a calculator and an indoor diversion for mathematicians? Above all, one should not wish to divest existence of its *ambiguous* character: that is a dictate of good taste, gentlemen, the taste of reverence for everything that lies beyond your horizon. That the only justifiable interpretation of the world should be one in which *you* are justified because one can continue to work and do research scientifically in *your* sense (you really mean, mechanistically?)—an interpretation that permits counting, calculating, weighing, seeing, and touching, and nothing more—that is a crudity and naiveté, assuming that it is not a mental illness, an idiocy.

Would it not be rather probable that, conversely, precisely the most superficial and external aspect of existence—what is most apparent, its skin and sensualization—would be grasped first—and might even be the only thing that allowed itself to be grasped? A "scientific" interpretation of the world, as you understand it, might therefore still be one of the *most stupid* of all possible interpretations of the world, meaning that it would be one of the poorest in meaning. This thought is intended for the ears and consciences of our mechanists who nowadays like to pass as philosophers and insist that mechanics is the doctrine of the first and last laws on which all existence must be based as on a ground floor. But an essentially mechanical world would be an essentially *meaningless* world. Assuming that one estimated the *value* of a piece of music according to how much of it could be counted, calculated, and expressed in formulas: how absurd would such a "scientific" estimation of music be! What would one have comprehended, understood, grasped of it? Nothing, really nothing of what is "music" in it!

Translated by Walter Kaufmann

From *Beyond Good and Evil:*
Prelude to a Philosophy
of the Future (1886)

Preface

Supposing truth is a woman—what then? Are there not grounds for the suspicion that all philosophers, insofar as they were dogmatists, have been very inexpert about women? That the gruesome seriousness, the clumsy obtrusiveness with which they have usually approached truth so far have been awkward and very improper methods for winning a woman's heart? What is certain is that she has not allowed herself to be won—and today every kind of dogmatism is left standing dispirited and discouraged. *If* it is left standing at all! For there are scoffers who claim that it has fallen, that all dogmatism lies on the ground—even more, that all dogmatism is dying.

Speaking seriously, there are good reasons why all philosophical dogmatizing, however solemn and definitive its airs used to be, may nevertheless have been no more than a noble childishness and tyronism. And perhaps the time is at hand when it will be comprehended again and again *how little* used to be sufficient to furnish the cornerstone for such sublime and unconditional philosophers' edifices as the dogmatists have built so far: any old popular superstition from time immemorial (like the soul superstition which, in the form of the subject and ego superstition, has not even yet ceased to do mischief); some play on words perhaps, a seduction by grammar, or an audacious generalization of very narrow, very personal, very human, all too human facts.

The dogmatists' philosophy was, let us hope, only a promise across millennia—as astrology was in still earlier times when perhaps more work, money, acuteness, and patience were lavished in its service than for any real science so far: to astrology and its "supraterrestrial" claims we owe the grand style of architecture in Asia and Egypt. It seems that all great things first have to bestride the earth in monstrous and frightening masks in order to inscribe themselves in the hearts of humanity with eternal demands: dogmatic philosophy was such a mask; for example, the Vedanta doctrine in Asia and Platonism in Europe.

Let us not be ungrateful to it, although it must certainly be conceded that the worst, most durable, and most dangerous of all errors so far was a dogmatist's error—namely, Plato's invention of the pure spirit and the good as such. But now that it is overcome, now that Europe is breathing freely again after this nightmare and at least can enjoy a healthier—sleep, we, *whose task is wakefulness itself*, are the heirs of all that strength which has been fostered[37] by the fight against this error. To be sure, it meant standing truth on her head and denying *perspective,* the basic condition of all life, when one spoke of spirit and the good as Plato did. Indeed, as a physician one might ask: "How could the most beautiful growth of antiquity, Plato, contract such a disease? Did the wicked Socrates corrupt him after all? Could Socrates have been the corrupter of youth after all? And did he deserve his hemlock?"

But the fight against Plato or, to speak more clearly and for "the people," the fight against the Christian-ecclesiastical pressure of millennia—for Christianity is Platonism for "the people"—has created in Europe a magnificent tension of the spirit the like of which had never yet existed on earth: with so tense a bow we can now shoot for the most distant goals. To be sure, European man experiences this tension as need and distress; twice already attempts have been made in the grand style to unbend the bow—once by means of Jesuitism, the second time by means of the democratic enlightenment which, with the aid of freedom of the press and newspaper reading, might indeed bring it about that the spirit would no longer experience itself so easily as a "need." (The Germans invented gunpowder—all due respect for that!—but then they made up for that: they invented the press.) But we who are neither Jesuits nor democrats, nor even German enough, we *good Europeans*[38] and free, *very* free spirits—we still feel it, the whole need of the spirit and the whole tension of its bow. And perhaps also the arrow, the task, and—who knows?—the *goal*—

Sils Maria, Upper Engadine,
June 1885

Translated by Walter Kaufmann

On the Prejudices of Philosophers
(Selections)
6.

Gradually it has become clear to me what every great philosophy so far has been: namely, the personal confession of its author and a kind of involuntary and unconscious memoir; also that the moral (or immoral) intentions in every philosophy have constituted the real germ of life from which the whole plant has grown.

Indeed, if one is to explain how the abstrusest metaphysical claims of a philosopher really came about, it is always well (and wise) to ask first: at what morality does all this (does *he*) aim? Accordingly, I do not believe that a "drive to knowledge" is the father of philosophy; but rather that another drive has, here as elsewhere, employed understanding (and misunderstanding) as a mere instrument. But anyone who considers the basic drives of man to see to what extent they may have been at play just here as *inspiring* spirits (or demons and kobolds) will find that all of them have done philosophy at some time—and that every single one of them would like only too well to represent just *itself* as the ultimate purpose of existence and the legitimate *master* of all the other drives. For every drive wants to be master—and it attempts to philosophize in *that spirit.*

To be sure: among scholars who are really scientific men, things may be different—"better," if you like—there you may really find something like a drive for knowledge, some small, independent clockwork that, once well wound, works on vigorously *without* any essential participation from all the other drives of the scholar. The real "interests" of the scholar therefore lie usually somewhere else—say, in his family, or in making money, or in politics. Indeed, it is almost a matter of total indifference whether his little machine is placed at this or that spot in science, and whether the "promising" young worker turns himself into a good philologist or an expert on fungi or a chemist: it does not *characterize* him that he becomes this or that. In the philosopher, conversely, there is nothing whatever that is impersonal; and above all, his morality bears decided and decisive witness to *who he is*—that is, in what order of rank the innermost drives of his nature stand in relation to each other.

16.

There are still harmless self-observers who believe that there are "immediate certainties"; for example, "I think," or as the superstition of Schopenhauer put it, "I will"; as though knowledge here got hold of its object purely and nakedly as "the thing in itself," without any falsification on the part of either the subject or the object. But that "immediate certainty," as well as "absolute knowledge" and the "thing in itself," involve a *contradictio in adjecto,*[39] I shall repeat a hundred times; we really ought to free ourselves from the seduction of words!

Let the people suppose that knowledge means knowing things entirely; the philosopher must say to himself: When I analyze the process that is expressed in the sentence, "I think," I find a whole series of daring assertions that would be difficult, perhaps impossible, to prove; for example, that it is *I* who think, that there must necessarily be something that thinks, that thinking is an activity and operation on the part of a being who is thought of as a cause, that there is an "ego," and, finally, that it is already determined what is to be designated by thinking—that I *know* what thinking is. For if I had not already decided within myself what it is, by what standard could I determine whether that which is just happening is not perhaps "willing" or "feeling"? In short, the assertion "I think" assumes that I *compare* my state at the present moment with other states of myself which I know, in order to determine what it is; on account of this retrospective connection with further "knowledge," it has, at any rate, no immediate certainty for me.

In place of the "immediate certainty" in which the people may believe in the case at hand, the philosopher thus finds a series of metaphysical questions presented to him, truly searching questions of the intellect; to wit: "From where do I get the concept of thinking? Why do I believe in cause and effect? What gives me the right to speak of an ego, and even of an ego as cause, and finally of an ego as the cause of thought?" Whoever ventures to answer these metaphysical questions at once by an appeal to a sort of *intuitive* perception, like the person who says, "I think, and know that this, at least, is true, actual, and certain"—will encounter a smile and two question marks from a philosopher nowadays. "Sir," the philosopher will perhaps give him to understand, "it is improbable that you are not mistaken; but why insist on the truth?"

20.

That individual philosophical concepts are not anything capricious or autonomously evolving, but grow up in connection and relationship with each other; that, however suddenly and arbitrarily they seem to appear in the history of thought, they nevertheless belong just as much to a system as all the members of the fauna of a continent—is betrayed in the end also by the fact that the most diverse philosophers keep filling in a definite fundamental scheme of possible philosophies. Under an invisible spell, they always revolve once more in the same orbit; however independent of each other they may feel themselves with their critical or systematic wills, something within them leads them, something impels them in a definite order, one after the other—to wit, the innate systematic structure and relationship of their concepts. Their thinking is, in fact, far less a discovery than a recognition, a remembering, a return and a homecoming to a remote, primordial, and inclusive household of the soul, out of which those concepts grew originally: philosophizing is to this extent a kind of atavism of the highest order.

The strange family resemblance of all Indian, Greek, and German philosophizing is explained easily enough. Where there is affinity of languages, it cannot fail, owing to the common philosophy of grammar—I mean, owing to the unconscious domination and guidance by similar grammatical functions—that everything is prepared at the outset for a similar development and sequence of philosophical systems; just as the way seems barred against certain other possibilities of world-interpretation. It is highly probable that philosophers within the domain of the Ural-Altaic languages (where the concept of the subject is least developed) look otherwise "into the world," and will be found on paths of thought different from those of the Indo-Germanic peoples and the Muslims: the spell of certain grammatical functions is ultimately also the spell of *physiological* valuations and racial conditions.

So much by way of rejecting Locke's superficiality regarding the origin of ideas.

Translated by Walter Kaufmann

The Free Spirit
(Selections)

24.

O sancta simplicitas![40] In what strange simplification and falsification man lives! One can never cease wondering once one has acquired eyes for this marvel! How we have made everything around us clear and free and easy and simple! how we have been able to give our senses a passport to everything superficial, our thoughts a divine desire for wanton leaps and wrong inferences! how from the beginning we have contrived to retain our ignorance in order to enjoy an almost inconceivable freedom, lack of scruple and caution, heartiness, and gaiety of life—in order to enjoy life! And only on this now solid granite foundation of ignorance could knowledge rise so far—the will to knowledge on the foundation of a far more powerful will: the will to ignorance, to the uncertain, to the untrue! Not as its opposite, but—as its refinement!

Even if *language,* here as elsewhere, will not get over its awkwardness, and will continue to talk of opposites where there are only degrees and many subtleties of gradation; even if the inveterate Tartuffery of morals, which now belongs to our unconquerable "flesh and blood," perverts the words even of those of us who know better—here and there we understand it and laugh at the way in which precisely science at its best seeks most to keep us in this *simplified,* thoroughly artificial, suitably constructed and suitably falsified world—at the way in which, willy-nilly, it loves error, because, being alive, it loves life.

39.

Nobody is very likely to consider a doctrine true merely because it makes people happy or virtuous—except perhaps the lovely "idealists" who become effusive about the good, the true, and the beautiful and allow all kinds of motley, clumsy, and benevolent desiderata to swim around in utter confusion in their pond. Happiness and virtue are no arguments. But people like to forget—even circumspect spirits—that making unhappy and evil are no counterarguments. Something might be true while being harmful and dangerous in the highest degree. Indeed, it might be a basic characteristic of existence that those who would know it completely would perish, in which case the strength of a spirit should be measured according to how much of the "truth" one could still barely endure—or to put it more clearly, to what degree one would *require* it to be thinned down, shrouded, sweetened, blunted, falsified.

But there is no doubt at all that the evil and unhappy are more favored when it comes to the discovery of certain *parts* of truth, and that the probability of their success here is greater—not to speak of the evil who are happy, a species the moralists pass over in silence. Perhaps hardness and cunning furnish more favorable conditions for the origin of the strong, independent spirit and philosopher than that gentle, fine conciliatory good-naturedness and art of taking things lightly which people prize, and prize rightly, in a scholar. Assuming first of all that the concept "philosopher" is not restricted to the philosopher who writes books—or makes books of *his* philosophy.

A final trait for the image of the free-spirited philosopher is contributed by Stendhal whom, considering German taste, I do not want to fail to stress—for he goes against the German taste. *"Pour être bon philosophe,"* says this last great psychologist, *"il faut être sec, clair, sans illusion. Un banquier, qui a fait fortune, a une partie du caractère requis pour faire des découveries en philosophie, c'est-à-dire pour voir clair dans ce qui est."*[41]

41.

One has to test oneself to see that one is destined for independence and command—and do it at the right time. One should not dodge one's tests, though they may be the most dangerous game one could play and are tests that are taken in the end before no witness or judge but ourselves.

Not to remain stuck to a person—not even the most loved—every person is a prison, also a nook.[42] Not to remain stuck to a fatherland—not even if it suffers most and needs help most—it is less difficult to sever one's heart from a victorious fatherland. Not to remain stuck to some pity—not even for higher men into whose rare torture and helplessness some accident allowed us to look. Not to remain stuck to a science—even if it should lure us with the most precious finds that seem to have been saved up precisely for us. Not to remain stuck to one's own detachment, to that voluptuous remoteness and strangeness of the bird who flees ever higher to see ever more below him—the danger of the flier. Not to remain stuck to our own virtues and become as a whole the victim of some detail in us, for example, our "hospitality," which is the danger of dangers for superior and rich souls who spend themselves lavishly, almost indifferently, and exaggerate the virtue of generosity into a vice. One must know how *to conserve oneself:* the hardest test of independence.

44.

Need I still say expressly after all this that they, too, will be free, *very* free spirits, these philosophers of the future—though just as certainly they will not be merely free spirits but something more, higher, greater, and thoroughly different that does not want to be misunderstood and mistaken for something else. But saying this I feel an *obligation*—almost as much to them as to ourselves who are their heralds and precursors, we free spirits—to sweep away a stupid old prejudice and misunderstanding about the lot of us: all too long it has clouded the concept "free spirit" like a fog.

In all the countries of Europe, and in America, too, there now is something that abuses this name: a very narrow, imprisoned, chained type of spirits who want just about the opposite of what accords with our intentions and instincts—not to speak of the fact that regarding the *new* philosophers who are coming up they must assuredly be closed windows and bolted doors. They belong, briefly and sadly, among the *levelers*—these falsely so-called "free spirits"—being eloquent and prolifically scribbling slaves of the democratic taste and its "modern ideas"; they are all human beings without solitude, without their own solitude, clumsy good fellows whom one should not deny either courage or respectable decency— only they are unfree and ridiculously superficial, above all in their basic inclination to find in the forms of the old society as it has existed so far just about the cause of *all* human misery and failure—which is a way of standing truth happily upon her head!

What they would like to strive for with all their powers is the universal green-pasture happiness of the herd, with security, lack of danger, comfort, and an easier life for everyone; the two songs and doctrines which they repeat most often are "equality of rights" and "sympathy for all that suffers"—and suffering itself they take for something that must be *abolished*.

We opposite men, having opened our eyes and conscience to the question where and how the plant "man" has so far grown most vigorously to a height—we think that this has happened every time under the opposite conditions, that to this end the dangerousness of his situation must first grow to the point of enormity, his power of invention and simulation (his "spirit") had to develop under prolonged pressure and constraint into refinement and audacity, his life-will had to be enhanced into an unconditional power-will. We think that hardness, forcefulness, slavery, danger in the alley and the heart, life in hiding, stoicism, the art of experiment and devilry of every kind, that everything evil, terrible, tyrannical in man, everything in him that is kin to beasts of prey and serpents, serves the enhancement of the species "man" as much as its opposite does. Indeed, we do not even say enough when we say only that much; and at any rate we are at this point, in what we say and keep silent about, at the *other* end from all modern ideology and herd desiderata—as their antipodes perhaps?

Is it any wonder that we "free spirits" are not exactly the most communicative spirits? that we do not want to betray in every particular *from what* a spirit can liberate himself and *to what* he may then be driven? And as for the meaning of the dangerous formula "beyond good and evil," with which we at least guard against being mistaken for others: we *are* something different from *"libres penseurs," "liberi pensatori," "Freidenker,"*[43] and whatever else all these goodly advocates of "modern ideas" like to call themselves.

At home, or at least having been guests, in many countries of the spirit; having escaped again and again from the musty agreeable nooks into which preference and prejudice, youth, origin, the accidents of people and books, or even exhaustion from wandering seemed to have banished us; full of malice against the lures of dependence that lie hidden in honors, or money, or offices, or enthusiasms of the senses; grateful even to need and fluctuating sickness because they always rid us from some rule and its "prejudice," grateful to god, devil, sheep, and worm in us; curious to a vice, investigators to the point of cruelty, with uninhibited fingers for the unfathomable, with teeth and stomachs for the most indigestible, ready for every feat that requires a sense of acuteness and acute senses, ready for every venture, thanks to an excess of "free will," with fore- and back-souls into whose ultimate intentions nobody can look so easily, with fore- and backgrounds which no foot is likely to explore to the end; concealed under cloaks of light, conquerors even if we look like heirs and prodigals, arrangers and collectors from morning until late, misers of our riches and our crammed drawers, economical in learning and forgetting, inventive in schemas, occasionally proud of tables of categories, occasionally pedants, occasionally night owls of work even in broad daylight; yes, when it is necessary even scarecrows—and today it is necessary; namely, insofar as we are born, sworn, jealous friends of *solitude,* of our own most profound, most midnightly, most middaily solitude: that is the type of man we are, we free spirits! And perhaps *you* have something of this, too, you that are coming, you *new* philosophers?

Translated by Walter Kaufmann

Maxims and Interludes
(Selections)

80.

A matter that becomes clear ceases to concern us.—What was on the mind of that god who counseled: "Know thyself!" Did he mean: "Cease to concern yourself! Become objective!"—And Socrates?—And "scientific men"?—

155.

The sense of the tragic gains and wanes with sensuality.

Translated by Walter Kaufmann

Concerning the Natural History of Morals
(Selections)

190.

There is something in the morality of Plato that does not really belong to Plato but is merely encountered in his philosophy—one might say, in spite of Plato: namely, the Socratism for which he was really too noble. "Nobody wants to do harm to himself, therefore all that is bad is done involuntarily. For the bad do harm to themselves: this they would not do if they knew that the bad is bad. Hence the bad are bad only because of an error; if one removes the error, one necessarily makes them—good."

This type of inference smells of the *rabble* that sees nothing in bad actions but the unpleasant consequences and really judges, "it is *stupid* to do what is bad," while "good" is taken without further ado to be identical with "useful and agreeable." In the case of every moral utilitarianism one may immediately infer the same origin and follow one's nose: one will rarely go astray.

Plato did everything he could in order to read something refined and noble into the proposition of his teacher—above all, himself. He was the most audacious of all interpreters and took the whole Socrates only the way one picks a popular tune and folk song from the streets in order to vary it into the infinite and impossible— namely, into all of his own masks and multiplicities. In a jest, Homeric at that: what is the Platonic Socrates after all if not *prosthe Platōn opithen te Platōn messē te Chimaira.*[44]

191.

The ancient theological problem of "faith" and "knowledge"—or, more clearly, of instinct and reason—in other words, the question whether regarding the valuation of things instinct deserves more authority than rationality, which wants us to evaluate and act in accordance with reasons, with a "why?"—in other words, in accordance with expedience and utility—this is still the ancient moral problem that first emerged in the person of Socrates and divided thinking people long before Christianity. Socrates himself, to be sure, with the taste of his talent—that of a superior dialectician— had initially sided with reason; and in fact, what did he do his life long but laugh at the awkward incapacity of noble Athenians who, like all noble men, were men of instinct and never could give sufficient information about the reasons for their actions? In the end, however, privately and secretly, he laughed at himself, too: in himself he found, before his subtle conscience and self-examination, the same difficulty and incapacity. But is that any reason, he encouraged himself, for giving up the instincts? One has to see to it that they as well as reason receive their due—one must follow the instincts but persuade reason to assist them with good reasons.

This was the real *falseness* of that great ironic, so rich in secrets; he got his conscience to be satisfied with a kind of self-trickery: at bottom, he had seen through the irrational element in moral judgments.

Plato, more innocent in such matters and lacking the craftiness of the plebeian, wanted to employ all his strength—the greatest strength any philosopher so far has had at his disposal—to prove to himself that reason and instinct of themselves tend toward one goal, the good, "God." And since Plato, all theologians and philosophers are on the same track—that is, in moral matters it has so far been instinct, or what the Christians call "faith," or "the herd," as I put it, that has triumphed. Perhaps Descartes should be excepted, as the father of rationalism (and hence the grandfather of the Revolution) who conceded authority to reason alone: but reason is merely an instrument, and Descartes was superficial.

202.

Let us immediately say once more what we have already said a hundred times, for today's ears resist such truths—*our* truths. We know well enough how insulting it sounds when anybody counts man, unadorned and without metaphor, among the animals; but it will be charged against us as almost a *guilt* that precisely for the men of "modern ideas" we constantly employ such expressions as "herd," "herd instincts," and so forth. What can be done about it? We cannot do anything else; for here exactly lies our novel insight. We have found that in all major moral judgments Europe is now of one mind, including even the countries dominated by the influence of Europe: plainly, one now *knows* in Europe what Socrates thought he did not know and what that famous old serpent once promised to teach—today one "knows" what is good and evil.

Now it must sound harsh and cannot be heard easily when we keep insisting: that which here believes it knows, that which here glorifies itself with its praises and reproaches, calling itself good, that is the instinct of the herd animal, man, which has scored a breakthrough and attained preponderance and predominance over other instincts—and this development is continuing in accordance with the growing physiological approximation and assimilation of which it is the symptom. *Morality in Europe today is herd animal morality*—in other words, as we understand it, merely *one* type of human morality beside which, before which, and after which many other types, above all *higher* moralities, are, or ought to be, possible. But this morality resists such a "possibility," such an "ought" with all its power: it says stubbornly and inexorably, "I am morality itself, and nothing else is morality." Indeed, with the help of a religion which indulged and flattered the most sublime herd-animal desires, we have reached the point where we find even in political and social institutions an ever more visible expression of this morality: the *democratic* movement is the heir of the Christian movement.

But there are indications that its tempo is still much too slow and sleepy for the more impatient, for the sick, the sufferers of the instinct mentioned: witness the ever madder howling of the anarchist dogs who are baring their fangs more and more obviously and roam through the alleys of European culture. They seem opposites of the peacefully industrious democrats and ideologists of revolution, and even more so of the doltish philosophasters and brotherhood enthusiasts who call themselves socialists and want a "free society"; but in fact they are at one with the lot in their thorough and instinctive hostility to every other form of society except that of the *autonomous* herd (even to the point of repudiating the very concepts of "master" and "servant"—*ni dieu ni maître*[45] runs a socialist formula). They are at one in their tough resistance to every special claim, every special right and privilege (which means in the last analysis, *every* right: for once all are equal, nobody needs "rights" anymore). They are at one in their mistrust of punitive justice (as if it were a violation of those who are weaker, a wrong against the *necessary* consequence of all previous society). But they are also at one in the religion of pity, in feeling with all who feel, live, and suffer (down to the animal, up to "God"—the excess of a "pity with God" belongs in a democratic age). They are at one, the lot of them, in the cry and the impatience of pity, in their deadly hatred of suffering generally, in their almost feminine inability to remain spectators, to *let* someone suffer. They are at one in their involuntary plunge into gloom and unmanly tenderness under whose spell Europe seems threatened by a new Buddhism. They are at one in their faith in the morality of *shared* pity, as if that were morality in itself, being the height, the *attained* height of man, the sole hope of the future, the consolation of present man, the great absolution from all former guilt. They are at one, the lot of them, in their faith in the community as the *savior,* in short, in the herd, in "themselves"—

Translated by Walter Kaufmann

We Scholars
(Selections)

205.

The dangers for a philosopher's development are indeed so manifold today that one may doubt whether this fruit can still ripen at all. The scope and the tower-building of the sciences has grown to be enormous, and with this also the probability that the philosopher grows weary while still learning or allows himself to be detained somewhere to become a "specialist"—so he never attains his proper level, the height for a comprehensive look, for looking around, for looking *down.* Or he attains it too late, when his best time and strength are spent—or impaired, coarsened, degenerated, so his view, his overall value judgment does not mean much anymore. It may be precisely the sensitivity of his intellectual conscience that leads him to delay somewhere along the way and to be late: he is afraid of the seduction to become a dilettante, a millipede, an insect with a thousand antennae; he knows too well that whoever has lost his self-respect cannot command or *lead* in the realm of knowledge—unless he would like to become a great actor, a philosophical Cagliostro[45a] and pied piper, in short, a seducer. This is in the end a question of taste, even if it were not a question of conscience.

Add to this, by way of once more doubling the difficulties for a philosopher, that he demands of himself a judgment, a *yes* or *no,* not about the sciences but about life and the value of life—that he is reluctant to come to believe that he has a right, or even a duty, to such a judgment, and must seek his way to this right and faith only from the most comprehensive—perhaps most disturbing and destructive[46]—experiences, and frequently hesitates, doubts, and lapses into silence.

Indeed, the crowd has for a long time misjudged and mistaken the philosopher, whether for a scientific man and ideal scholar or for a religiously elevated, desensualized,[47] "desecularized" enthusiast and sort of God.[48] And if a man is praised today for living "wisely" or "as a philosopher," it hardly means more than "prudently and apart." Wisdom seems to the rabble a kind of escape, a means and trick for getting well out of a wicked game. But the genuine philosopher—as it seems to *us*, my friends?—lives "unphilosophically" and "unwisely," above all *imprudently*, and feels the burden and the duty of a hundred attempts and temptations of life—he risks *himself* constantly, he plays the wicked game.

206.

Compared to a genius—that is, to one who either *begets* or *gives birth*, taking both terms in their most elevated sense—the scholar, the average scientific man, always rather resembles an old maid: like her he is not conversant with the two most valuable functions of man. Indeed, one even concedes to both, to the scholars and to old maids, as it were, by way of a compensation, that they are respectable—one stresses their respectability—and yet feels annoyed all over at having to make this concession.

Let us look more closely: what is the scientific man? To begin with, a type of man that is not noble, with the virtues of a type of man that is not noble, which is to say, a type that does not dominate and is neither authoritative nor self-sufficient: he has industriousness, patient acceptance of his place in rank and file, evenness and moderation in his abilities and needs, an instinct for his equals and for what they need; for example, that bit of independence and green pasture without which there is no quiet work, that claim to honor and recognition (which first of all presupposes literal recognition and recognizability), that sunshine of a good name, that constant attestation of his value and utility which is needed to overcome again and again the internal *mistrust* which is the sediment in the hearts of all dependent men and herd animals.

The scholar also has, as is only fair, the diseases and bad manners of a type that is not noble: he is rich in petty envy and has lynx eyes for what is base in natures to whose heights he cannot attain. He is familiar, but only like those who let themselves go, not *flow*; and precisely before those who flow like great currents he freezes and becomes doubly reserved: his eye becomes like a smooth and reluctant lake with not a ripple of delight or sympathy. The worst and most dangerous thing of which scholars are capable comes from their sense of the mediocrity of their own type—from that Jesuitism of mediocrity which instinctively works at the anni-hilation of the uncommon man and tries to break every bent bow or, preferably, to unbend it. Unbending—considerately, of course, with a solicitous hand—*unbending* with familiar pity, that is the characteristic art of Jesuitism which has always known how to introduce itself as a religion of pity.

211.

I insist that people should finally stop confounding philosophical laborers, and scientific men generally, with philosophers; precisely at this point we should be strict about giving "each his due," and not far too much to those and far too little to these.

It may be necessary for the education of a genuine philosopher that he himself has also once stood on all these steps on which his servants, the scientific laborers of philosophy, remain standing—*have to* remain standing. Perhaps he himself must have been critic and skeptic and dogmatist and historian and also poet and collector and traveler and solver of riddles and moralist and seer and "free spirit" and almost everything in order to pass through the whole range of human values and value feelings and to be *able* to see with many different eyes and consciences, from a height and into every distance, from the depths into every height, from a nook into every expanse. But all these are merely preconditions of his task: this task itself demands something different—it demands that he *create values*.

Those philosophical laborers after the noble model of Kant and Hegel have to determine and press into formulas, whether in the realm of *logic* or *political* (moral) thought or *art,* some great data of valuations—that is, former *positings* of values, creations of value which have become dominant and are for a time called "truths." It is for these investigators to make everything that has happened and been esteemed so far easy to look over, easy to think over, intelligible and manageable, to abbreviate everything long, even "time," and to *overcome* the entire past—an enormous and won-derful task in whose service every subtle pride, every tough will can certainly find satisfaction. *Genuine philosophers, however, are commanders and legislators:* they say "*thus* it *shall* be!" They first determine the whither and for what of man, and in so doing have at their disposal the preliminary labor of all philosophical laborers, all who have overcome the past. With a creative hand they reach for the future, and all that is and has been becomes a means for them, an instrument, a hammer. Their "knowing" is *creating*, their creating is a legislation, their will to truth is—*will to power*.

Are there such philosophers today? Have there been such philosophers yet? *Must* there not be such philosophers?

213.

What a philosopher is, that is hard to learn because it cannot be taught: one must "know" it, from experience—or one should have the pride *not* to know it. But nowadays all the world talks of things of which it *cannot* have any experience, and this is most true, and in the worst way, concerning philosophers and philosophical states: exceedingly few know them, may know them, and all popular opinions about them are false.

That genuinely philosophical combination, for example, of a bold and exuberant intellectuality that runs *presto* and a dialectical severity and necessity that takes no false step is unknown to most thinkers and scholars from their own experience, and therefore would seem incredible to them if somebody should speak of it in their presence. They picture every necessity as a kind of need, as a painstaking having-to-follow and being-compelled. And thinking itself they regard as something slow and hesitant, almost as toil, and often enough as "worthy of the *sweat* of the noble"—but not in the least as something light, divine, closely related to dancing and high spirits. "Thinking" and taking a matter "seriously," considering it "grave"—for them all this belongs together: that is the only way they have "experienced" it.

Artists seem to have more sensitive noses in these matters, knowing only too well that precisely when they no longer do anything "voluntarily" but do everything of necessity, their feeling of freedom, subtlety, full power, of creative placing, disposing, and forming reaches its peak—in short, that necessity and "freedom of the will" then become one in them.

Ultimately, there is an order of rank among states of the soul, and the order of rank of problems accords with this. The highest problems repulse everyone mercilessly who dares approach them without being predestined for their solution by the height and power of his intellectuality. What does it avail when nimble smarties or clumsy solid mechanics and empiricists push near them, as is common today, trying with their plebeian ambition to enter the "court of courts." Upon such carpets coarse feet may never step: the primeval law of things takes care of that; the doors remain closed to such obtrusiveness, even if they crash and crush their heads against them.

For every high world one must be born; or to speak more clearly, one must be *cultivated* for it: a right to philosophy—taking that word in its great sense—one has only by virtue of one's origins; one's ancestors, one's "blood"[49] decide here, too. Many generations must have labored to prepare the origin of the philosopher; every one of his virtues must have been acquired, nurtured, inherited, and digested singly, and not only the bold, light, delicate gait and course of his thoughts but, above all, the readiness for great responsibilities, the loftiness of glances that dominate and look down, feeling separated from the crowd and its duties and virtues, the affable protection and defense of whatever is misunderstood and slandered, whether it be god or devil, the pleasure and exercise of the great justice, the art of command, the width of the will, the slow eye that rarely admires, rarely looks up, rarely loves.

Translated by Walter Kaufmann

What Is Noble?
(Selections)
289.

In the writings of a hermit one always also hears something of the echo of the desolate regions, something of the whispered tones and the furtive look of solitude; in his strongest words, even in his cry, there still vibrates a new and dangerous kind of silence—of burying something in silence. When a man has been sitting alone with his soul in confidential discord and discourse, year in and year out, day and night; when in his cave—it may be a labyrinth or a gold mine—he has become a cave bear or a treasure digger or a treasure guard and dragon; then even his concepts eventually acquire a peculiar twilight color, an odor just as much of depth as of must, something incommunicable and recalcitrant that blows at every passerby like a chill.

The hermit does not believe that any philosopher—assuming that every philosopher was first of all a hermit—ever expressed his real and ultimate opinions in books: does one not write books precisely to conceal what one harbors?[50] Indeed, he will doubt whether a philosopher could *possibly* have "ultimate and real" opinions, whether behind every one of his caves there is not, must not be, another deeper cave—a more comprehensive, stranger, richer world beyond the surface, an abysmally deep ground behind every ground, under every attempt to furnish "grounds."[51] Every philosophy is a foreground philosophy—that is a hermit's judgment: "There is something arbitrary in his stopping *here* to look back and look around, in his not digging deeper *here* but laying his spade aside; there is also something suspicious about it." Every philosophy also *conceals* a philosophy; every opinion is also a hideout, every word also a mask.

292.

A philosopher is a human being who constantly experiences, sees, hears, suspects, hopes, and dreams extraordinary things; who is struck by his own thoughts as from outside, as from above and below, as by *his* type of experiences and lightning bolts; who is perhaps himself a storm pregnant with new lightnings; a fatal human being around whom there are constant rumblings and growlings, crevices, and uncanny doings. A philosopher—alas, a being that often runs away from itself, often is afraid of itself—but too inquisitive not to "come to" again—always back to himself.

295.

The genius of the heart, as that great concealed one possesses it, the tempter god and born pied piper of consciences whose voice knows how to descend into the netherworld of every soul; who does not say a word or cast a glance in which there is no consideration and secret enticement;[52] whose mastery includes the knowledge of how to seem—not what he is but what is to those who follow him one *more* constraint to press ever closer to him in order to follow him ever more inwardly and thoroughly—the genius of the heart who silences all that is loud and self-satisfied, teaching it to listen; who smooths rough souls and lets them taste a new desire—to lie still as a mirror, that the deep sky may mirror itself in them—the genius of the heart who teaches the doltish and rash hand to hesitate and reach out more delicately; who guesses the concealed and forgotten treasure, the drop of graciousness and sweet spirituality[53] under dim and thick ice, and is a divining rod for every grain of gold that has long lain buried in the dungeon of much mud and sand; the genius of the heart from whose touch everyone walks away richer, not having received grace and surprised, not as blessed and oppressed by alien goods, but richer in himself, newer to himself than before, broken open, blown at and sounded out by a thawing wind, perhaps more unsure, tenderer, more fragile, more broken, but full of hopes that as yet have no name, full of new will and currents, full of new dissatisfaction and undertows—but what am I doing, my friends? Of whom am I speaking to you? Have I forgotten myself so far that I have not even told you his name? Unless you have guessed by yourselves who this questionable spirit and god is who wants to be *praised* in such fashion. For just as happens to everyone who from childhood has always been roaming and in foreign parts, many strange and not undangerous spirits have crossed my path, too, but above all he of whom I was speaking just now, and he again and again— namely, no less a one than the god *Dionysus*, that great ambiguous one and tempter god to whom I once offered, as you know, in all secrecy and reverence, my firstborn—as the last, it seems to me, who offered him a *sacrifice:* for I have found no one who understood what I was doing then.[54]

Meanwhile I have learned much, all too much, more about the philosophy of this god, and, as I said, from mouth to mouth—I, the last disciple and initiate of the god Dionysus—and I suppose I might begin at long last to offer you, my friends, a few tastes of this philosophy, insofar as this is permitted to me? In an undertone, as is fitting, for it concerns much that is secret, new, strange, odd, uncanny.

Even that Dionysus is a philosopher, and that gods, too, thus do philosophy, seems to me to be a novelty that is far from innocuous and might arouse suspicion precisely among philosophers. Among you, my friends, it will not seem so offensive, unless it comes too late and not at the right moment; for today, as I have been told, you no longer like to believe in God and gods. Perhaps I shall also have to carry frankness further in my tale than will always be pleasing to the strict habits of your ears? Certainly the god in question went farther, very much farther, in dialogues of this sort and was always many steps ahead of me.

Indeed, if it were permitted to follow human custom in according to him many solemn pomp-and-virtue names, I should have to give abundant praise to his exploring and discovering courage, his daring honesty, truthfulness, and love of wisdom. But such a god has no use whatever for all such venerable junk and pomp. "Keep that," he would say, "for yourself and your likes and whoever else has need of it! I—have no reason for covering my nakedness."

One guesses: this type of deity and philosopher is perhaps lacking in shame?

Thus he once said: "Under certain circumstances I love what is human"—and with this he alluded to Ariadne, who was present. "Man is to my mind an agreeable, courageous, inventive animal that has no equal on earth; it finds its way in any labyrinth. I am well disposed towards him: I often reflect how I might yet advance him and make him stronger, more evil, and more profound than he is."

"Stronger, more evil, and more profound?" I asked startled. "Yes," he said once more; "stronger, more evil, and more profound; also more beautiful"—and at that the tempter god smiled with his halcyon smile as though he had just paid an enchanting compliment. Here we also see: what this divinity lacks is not only a sense of shame—and there are also other good reasons for conjecturing that in several respects all of the gods could learn from us humans. We humans are—more humane.[55]

Translated by Walter Kaufmann

From *On the Genealogy of Morals: A Polemic* (1887)

Preface

(Selection)

7.

L et it suffice that, after this prospect had opened up before me, I had reasons to look about me for scholarly, bold, and industrious comrades (I am still looking). The project is to traverse with quite novel questions, and as though with new eyes, the enormous, distant, and so well hidden land of morality—of morality that has actually existed, actually been lived; and does this not mean virtually to *discover* this land for the first time?

If I considered in this connection the above-mentioned Dr. Rée,[56] among others, it was because I had no doubt that the very nature of his inquiries would compel him to adopt a better method for reaching answers. Have I deceived myself in this? My desire, at any rate, was to point out to so sharp and disinterested an eye as his a better direction in which to look, in the direction of an actual *history of morality,* and to warn him in time against gazing around haphazardly in the blue after the English fashion. For it must be obvious which color is a hundred times more vital for a genealogist of morals than blue: namely *gray,* that is, what is documented, what can actually be confirmed and has actually existed, in short the entire long hieroglyphic record, so hard to decipher, of the moral past of mankind!

This was unknown to Dr. Rée; but he had read Darwin—so that in his hypotheses, and after a fashion that is at least entertaining, the Darwinian beast and the ultramodern unassuming moral milk-sop who "no longer bites" politely link hands, the latter wearing an expression of a certain good-natured and refined indolence, with which is mingled even a grain of pessimism and weariness, as if all these things—the problems of morality—were really not worth taking quite so seriously. But to me, on the contrary, there seems to be nothing *more* worth taking seriously, among the rewards for it being that some day one will perhaps be allowed to take them *cheerfully.* For cheerfulness—or, in my own language, *gay science*—is a reward: the reward of a long, brave, industrious, and subterranean seriousness, of which, to be sure, not everyone is capable. But on the day we can say with all our hearts, "Onwards! our old morality, too, is part of the *comedy!*" we shall have discovered a new complication and possibility for the Dionysian drama of "The Destiny of the Soul"—and one can wager that the grand old eternal comic poet of our existence will be quick to make use of it!

Translated by Walter Kaufmann
and R. J. Hollingdale

What Is the Meaning of Ascetic Ideals?
(Selections)

Unconcerned, mocking, violent—thus wisdom wants *us:* she is a woman and always loves only a warrior.
Thus Spoke Zarathustra[57]

1.

What is the meaning of ascetic ideals? In the case of artists, they mean nothing or too many things; in the case of philosophers and scholars, something like a sense and instinct for the most favorable preconditions of higher intellectuality; in the case of women, at best one *more* seductive charm, a touch of *morbidezza* in fair flesh, the angelic look of a plump pretty animal; in the case of the physiologically deformed and disgruntled[58] (the *majority* of mortals), an attempt to see themselves as "too good" for this world, a saintly form of debauch, their chief weapon in the struggle against slow pain and boredom; in the case of priests, the distinctive priestly faith, their best instrument of power, also the "supreme" license for power; in the case of saints, finally, a pretext for hibernation, their *novissima gloriae cupido*,[59] their repose in nothingness ("God"), their form of madness. *That* the ascetic ideal has meant so many things to man, however, is an expression of the basic fact of the human will, its *horror vacui:*[60] *It needs a goal*—and it will rather will *nothingness* than *not* will.—Am I understood? . . . Have I been understood? . . . *"Not at all, my dear sir!"*—Then let us start again, from the beginning.

7.

Let us not become gloomy as soon as we hear the word "torture": in this particular case there is plenty to offset and mitigate that word—even something to laugh at. Above all, we should not underestimate the fact that Schopenhauer, who treated sexuality as a personal enemy (including its tool, woman, that *"instrumentum diaboli"*[61]), *needed* enemies in order to keep in good spirits; that he loved grim, bilious, black-green words, that he raged for the sake of raging, out of passion; that he would have become ill, become a *pessimist* (for he was not one, however much he desired it), if deprived of his enemies, of Hegel, of woman, of sensuality and the whole will to existence, to persistence. Without these, Schopenhauer would *not* have persisted, one may wager on that; he would have run away: but his enemies held him fast, his enemies seduced him ever again to existence; his anger was, just as in the case of the Cynics of antiquity, his balm, his refreshment, his reward, his specific against disgust, his *happiness*. So much in regard to what is most personal in the case of Schopenhauer; on the other hand, there is also something typical in him—and here we finally come back to our problem.

As long as there are philosophers on earth, and wherever there have been philosophers (from India to England, to take the antithetical poles of philosophical endowment), there unquestionably exists a peculiar philosophers' irritation at and rancor against sensuality: Schopenhauer is merely its most eloquent and, if one has ears for this, most ravishing and delightful expression. There also exists a peculiar philosophers' prejudice and affection in favor of the whole ascetic ideal; one should not overlook that. Both, to repeat, pertain to the type; if both are lacking in a philosopher, then—one can be sure of it—he is always only a "so-called" philosopher. What does that *mean?* For this fact has to be interpreted: *in itself* it just stands there, stupid to all eternity, like every "thing-in-itself."

Every animal—therefore *la bête philosophe,*[62] too—instinctively strives for an optimum of favorable conditions under which it can expend all its strength and achieve its maximal feeling of power; every animal abhors, just as instinctively and with a subtlety of discernment that is "higher than all reason," every kind of intrusion or hindrance that obstructs or could obstruct this path to the optimum (I am *not* speaking of its path to happiness, but its path to power, to action, to the most powerful activity, and in most cases actually its path to unhappiness). Thus the philosopher abhors *marriage,* together with that which might persuade to it—marriage being a hindrance and calamity on his path to the optimum. What great philosopher hitherto has been married? Heraclitus, Plato, Descartes, Spinoza, Leibniz, Kant, Schopenhauer—they were not; more, one cannot even *imagine* them married. A married philosopher belongs *in comedy,* that is my proposition—and as for that exception, Socrates[63]—the malicious Socrates, it would seem, married *ironically,* just to demonstrate *this* proposition.

Every philosopher would speak as Buddha did when he was told of the birth of a son: "Rahula has been born to me, a fetter has been forged for me" (Rahula here means "a little demon"); every "free spirit" would experience a thoughtful moment, supposing he had previously experienced a thoughtless one, of the kind that once came to the same Buddha—"narrow and oppressive," he thought to himself, "is life in a house, a place of impurity; freedom lies in leaving the house": "thinking thus, he left the house." Ascetic ideals reveal so many bridges to *independence* that a philosopher is bound to rejoice and clap his hands when he hears the story of all those resolute men who one day said No to all servitude and went into some *desert:* even supposing they were merely strong asses and quite the reverse of a strong spirit.

What, then, is the meaning of the ascetic ideal in the case of a philosopher? My answer is—you will have guessed it long ago: the philosopher sees in it an optimum condition for the highest and boldest intellectuality and smiles—he does *not* deny "existence," he rather affirms *his* existence and *only* his existence, and this perhaps to the point at which he is not far from harboring the outrageous wish: *pereat mundus, fiat philosophia, fiat philosophus, f i a m!*[64]

23.

The ascetic ideal has not only ruined health and taste, it has also ruined a third, fourth, fifth, sixth thing as well—I beware of enumerating everything (I'd never finish). It is my purpose here to bring to light, not what this ideal has *done,* but simply what it *means;* what it indicates; what lies hidden behind it, beneath it, in it; of what it is the provisional, indistinct expression, overlaid with question marks and misunderstandings. And it is only in pursuit of *this* end that I could not spare my readers a glance at its monstrous and calamitous effects, to prepare them for the ultimate and most terrifying aspect of the question concerning the meaning for me of this ideal. What is the meaning of the *power* of this ideal, the monstrous nature of its power? Why has it been allowed to flourish to this extent? Why has it not rather been resisted? The ascetic ideal expresses a will: *where* is the opposing will that might express an *opposing ideal?* The ascetic ideal has a *goal*—this goal is so universal that all the other interests of human existence seem, when compared with it, petty and narrow; it interprets epochs, nations, and men inexorably with a view to this one goal; it permits no other interpretation, no other goal; it rejects, denies, affirms, and sanctions solely from the point of view of *its* interpretation (and has there ever been a system of interpretation more thoroughly thought through?); it submits to no power, it believes in its own predominance over every other power, in its absolute *superiority of rank* over every other power—it believes that no power exists on earth that does not first have to receive a meaning, a right to exist, a value, as a tool of the ascetic ideal, as a way and means to *its* goal, to *one* goal.—Where is the match of this closed system of will, goal, and interpretation? Why has it not found its match?— Where is the *other* "*one* goal"?

But they tell me it is *not* lacking, it has not merely waged a long and successful fight against this ideal, it has already conquered this ideal in all important respects: all of modern *science*[65] is supposed to bear witness to that—modern science which, as a genuine philosophy of reality, clearly believes in itself alone, clearly possesses the courage for itself and the will to itself, and has up to now survived well enough without God, the beyond, and the virtues of denial. Such noisy agitators' chatter, however, does not impress me: these trumpeters of reality are bad musicians, their voices obviously do *not* come from the depths, the abyss of the scientific conscience does *not* speak through them—for today the scientific conscience is an abyss—the word "science" in the mouths of such trumpeters is simply an indecency, an abuse, and a piece of impudence. The truth is precisely the opposite of what is asserted here: science today has absolutely *no* belief in itself, let alone an ideal above it—and where it still inspires passion, love, ardor, and *suffering* at all, it is not the opposite of the ascetic ideal but rather *the latest and noblest form of it*. Does that sound strange to you?

Today there are plenty of modest and worthy laborers[66] among scholars, too, who are happy in their little niches; and because they are happy there, they sometimes demand rather immodestly that one ought to be content with things today, generally—especially in the domain of science, where so much that is useful remains to be done. I am not denying that; the last thing I want is to destroy the pleasure these honest workers[67] take in their craft: for I approve of their work. But that one works rigorously in the sciences, and that there are contented workers, certainly does *not* prove that science as a whole possesses a goal, a will, an ideal, or the passion of a great faith. The opposite is the case; to repeat: where it is not the latest expression of the ascetic ideal—and the exceptions are too rare, noble, and atypical to refute the general proposition— science today is a *hiding place* for every kind of discontent, disbelief, gnawing worm, *despectio sui*,[67a] bad conscience—it is the unrest of the *lack* of ideals, the suffering from the *lack* of any great love, the discontent in the face of involuntary contentment.

Oh, what does science not conceal today! How much, at any rate, is it *meant* to conceal! The proficiency of our finest scholars, their heedless industry, their heads smoking day and night, their very craftsmanship—how often the real meaning of all this lies in the desire to keep something hidden from oneself! Science as a means of self-narcosis: *do you have experience of that?*

Whoever associates with scholars knows that one occasionally wounds them to the marrow with some harmless word; one incenses one's scholarly friends just when one means to honor them, one can drive them beside themselves merely because one has been too coarse to realize with whom one was really dealing—with *sufferers* who refuse to admit to themselves what they are, with drugged and heedless men who fear only one thing: *regaining consciousness.*

25.

No! Don't come to me with science when I ask for the natural antagonist of the ascetic ideal, when I demand: "where is the opposing will expressing the *opposing ideal?*" Science is not nearly self-reliant enough to be that; it first requires in every respect an ideal of value, a value-creating power, in the *service* of which it could *believe* in itself—it never creates values. Its relation to the ascetic ideal is by no means essentially antagonistic; it might even be said to represent the driving force in the latter's inner development. It opposes and fights, on closer inspection, not the ideal itself but only its exteriors, its guise and masquerade, its temporary dogmatic hardening and stiffening, and by denying what is exoteric in this ideal, it liberates what life is in it. This pair, science and the ascetic ideal, both rest on the same foundation—I have already indicated it: on the same overestimation of truth (more exactly: on the same belief that truth is inestimable and cannot be criticized). Therefore they are *necessarily* allies, so that if they are to be fought they can only be fought and called in question together. A depreciation of the ascetic ideal unavoidably involves a depreciation of science: one must keep one's eyes and ears open to this fact!

(*Art*—to say it in advance, for I shall some day return to this subject at greater length—art, in which precisely the *lie* is sanctified and the *will to deception* has a good conscience, is much more fundamentally opposed to the ascetic ideal than is science: this was instinctively sensed by Plato, the greatest enemy of art Europe has yet produced. Plato versus Homer: that is the complete, the genuine antagonism—there the sincerest advocate of the "beyond," the great slanderer of life; here the instinctive deifier, the *golden* nature. To place himself in the service of the ascetic ideal is therefore the most distinctive *corruption* of an artist that is at all possible; unhappily, also one of the most common forms of corruption, for nothing is more easily corrupted than an artist.)

Physiologically, too, science rests on the same foundation as the ascetic ideal: a certain *impoverishment of life* is a presupposition of both of them—the affects grown cool, the tempo of life slowed down, dialectics in place of instinct, seriousness imprinted on faces and gestures (seriousness, the most unmistakable sign of a labored metabolism, of struggling, laborious life). Observe the ages in the history of people when the scholar steps into the foreground: they are ages of exhaustion, often of evening and decline; overflowing energy, certainty of life and of the *future,* are things of the past. A predominance of mandarins always means something is wrong; so do the advent of democracy, international courts in place of war, equal rights for women, the religion of pity, and whatever other symptoms of declining life there are. (Science posed as a problem; what is the meaning of science?—cf. the preface to *The Birth of Tragedy.*)

No! this "modern science"—let us face this fact!—is the *best* ally the ascetic ideal has at present, and precisely because it is the most unconscious, involuntary, hidden, and subterranean ally! They have played the same game up to now, the "poor in spirit" and the scientific opponents of this ideal (one should not think, by the way, that they are their opposites, the *rich* in spirit perhaps— they are *not;* I have called them the hectics of the spirit). As for the famous *victories* of the latter, they undoubtedly are victories— but over what? The ascetic ideal has decidedly not been conquered: if anything, it became stronger, which is to say, more elusive, more spiritual, more captious, as science remorselessly detached and broke off wall upon wall, external additions that had coarsened its appearance. Does anyone really believe that the defeat of theological astronomy represented a defeat for that ideal?

Has man perhaps become *less desirous* of a transcendent solution to the riddle of his existence, now that this existence appears more arbitrary, idler,[68] more dispensable in the *visible* order of things? Has the self-belittlement of man, his *will* to self-belittlement, not progressed irresistibly since Copernicus? Alas, the faith in the dignity and uniqueness of man, in his irreplaceability in the great chain of being,[69] is a thing of the past—he has become an *animal,* literally and without reservation or qualification, he who was, according to his old faith, almost God ("child of God," "God-man").

Since Copernicus, man seems to have got himself on an inclined plane—now he is slipping faster and faster away from the center into—what? into nothingness? into a *"penetrating* sense of his nothingness"? Very well! hasn't this been the straightest route to— the *old* ideal?

All science (and by no means only astronomy, on the humiliating and degrading effect of which Kant made the noteworthy confession: "it destroys my importance" . . .), all science, natural as well as *unnatural*—which is what I call the self-critique of knowledge—has at present the object of dissuading man from his former respect for himself, as if this had been nothing but a piece of bizarre conceit. One might even say that its own pride, its own austere form of stoical ataraxy, consists in sustaining this hard-won *self-contempt* of man as his ultimate and most serious claim to self-respect (and quite rightly, indeed: for he that despises is always one who "has not forgotten how to respect"). Is this really to *work against* the ascetic ideal? Does one still seriously believe (as theologians imagined for a while) that Kant's *victory* over the dogmatic concepts of theology ("God," "soul," "freedom," "immortality") damaged that ideal?—it being no concern of ours for the present whether Kant ever had any intention of doing such a thing. What is certain is that, since Kant, transcendentalists of every kind have once more won the day—they have been emancipated from the theologians: what joy!—Kant showed them a secret path by which they may, on their own initiative and with all scientific respectability, from now on follow their "heart's desire."

In the same vein: who could hold it against the agnostics if, as votaries of the unknown and mysterious as such, they now worship the *question mark itself* as God? (Xaver Doudan[70] once spoke of the *ravages* worked by *"l'habitude d'admirer l'inintelligible au lieu de rester tout simplement dans l'inconnu";*[71] he thought the ancients had avoided this.) Presuming that everything man "knows" does not merely fail to satisfy his desires but rather contradicts them and produces a sense of horror, what a divine way out to have the right to seek the responsibility for this not in "desire" but in "knowledge"!

"There is no knowledge: *consequently*—there is a God"; what a new *elegantia syllogismi!*[72] what a *triumph* for the ascetic ideal!

28.

Apart from the ascetic ideal, man, the human *animal,* had no meaning so far. His existence on earth contained no goal; "why man at all?" was a question without an answer; the *will* for man and earth was lacking; behind every great human destiny there sounded as a refrain a yet greater "in vain!" *This* is precisely what the ascetic ideal means: that something was *lacking,* that man was surrounded by a fearful *void*—he did not know how to justify, to account for, to affirm himself; he *suffered* from the problem of his meaning. He also suffered otherwise, he was in the main a sickly animal: but his problem was *not* suffering itself, but that there was no answer to the crying question, *"why* do I suffer?"

Man, the bravest of animals and the one most accustomed to suffering, does *not* repudiate suffering as such; he *desires* it, he even seeks it out, provided he is shown a *meaning* for it, a *purpose* of suffering. The meaninglessness of suffering, *not* suffering itself, was the curse that lay over mankind so far—*and the ascetic ideal offered man meaning!* It was the only meaning offered so far; any meaning is better than none at all; the ascetic ideal was in every sense the *"faute de mieux"* par excellence so far. In it, suffering was *interpreted;* the tremendous void seemed to have been filled; the door was closed to any kind of suicidal nihilism. This interpretation—there is no doubt of it—brought fresh suffering with it, deeper, more inward, more poisonous, more life-destructive suffering: it placed all suffering under the perspective of *guilt.*

But all this notwithstanding—man was *saved* thereby, he possessed a meaning, he was henceforth no longer like a leaf in the wind, a plaything of nonsense—the "sense-less"—he could now *will* something; no matter at first to what end, why, with what he willed: *the will itself was saved.*

We can no longer conceal from ourselves *what* is expressed by all that willing which has taken its direction from the ascetic ideal: this hatred of the human, and even more of the animal, and more still of the material, this horror of the senses, of reason itself, this fear of happiness and beauty, this longing to get away from all appearance, change, becoming, death, wishing, from longing itself—all this means—let us dare to grasp it—*a will to nothingness,* an aversion[73] to life, a rebellion against the most fundamental presuppositions of life; but it is and remains a *will!* . . . And, to repeat in conclusion what I said at the beginning: man would rather will *nothingness* than *not* will.[74]

*Translated by Walter Kaufmann
and R. J. Hollingdale*

penhauer, including all of modern "humaneness." A profound estrangement, cold, sobering up—against everything that is of this time, everything timely—and most desirable of all, the eye of Zarathustra, an eye that beholds the whole fact of man at a tremendous distance—below. For such a goal, what sacrifice wouldn't be fitting? what "self-overcoming"? what "self-denial"?

My greatest experience was a recovery. Wagner is merely one of my sicknesses.

Not that I wish to be ungrateful to this sickness. When in this essay I assert the proposition that Wagner is harmful, I wish no less to assert for whom he is nevertheless indispensable—for the philosopher. Others may be able to get along without Wagner; but the philosopher is not free to do without Wagner. He has to be the bad conscience of his time: for that he needs to understand it best. But confronted with the labyrinth of the modern soul, where could he find a guide more initiated, a more eloquent prophet of the soul, than Wagner? Through Wagner modernity speaks most intimately, concealing neither its good nor its evil—having forgotten all sense of shame. And conversely: one has almost completed an account of the value of what is modern once one has gained clarity about what is good and evil in Wagner.

I understand perfectly when a musician says today: "I hate Wagner, but I can no longer endure any other music." But I'd also understand a philosopher who would declare: "Wagner sums up modernity. There is no way out, one must first become a Wagnerian."

Translated by Walter Kaufmann

From *The Case of Wagner:*
A Musician's Problem (1888)[75]

Preface

I have granted myself some small relief. It is not merely pure malice when I praise Bizet in this essay at the expense of Wagner. Interspersed with many jokes, I bring up a matter that is no joke. To turn my back on Wagner was for me a fate; to like anything at all again after that, a triumph. Perhaps nobody was more dangerously attached to—grown together with—Wagnerizing; nobody tried harder to resist it; nobody was happier to be rid of it. A long story!—You want a word for it?—If I were a moralist, who knows what I might call it? Perhaps self-overcoming.—But the philosopher has no love for moralists. Neither does he love pretty words.

What does a philosopher demand of himself first and last? To overcome his time in himself, to become "timeless." With what must he therefore engage in the hardest combat? With whatever marks him as the child of his time. Well, then! I am, no less than Wagner, a child of this time; that is, a decadent: but I comprehended this, I resisted it. The philosopher in me resisted.

Nothing has preoccupied me more profoundly than the problem of decadence—I had reasons. "Good and evil" is merely a variation of that problem. Once one has developed a keen eye for the symptoms of decline, one understands morality, too—one understands what is hiding under its most sacred names and value formulas: impoverished life, the will to the end, the great weariness. Morality negates life.

For such a task I required a special self-discipline: to take sides against everything sick in me, including Wagner, including Scho-

From *Twilight of the Idols; or, How One Philosophizes with a Hammer* (1888)

Maxims and Arrows

(Selection)

11.

Can an *ass* be tragic? To perish under a burden one can neither bear nor throw off? The case of the philosopher.

Translated by Walter Kaufmann

The Problem of Socrates

1.

Concerning life, the wisest men of all ages have judged alike: *it is no good*. Always and everywhere one has heard the same sound from their mouths—a sound full of doubt, full of melancholy, full of weariness of life, full of resistance to life. Even Socrates said, as he died: "To live—that means to be sick a long time: I owe Asclepius the Savior[76] a rooster." Even Socrates was tired of it. What does that evidence? What does it evince? Formerly one would have said (—oh, it has been said, and loud by enough, and especially by our pessimists): "At least something of all this must be true! The *consensus sapientium*[77] evidences the truth." Shall we still talk like that today? *May* we? "At least something must be *sick* here," *we* retort. These wisest men of all ages—they should first be scrutinized closely. Were they all perhaps shaky on their legs? late? tottery? decadents? Could it be that wisdom appears on earth as a raven, inspired by a little whiff of carrion?

2.

This irreverent thought that the great sages are *types of decline* first occurred to me precisely in a case where it is most strongly opposed by both scholarly and unscholarly prejudice: I recognized Socrates and Plato to be symptoms of degeneration, tools of the Greek dissolution, pseudo-Greek, anti-Greek (*The Birth of Tragedy,* 1872). That *consensus sapientium*—I comprehended this ever more clearly—proves least of all that they were right in what they agreed on: it shows rather that they themselves, these wisest men, agreed in some *physiological* respect, and hence adopted the same negative attitude to life—*had to* adopt it. Judgments, value judgments concerning life, for it or against it, can, in the end, never be true: they have value only as symptoms, they are worthy of consideration only as symptoms; in themselves such judgments are stupidities. One must by all means stretch out one's fingers and make the attempt to grasp this amazing finesse, *that the value of life cannot be estimated.* Not by the living, for they are an interested party, even a bone of contention, and not judges; not by the dead, for a different reason. For a philosopher to see a problem in the value of life is thus an objection to him, a question mark concerning his wisdom, an unwisdom. What? All these great wise men—they were not only decadents, they weren't even wise? But I return to the problem of Socrates.

3.

In origin, Socrates belonged to the lowest class: Socrates was plebs. We know, we can still see for ourselves, how ugly he was. But ugliness, in itself an objection, is among the Greeks almost a refutation. Was Socrates a Greek at all? Ugliness is often enough the expression of a development that has been crossed, *thwarted* by crossing. Or it appears as *declining* development. The anthropologists among the criminologists tell us that the typical criminal is ugly: *monstrum in fronte, monstrum in animo.*[78] But the criminal is a decadent. Was Socrates a typical criminal? At least that would not be contradicted by the famous judgment of the physiognomist which sounded so offensive to the friends of Socrates. A foreigner who knew about faces once passed through Athens and told Socrates to his face that he *was a monstrum*—that he harbored in himself all the bad vices and appetites. And Socrates merely answered: "You know me, sir!"

4.

Socrates's decadence is suggested not only by the admitted wantonness and anarchy of his instincts, but also by the hypertrophy of the logical faculty and that *malice of the rachitic* which distinguishes him. Nor should we forget those auditory hallucinations which, as "the *daimonion* of Socrates," have been interpreted religiously. Everything in him is exaggerated, *buffo,* a caricature; everything is at the same time concealed, ulterior, subterranean. I seek to comprehend what idiosyncrasy begot that Socratic equation of reason = virtue = happiness: that most bizarre of all equations, which, moreover, is opposed to all the instincts of the earlier Greeks.

5.

With Socrates, Greek taste changes in favor of dialectics. What really happened there? Above all, a *noble* taste is thus vanquished; with dialectics the plebs come to the top. Before Socrates, dialectic manners were repudiated in good society: they were considered bad manners, they were compromising. The young were warned against them. Furthermore, all such presentations of one's reasons were distrusted. Honest things, like honest men, do not carry their reasons in their hands like that. It is indecent to show all five fingers. What must first be proved is worth little. Wherever authority still forms part of good bearing, where one does not give reasons but commands, the dialectician is a kind of buffoon: one laughs at him, one does not take him seriously. Socrates was the buffoon who *got himself taken seriously:* what really happened there?

6.

One chooses dialectic only when one has no other means. One knows that one arouses mistrust with it, that it is not very persuasive. Nothing is easier to erase than a dialectical effect: the experience of every meeting at which there are speeches proves this. It can only be *self-defense* for those who no longer have other weapons. One must have to *enforce* one's right: until one reaches that point, one makes no use of it. The Jews were dialecticians for that reason; Reynard the Fox was one—and Socrates, too?

7.

Is the irony of Socrates an expression of revolt? Of plebeian resentment? Does he, as one oppressed, enjoy his own ferocity in the knife-thrusts of his syllogisms? Does he *avenge* himself on the noble people whom he fascinates? As a dialectician, one holds a merciless tool in one's hand; one can become a tyrant by means of it; one exposes those one conquers. The dialectician leaves it to his opponent to prove that he is no idiot: he makes one furious and helpless at the same time. The dialectician renders the intellect of his opponent powerless. What? Is dialectic only a form of *revenge* in Socrates?

8.

I have given to understand how it was that Socrates could repel: it is therefore all the more necessary to explain his fascination. That he discovered a new kind of *agon*,[79] that he became its first fencing master for the noble circles of Athens, is one point. He fascinated by appealing to the agonistic impulse of the Greeks— he introduced a variation into the wrestling match between young men and youths. Socrates was also a great *erotic*.

9.

But Socrates guessed even more. He saw *through* his noble Athenians; he comprehended that his own case, his idiosyncrasy, was no longer exceptional. The same kind of degeneration was quietly developing everywhere: old Athens was coming to an end. And Socrates understood that all the world *needed* him—his means, his cure, his personal artifice of self-preservation. Everywhere the instincts were in anarchy; everywhere one was within five paces of excess: *monstrum in animo* was the general danger. "The impulses want to play the tyrant; one must invent a *counter-tyrant* who is stronger." When the physiognomist had revealed to Socrates who he was—a cave of bad appetites—the great master of irony let slip another word which is the key to his character. "This is true," he said, "but I mastered them all." *How* did Socrates become master over *himself*? His case was, at bottom, merely the extreme case, only the most striking instance of what was then beginning to be a universal distress: no one was any longer master over himself, the instincts were turning *against* each other. He fascinated, being this extreme case; his fearsome ugliness proclaimed him as such to all who could see: he fascinated, of course, even more as an answer, a solution, an apparent *cure* of this case.

10.

When one finds it necessary to turn *reason* into a tyrant, as Socrates did, the danger cannot be slight that something else will play the tyrant. Rationality was then hit upon as the savior; neither Socrates nor his "patients" had any choice about being rational: it was *de rigueur,*[79a] it was their last resort. The fanaticism with which all Greek reflection throws itself upon rationality betrays a desperate situation; there was danger, there was but one choice: either to perish or—to be *absurdly rational*. The moralism of the Greek philosophers from Plato on is pathologically conditioned; so is their esteem of dialectics. Reason = virtue = happiness: which means merely that one must imitate Socrates and counter the dark appetites with a permanent daylight—the daylight of reason. One must be clever, clear, bright at any price: any concession to the instincts, to the unconscious, leads *downward*.

11.

I have given to understand how it was that Socrates fascinated: he seemed to be a physician, a savior. Is it necessary to go on to demonstrate the error in his faith in "rationality at any price"? It is a self-deception on the part of philosophers and moralists if they believe that they are extricating themselves from decadence when they merely wage war against it. Extrication lies beyond their strength: what they choose as a means, as salvation, is itself but another expression of decadence; they change its expression, but they do not get rid of decadence itself. Socrates was a misunderstanding: *the whole improvement-morality, including its Christian version, was a misunderstanding*. The most blinding daylight; rationality at any price; life, bright, cold, cautious, conscious, without instinct, in opposition to the instincts—all this, too, was a mere disease, another disease, and by no means a return to "virtue," to "health," to happiness. To *have* to fight the instincts—that is the formula of decadence: as long as life is *ascending*, happiness equals instincts.

12.

Did he himself still comprehend this, this most brilliant of all self-outwitters? Was this what he said to himself in the end, in the *wisdom* of his courage to die? Socrates *wanted* to die: not Athens, but he himself chose the hemlock; he forced Athens to sentence him. "Socrates is no physician," he said softly to himself; "here death alone is the physician. Socrates himself has merely been sick a long time."

Translated by Walter Kaufmann

"Reason" in Philosophy

1.

You ask me which of the philosophers' traits are really idiosyncrasies? For example, their lack of historical sense, their hatred of the very idea of becoming, their Egypticism. They think that they show their *respect* for a subject when they dehistoricize it, *sub specie aeterni*[80]—when they turn it into a mummy. All that philosophers have handled for thousands of years have been concept-mummies; nothing real escaped their grasp alive. When these honorable idolators of concepts worship something, they kill it and stuff it; they threaten the life of everything they worship. Death, change, old age, as well as procreation and growth, are to their minds objections—even refutations. Whatever has being does not become; whatever becomes does not have being. Now they all believe, desperately even, in what has being. But since they never grasp it, they seek for reasons why it is kept from them. "There must be mere appearance, there must be some deception which prevents us from perceiving that which has being: where is the deceiver?"

"We have found him," they cry ecstatically; "it is the senses! These senses, which are so immoral in other ways, too, deceive us concerning the *true* world. Moral: let us free ourselves from the deception of the senses, from becoming, from history, from lies; history is nothing but faith in the senses, faith in lies. Moral: let us say No to all who have faith in the senses, to all the rest of mankind; they are all 'mob.' Let us be philosophers! Let us be mummies! Let us represent monotono-theism by adopting the expression of a gravedigger! And above all, away with the body, this wretched *idée fixe* of the senses, disfigured by all the fallacies of logic, refuted, even impossible, although it is impudent enough to behave as if it were real!"

2.

With the highest respect, I except the name of *Heraclitus*. When the rest of the philosophic folk rejected the testimony of the senses because they showed multiplicity and change, he rejected their testimony because they showed things as if they had permanence and unity. Heraclitus, too, did the senses an injustice. They lie neither in the way the Eleatics[81] believed, nor as he believed—they do not lie at all. What we *make* of their testimony, that alone introduces lies; for example, the lie of unity, the lie of thinghood, of substance, of permanence. "Reason" is the cause of our falsification of the testimony of the senses. Insofar as the senses show becoming, passing away, and change, they do not lie. But Heraclitus will remain eternally right with his assertion that being is an empty fiction. The "apparent" world is the only one: the "true" world is merely added by a lie.

3.

And what magnificent instruments of observation we possess in our senses! This nose, for example, of which no philosopher has yet spoken with reverence and gratitude, is actually the most delicate instrument so far at our disposal: it is able to detect minimal differences of motion which even a spectroscope cannot detect. Today we possess science precisely to the extent to which we have decided to *accept* the testimony of the senses—to the extent to which we sharpen them further, arm them, and have learned to think them through. The rest is miscarriage and not-yet-science—in other words, metaphysics, theology, psychology, epistemology—or formal science, a doctrine of signs, such as logic and that applied logic which is called mathematics. In them, reality is not encountered at all, not even as a problem—no more than the question of the value of such a sign-convention as logic.

4.

The other idiosyncrasy of the philosophers is no less dangerous; it consists in confusing the last and the first. They place that which comes at the end—unfortunately! for it ought not to come at all!—namely, the "highest concepts"—which means the most general, the emptiest concepts, the last smoke of evaporating reality—in the beginning, *as* the beginning. This again is nothing but their way of showing reverence: the higher *must* not grow out of the lower, *must* not have grown at all. Moral: whatever is of the first rank must be *causa sui*.[82] Origin out of something else is considered an objection, a questioning of value. All the highest values are of the first rank; all the highest concepts, that which has being, the unconditional, the good, the true, the perfect—all these cannot have become and must therefore be *causa sui*. All these, moreover, cannot be unlike each other or in contradiction to each other. Thus they arrive at their stupendous concept, "God." That which is last, thinnest, and emptiest is put first, as *the* cause, as *ens realissimum*.[83] Why did mankind have to take seriously the brain afflictions of sick web-spinners? They have paid dearly for it!

5.

At long last, let us contrast the very different manner in which we conceive the problem of error and appearance. (I say "we" for politeness' sake.) Formerly, alteration, change, any becoming at all, were taken as proof of mere appearance, as an indication that there must be something which led us astray. Today, conversely—precisely insofar as the prejudice of reason forces us to posit unity, identity, permanence, substance, cause, thinghood, being—we see ourselves somehow caught in error, compelled into error. So certain are we, on the basis of rigorous examination, that this is where the error lies.

It is no different in this case than with the movement of the sun: there our eye is the constant advocate of error, here it is our language. In its origin language belongs in the age of the most rudimentary form of psychology. We enter a realm of crude fetishism when we summon before consciousness the basic presuppositions of the metaphysics of language, in plain talk, the presuppositions of reason. Everywhere it sees a doer and doing; it believes in will as *the* cause; it believes in the ego, in the ego as being, in the ego as substance, and it projects this faith in the ego-substance upon all things—only thereby does it first *create* the concept of "thing." Everywhere "being" is projected by thought, *smuggled in by it*, as the cause; the concept of being follows, and is a derivative of, the concept of ego. In the beginning there is that great calamity of an error that the will is something which is effective, that will is a capacity. Today we know that it is only a word.

Very much later, in a world which was in a thousand ways more enlightened, philosophers, to their great surprise, became aware of the sureness, the subjective certainty, in our handling of the categories of reason: they concluded that these categories could not be derived from anything empirical—for everything empirical plainly contradicted them. Whence, then, were they derived?

And in India, as in Greece, the same mistake was made: "We must once have been at home in a higher world (instead of a very much lower one, which would have been the truth); we must have been divine, *for* we have reason!" Indeed, nothing has yet possessed a more naive power of persuasion than the error concerning being, as it has been formulated by the Eleatics, for example. After all, every word we say and every sentence speak in its favor. Even the opponents of the Eleatics still succumbed to the seduction of their concept of being: Democritus, among others, when he invented his atom. "Reason" in language—oh, what an old deceptive female she is! I am afraid we are not rid of God because we still have faith in grammar.

6.

It will be appreciated if I condense so essential and so new an insight into four theses. In that way I facilitate comprehension; in that way I provoke contradiction.

First proposition. The reasons for which "this" world has been characterized as "apparent" are the very reasons which indicate its reality; any other kind of reality is absolutely indemonstrable.

Second proposition. The criteria which have been bestowed on the "true being" of things are the criteria of not-being, of *naught;* the "true world" has been constructed out of contradiction to the actual world: indeed an apparent world, insofar as it is merely a moral-optical illusion.

Third proposition. To invent fables about a world "other" than this one has no meaning at all, unless an instinct of slander, detraction, and suspicion against life has gained the upper hand in us: in that case, we avenge ourselves against life with a phantasmagoria of "another," a "better" life.

Fourth proposition. Any distinction between a "true" and an "apparent" world—whether in the Christian manner or in the manner of Kant (in the end, an underhanded Christian)—is only a suggestion of decadence, a symptom of the *decline of life*. That the artist esteems appearance higher than reality is no objection to this proposition. For "appearance" in this case means reality *once more*, only by way of selection, reinforcement, and correction. The tragic artist is no pessimist: he is precisely the one who says *yes* to everything questionable, even to the terrible—he is *Dionysian*.

Translated by Walter Kaufmann

How the "True World" Finally Became a Fable: The History of an Error

1. The true world—attainable for the sage, the pious, the virtuous man; he lives in it, *he is it.*

   (The oldest form of the idea, relatively sensible, simple, and persuasive. A circumlocution for the sentence, "I, Plato, *am* the truth.")
2. The true world—unattainable for now, but promised for the sage, the pious, the virtuous man ("for the sinner who repents").

   (Progress of the idea: it becomes more subtle, insidious, in-comprehensible—*it becomes female,* it becomes Christian.)
3. The true world—unattainable, indemonstrable, unpromisable; but the very thought of it—a consolation, an obligation, an imperative.

   (At bottom, the old sun, but seen through mist and skepticism. The idea has become elusive, pale, Nordic, Königsbergian.[84])
4. The true world—unattainable? At any rate, unattained. And being unattained, also *unknown.* Consequently, not consoling, redeeming, or obligating: how could something unknown obli-gate us?

   (Gray morning. The first yawn of reason. The cockcrow of positivism.)
5. The "true" world—an idea which is no longer good for any-thing, no longer even obligating—an idea which has become useless and superfluous—*consequently,* a refuted idea: let us abolish it!

   (Bright day; breakfast; return of *bon sens* and cheerfulness; Plato's embarrassed blush; pandemonium of all free spirits.)

6. The true world—we have abolished. What world has remained? The apparent one perhaps? But no! *With the true world we have also abolished the apparent one.*

(Noon; moment of the shortest shadow; end of the longest error; high point of humanity; INCIPIT ZARATHUSTRA.[85])

Translated by Walter Kaufmann

Skirmishes of an Untimely Man

(Selections)

10.

What is the meaning of the conceptual opposites which I have introduced into aesthetics, *Apollonian* and *Dionysian,* both conceived as kinds of intoxication? The Apollonian intoxication excites the eye above all, so that it gains the power of vision. The painter, the sculptor, the epic poet are visionaries par excellence. In the Dionysian state, on the other hand, the whole affective system is excited and enhanced: so that it discharges all its means of expression at once and drives forth simultaneously the power of representation, imitation, transfiguration, transformation, and every kind of mimicking and acting. The essential feature here remains the ease of metamorphosis, the inability *not* to react (similar to certain hysterical types who also, upon any suggestion, enter into *any* role). It is impossible for the Dionysian type not to understand any suggestion; he does not overlook any sign of an affect; he possesses the instinct of understanding and guessing in the highest degree, just as he commands the art of communication in the highest degree. He enters into any skin, into any affect: he constantly transforms himself.

Music, as we understand it today, is also a total excitement and a total discharge of the affects, but even so only the remnant of a much fuller world of expression of the affects, a mere residue of the Dionysian histrionicism. To make music possible as a separate art, a number of senses, especially the muscle sense, have been immobilized (at least relatively, for to a certain degree all rhythm still appeals to our muscles); so that man no longer bodily imitates and represents everything he feels. Nevertheless, *that* is really the normal Dionysian state, at least the original state. Music is the specialization of this state attained slowly at the expense of those faculties which are most closely related to it.

19.

Beautiful and ugly. Nothing is more conditional—or, let us say, narrower—than our feeling for beauty. Whoever would think of it apart from man's joy in man would immediately lose any foothold. "Beautiful in itself" is a mere phrase, not even a concept. In the beautiful, man posits himself as the measure of perfection; in special cases he worships himself in it. A species cannot do otherwise but thus affirm itself alone. Its *lowest* instinct, that of self-preservation and self-expansion, still radiates in such sublimities. Man believes the world itself to be overloaded with beauty—and he forgets himself as the cause of this. He alone has presented the world with beauty—alas! only with a very human, all-too-human beauty. At bottom, man mirrors himself in things; he considers everything beautiful that reflects his own image: the judgment "beautiful" is the *vanity of his species*. For a little suspicion may whisper this question into the skeptic's ear: Is the world really beautified by the fact that man thinks it beautiful? He has anthropomorphized it, that is all. But nothing, absolutely nothing, guarantees that man should be the model of beauty. Who knows what he looks like in the eyes of a higher judge of beauty? Daring perhaps? Perhaps even amusing? Perhaps a little arbitrary?

"O Dionysus, divine one, why do you pull me by my ears?" Ariadne once asked her philosophic lover during one of those famous dialogues on Naxos. "I find a kind of humor in your ears, Ariadne: why are they not even longer?"

24.

L'art pour l'art. The fight against purpose in art is always a fight against the moralizing tendency in art, against its subordination to morality. *L'art pour l'art* means: "the devil take morality!" But even this hostility still betrays the overpowering force of the prejudice. When the purpose of moral preaching and of improving man has been excluded from art, it still does not follow by any means that art is altogether purposeless, aimless, senseless—in short, *l'art pour l'art,* a worm chewing its own tail. "Rather no purpose at all than a moral purpose!"—that is the talk of mere passion. A psychologist, on the other hand, asks: what does all art do? does it not praise? glorify? choose? prefer? With all this it strengthens or weakens certain valuations. Is this merely incidental? Merely accidental? Something in which the artist's instinct had no share? Or is it not the very presupposition of the artist's ability? Does his basic instinct aim at art, or rather at the sense of art, at life? at a desirability of life? Art is the great stimulus to life: how could one understand it as purposeless, as aimless, as *l'art pour l'art*?

One question remains: art also makes apparent much that is ugly, hard, and questionable in life; does it not thereby spoil life for us? And indeed there have been philosophers who attributed this sense to it: "liberation from the will" was what Schopenhauer taught as the overall end of art; and with admiration he found the great utility of tragedy in its "evoking resignation." But this, as I have already suggested, is the pessimist's perspective and "evil eye." We must appeal to the artists themselves. *What does the tragic artist communicate of himself?* Is it not precisely the state *without* fear in the face of the fearful and questionable that he is showing? This state itself is a great desideratum; whoever knows it honors it with the greatest honors. He communicates it—*must* communicate it, provided he is an artist, a genius of communication. Courage and freedom of feeling before a powerful enemy, before a sublime calamity, before a problem that arouses dread— this triumphant state is what the tragic artist chooses, what he glorifies. Before tragedy, what is warlike in our soul celebrates its Saturnalia; whoever is used to suffering, whoever seeks out suffering, the heroic man praises his own being through tragedy—to him alone the tragedian presents this drink of sweetest cruelty.

49.

Goethe—not a German event, but a European one: a magnificent attempt to overcome the eighteenth century by a return to nature, by an *ascent* to the naturalness of the Renaissance—a kind of self-overcoming on the part of that century. He bore its strongest instincts within himself: the sentimentality, the idolatry of nature, the antihistorical, the idealistic, the unreal and revolutionary (the latter being merely a form of the unreal). He sought help from history, natural science, antiquity, and also Spinoza, but, above all, from practical activity; he surrounded himself with clearly delineated horizons; he did not retire from life but put himself into the midst of it; he was not fainthearted but took as much as possible upon himself, over himself, into himself. What he wanted was *totality;* he fought the mutual exclusiveness of reason, senses, feeling, and will (preached with the most abhorrent scholasticism by *Kant,* the antipode of Goethe); he disciplined himself to wholeness, he *created* himself.

In the middle of an age with an unreal outlook, Goethe was a convinced realist: he said *yes* to everything that was related to him in this respect—and he had no greater experience than that *ens realissimum*[86] called Napoleon. Goethe conceived a human being who would be strong, highly educated, skillful in all bodily matters, self-controlled, reverent toward himself, and who might dare to allow himself the whole range and wealth of being natural, being strong enough for such freedom; the man of tolerance, not from weakness but from strength, because he knows how to use to his advantage even that from which the average nature would perish; the man for whom there is no longer anything that is forbidden—unless it be *weakness,* whether called vice or virtue.

Such a spirit who has *become free* stands amid the cosmos with a joyous and trusting fatalism, in the *faith* that only the particular is loathsome, and that all is redeemed and affirmed in the whole—*he does not negate any more.* Such a faith, however, is the highest of all possible faiths: I have baptized it with the name of *Dionysus.*

Translated by Walter Kaufmann

What I Owe to the Ancients

1.

In conclusion, a word about that world to which I sought approaches, to which I have perhaps found a new approach—the ancient world. My taste, which may be the opposite of a tolerant taste, is in this case, too, far from saying *yes* indiscriminately: it does not like to say *yes;* better *no;* but best of all, nothing. That applies to whole cultures, it applies to books—it also applies to places and regions. At bottom it is a very small number of ancient books that counts in my life; the most famous are not among them. My sense of style, for the epigram as a style, was awakened almost instantly when I came into contact with Sallust.[86a] I have not forgotten the surprise of my honored teacher, Corssen, when he had to give his worst Latin pupil the best grade: I had finished with one stroke. Compact, severe, with as much substance as possible,[87] a cold sarcasm against "beautiful words" and "beautiful sentiments"—here I found myself. And even in my *Zarathustra* one will recognize a very serious ambition for a *Roman* style, for the *aere perennius*[88] in style.

Nor was my experience any different in my first contact with Horace. To this day, no other poet has given me the same artistic delight that a Horatian ode gave me from the first. In certain languages that which has been achieved here could not even be *attempted*.[89] This mosaic of words, in which every word—as sound, as place, as concept—pours out its strength right and left and over the whole, this minimum in the extent and number of the signs, and the maximum thereby attained in the energy of the signs—all that is Roman and, if one will believe me, *noble* par excellence. All the rest of poetry becomes, in contrast, something too popular—a mere garrulity of feelings.

2.

To the Greeks I do not by any means owe similarly strong impressions; and—to come right out with it—they *cannot* be for us what the Romans are. One does not *learn* from the Greeks—their manner is too foreign, and also too fluid, to have an imperative, a "classical" effect. Who could ever have learned to write from a Greek? Who could ever have learned it *without* the Romans?

For heaven's sake, do not throw Plato at me. I am a complete skeptic about Plato, and I have never been able to join in the admiration for the *artist* Plato which is customary among scholars. In the end, the subtlest judges of taste among the ancients themselves are here on my side. Plato, it seems to me, throws all stylistic forms together and is thus the first decadent in style: his responsibility is thus comparable to that of the Cynics who invented the *satura Menippea*.[90] To be attracted by the Platonic dialogue, this horribly self-satisfied and childish kind of dialectic, one must never have read good French writers—Fontenelle, for example. Plato is boring. In the end, my mistrust of Plato goes deep: he represents such an aberration from all the basic instincts of the Hellene, is so "moralistic," so preexistently Christian—he already takes the concept "good" for the highest concept—that for the whole phenomenon Plato I would sooner use the harsh phrase "higher swindle," or, if it sounds better, "idealism," than any other. We have paid dearly for the fact that this Athenian got his schooling from the Egyptians (or from the Jews in Egypt?). In that great calamity, Christianity, Plato represents that ambiguity and fascination, called an "ideal," which made it possible for the nobler spirits of antiquity to misunderstand themselves and to set foot on the bridge leading to the cross. And how much Plato there still is in the concept "church," in the construction, system, and practice of the church!

My recreation, my preference, my *cure* from all Platonism has always been *Thucydides*. Thucydides and, perhaps, Machiavelli's *Principe* are most closely related to myself by the unconditional will not to gull oneself and to see reason in *reality*—not in "reason," still less in "morality." For the wretched embellishment of the Greeks into an ideal, which the "classically educated" youth carries into life as a prize for his classroom drill, there is no more complete cure than Thucydides. One must follow him line by line, but read no less clearly between them: there are few thinkers who say so much between the lines. With him the *culture of the Sophists,* by which I mean the *culture of the realists,* reaches its perfect expression—this inestimable movement amid the moralistic and idealistic swindle set loose on all sides by the Socratic schools. Greek philosophy: the decadence of the Greek instinct. Thucydides: the great sum, the last revelation of that strong, severe, hard factuality which was instinctive with the older Hellenes. In the end, it is *courage* in the face of reality that distinguishes a man like Thucydides from Plato: Plato is a coward before reality, consequently he flees into the ideal; Thucydides has control of *himself,* consequently he also maintains control of things.

3.

To sniff out "beautiful souls," "golden means," and other perfections in the Greeks, or to admire their calm in greatness, their ideal cast of mind, their noble simplicity—the psychologist in me protected me against such "noble simplicity," a *niaiserie allemande*[91] anyway. I saw their strongest instinct, the will to power; I saw them tremble before the indomitable force of this drive—I saw how all their institutions grew out of preventive measures taken to protect each other against their inner *explosives*. This tremendous inward tension then discharged itself in terrible and ruthless hostility to the outside world: the city-states tore each other to pieces so that the citizens of each might find peace from themselves. One needed to be strong: danger was near, it lurked everywhere. The splendidly supple physicality, the audacious realism and immoralism which distinguished the Hellene constituted a *need,* not "nature." It only resulted, it was not there from the start. And with festivals and the arts they also aimed at nothing other than to feel *on top,* to *show* themselves on top. These are means of glorifying oneself, and in certain cases, of inspiring fear of oneself.

How could one possibly judge the Greeks by their philosophers, as the Germans have done, and use the Philistine moralism[92] of the Socratic schools as a clue to what was basically Hellenic! After all, the philosophers are the decadents of Greek culture, the countermovement, the movement against the ancient, noble taste (against the agonistic instinct, against the polis, against the value of race, against the authority of tradition). The Socratic virtues were preached *because* the Greeks had lost them: excitable, timid, fickle comedians, every one of them, they had a few reasons too many for having morals preached to them. Not that it did any good—but big words and attitudes suit decadents so well.

4.

I was the first to take seriously, for the understanding of the older, the still rich and even overflowing Hellenic instinct, that wonderful phenomenon which bears the name of Dionysus: it is explicable only in terms of an *excess* of force. Whoever followed the Greeks, like that most profound student of their culture in our time, Jacob Burckhardt in Basel, knew immediately that something had been accomplished thereby; and Burckhardt added a special section on this phenomenon to his *Civilization of the Greeks.* To see the opposite, one should look at the almost amusing poverty of instinct among the German philologists when they approach the Dionysian. The famous Lobeck, above all, crawled into this world of mysterious states with all the venerable sureness of a worm dried up between books, and persuaded himself that it was scientific of him to be glib and childish to the point of nausea—and with the utmost erudition. Lobeck gave us to understand that all these curiosities really did not amount to anything. In fact, the priests could have told the participants in such orgies some not altogether worthless things; for example, that wine excites lust, that man can under certain circumstances live on fruit, that plants bloom in the spring and wilt in the fall. As regards the astonishing wealth of rites, symbols, and myths of an orgiastic origin, with which the ancient world is literally overrun, this gave Lobeck an opportunity to become still more ingenious. "The Greeks," he said (*Aglaophamus* I, 672), "when they had nothing else to do, laughed, jumped, and ran around; or, since man sometimes feels that urge, too, they sat down, cried, and lamented. *Others* came later on and sought some reason for this startling behavior; and thus there originated, as explanations for these customs, countless legends linked to festivals, and myths. On the other hand, it was believed that this *droll ado,* which took place on the feast days after all, must also form a necessary part of the festival and therefore it was maintained as an indispensable feature of the religious service." This is contemptible prattle; a Lobeck simply cannot be taken seriously for a moment.

We have quite a different feeling when we examine the concept "Greek" which was developed by Winckelmann and Goethe, and find it incompatible with that element out of which Dionysian art grows—the orgiastic. Indeed I do not doubt that as a matter of principle Goethe excluded anything of the sort from the possibilities of the Greek soul. *Consequently Goethe did not understand the Greeks.* For it is only in the Dionysian mysteries, in the psychology of the Dionysian state, that the *basic fact* of the Hellenic instinct finds expression—its "will to life." What was it that the Hellene guaranteed himself by means of these mysteries? *Eternal* life, the eternal return of life; the future promised and hallowed in the past; the triumphant *yes* to life beyond all death and change; *true* life as the overall continuation of life through procreation, through the mysteries of sexuality. For the Greeks the *sexual* symbol was therefore the venerable symbol par excellence, the real profundity in the whole of ancient piety. Every single element in the act of procreation, of pregnancy, and of birth aroused the highest and most solemn feelings. In the doctrine of the mysteries, *pain* is pronounced holy: the pangs of "her who gives birth" hallow all pain; all becoming and growing—all that guarantees a future— *involves* pain. That there may be the eternal joy of creating, that the will to life may eternally affirm itself, the agony of "her who gives birth" *must* also be there eternally.

All this is meant by the word Dionysus: I know no higher symbolism than this *Greek* symbolism of the Dionysian festivals. Here the most profound instinct of life, that directed toward the future of life, the eternity of life, is experienced religiously—and the way to life, procreation, as the *holy* way. It was Christianity, with its resentment *against* life at the bottom of its heart,[93] which first made something unclean of sexuality: it threw *filth* on the origin, on the presupposition of our life.

5.

The psychology of the orgiastic as an overflowing feeling of life and strength, within which even pain still has the effect of a stimulus, gave me the key to the concept of *tragic* feeling, which had been misunderstood both by Aristotle and, quite especially, by our modern pessimists. Tragedy is so far from proving anything about the pessimism of the Hellenes, in Schopenhauer's sense, that it may, on the contrary, be considered its decisive repudiation and *counterinstance*. Saying *yes* to life even in its strangest and hardest problems, the will to life rejoicing over its own inexhaustibility in the very *sacrifice* of its highest types—*that* is what I called Dionysian, *that* is what I guessed to be the bridge to the psychology of the *tragic* poet. *Not* in order to be liberated from terror and pity, not in order to purge oneself of a dangerous affect by its vehement discharge—Aristotle understood it that way—but in order to be *oneself* the eternal joy of becoming, beyond all terror and pity—that joy which included even *joy in destroying*.

And herewith I again touch that point from which I once went forth: *The Birth of Tragedy* was my first revaluation of all values. Herewith I again stand on the soil out of which my intention, my *ability* grows—I, the last disciple of the philosopher Dionysus—I, the teacher of the eternal recurrence.

Translated by Walter Kaufmann

From *Nietzsche contra Wagner:*
From the Files
of a Psychologist (1888)

We Antipodes

It may perhaps be recalled, at least among my friends, that at first I approached the modern world with a few errors and overestimations: in any case, full of *hopes*. I understood—who knows on the basis of what personal experiences?—the philosophic pessimism of the nineteenth century as a symptom of a greater strength of thought, of a more triumphant fullness of life, than had found expression in the philosophy of Hume, Kant, and Hegel: I took *tragic* insight for the most beautiful luxury of our culture, for its most precious, noblest, most dangerous kind of squandering—but nevertheless, in view of its excessive wealth, as a *permissible* luxury. Similarly, to suit my purposes, I interpreted[94] Wagner's music as an expression of a Dionysian power of the soul; I believed I heard in it the earthquake with which a primordial force of life, dammed up from time immemorial, finally vents itself, indifferent to the possibility that everything that calls itself culture today might start tottering. It is plain what I misunderstood in, equally plain what I read into, Wagner and Schopenhauer—myself.

Every art, every philosophy, may be considered a remedy and aid in the service of either growing or declining life: it always presupposes suffering and sufferers. But there are two kinds of sufferers: first, those who suffer from the *overfullness* of life and want a Dionysian art as well as a tragic insight and outlook on life—and then those who suffer from the *impoverishment* of life and demand of art and philosophy calm, stillness, smooth seas, or, on the other hand, frenzy, convulsion, and anesthesia. Revenge against life itself—the most voluptuous kind of frenzy for those so impoverished!

Wagner responds to this dual need of the latter no less than Schopenhauer: they negate life, they slander it, hence they are my antipodes. He that is richest in the fullness of life, the Dionysian god and man, can afford not only the *sight* of the terrible and the questionable, but even the terrible deed and any luxury of destruction, decomposition, and negation: in his case, what is evil, senseless, and ugly seems, as it were, permissible, as it seems permissible in nature, because of an excess of procreating, restoring powers which can yet turn every desert into luxurious farmland. Conversely, those who suffer most and are poorest in life would need mildness, peacefulness, and goodness most—what is today called humaneness—in thought as well as in deed, and, if possible, a god who would be truly a god for the sick, a healer and "savior";[95] also logic, the conceptual understandability of existence even for idiots—the typical "free spirits," like the "idealists" and "beautiful souls," are all decadents—in short, a certain warm, fear-repulsing narrowness and enclosure within optimistic horizons which permit *hebetation*.

Thus I gradually learned to understand Epicurus, the opposite of a Dionysian Greek; also the Christian, who is, in fact, only a kind of Epicurean, and, with his "faith makes blessed," follows the principle of hedonism as far as possible—far beyond any intellectual integrity. If there is anything in which I am ahead of all psychologists, it is that my eye is sharper for that most difficult and captious kind of *backward inference* in which the most mistakes are made: the backward inference from the work to the maker, from the deed to the doer, from the ideal to him who *needs* it, from every way of thinking and valuing to the *want* behind it that prompts it.

Regarding artists of all kinds, I now avail myself of this main distinction: is it the *hatred* against life or the *excess* of life which has here become creative? In Goethe, for example, the excess became creative; in Flaubert, hatred: Flaubert—a new edition of Pascal, but as an artist, with the instinctive judgment deep down: "*Flaubert est toujours haïssable, l'homme n'est rien, l'œuvre est tout.*"[96] He tortured himself when he wrote, just as Pascal tortured himself when he thought; they were both unegoistic. "Selflessness"—the principle of decadence, the will to the end, in art as well as in morals.

Translated by Walter Kaufmann

Epilogue

1.

I have often asked myself whether I am not more heavily obligated to the hardest years of my life than to any others. As my inmost nature teaches me, whatever is necessary—as seen from the heights and in the sense of a *great* economy—is also the useful par excellence: one should not only bear it, one should *love* it. *Amor fati:*[97] that is my inmost nature. And as for my long sickness, do I not owe it indescribably more than I owe to my health? I owe it a *higher* health—one which is made stronger by whatever does not kill it. *I also owe my philosophy to it.* Only great pain is the ultimate liberator of the spirit, as the teacher of great suspicion which turns every U into an X,[98] a real, genuine X: that is, the letter before the *penultimate* one. Only great pain, that long, slow pain in which we are burned with green wood, as it were—pain which takes its time—only this forces us philosophers to descend into our ultimate depths and to put away all trust, all good-naturedness, all that would veil, all mildness, all that is medium—things in which formerly we may have found our humanity. I doubt that such a pain makes us "better," but I know that it makes us more *profound.*

Whether we learn to pit our pride, our scorn, our will power against it, equaling the American Indian who, however tortured, evens the score with his torturer by the malice of his tongue; or whether we withdraw from pain into that Nothing, into mute, rigid, deaf resignation, self-forgetting, self-extinction: out of such long and dangerous exercises of self-mastery one emerges as a different person, with a few *more* question marks—above all, with the will to question more persistently, more deeply, severely, harshly, evilly, and quietly than has ever been questioned on this earth before. The trust in life is gone; life itself has become a problem. Yet one should not jump to the conclusion that with all this a man has necessarily become gloomy, a barn owl. Even the love of life is still possible—only, one loves differently. It is the love for a woman who raises doubts in us.

2.

What is strangest is this: afterward one has a different taste—a *second* taste. Out of such abysses, also out of the abyss of *great suspicion,* one returns newborn, having shed one's skin, more ticklish and sarcastic, with a more delicate taste for joy, with a more tender tongue for all good things, with gayer senses, with a second dangerous innocence in joy, more childlike and yet a hundred times more subtle than one has ever been before.

How repulsive pleasure is now, that crude, musty, brown pleasure as it is understood by those who like pleasure, our "educated" people, our rich people, and our rulers! How sarcastically we listen now to the big county-fair boom-boom with which the "educated" person and city dweller today permits art, books, and music to rape him and provide "spiritual pleasures"—with the aid of spirituous liquors! How the theatrical scream of passion now hurts our ears, how strange to our taste the whole romantic uproar and tumult of the senses have become, which the educated rabble loves, and all its aspirations after the elevated, inflated, and exaggerated! No, if we who have recovered still need art, it is another kind of art—a mocking, light, fleeting, divinely untroubled, divinely artificial art, which, like a pure flame, licks into unclouded skies. Above all, an art for artists, *for artists only!* We know better afterward what above all is needed for this: cheerfulness, *any* cheerfulness, my friends. There are a few things we now know too well, we knowing ones: oh, how we learn now to forget well, and to be good at *not* knowing, as artists!

And as for our future, one will hardly find us again on the paths of those Egyptian youths who endanger temples by night, embrace statues, and want by all means to unveil, uncover, and put into a bright light whatever is kept concealed for good reasons.[99] No, this bad taste, this will to truth, to "truth at any price," this youthful madness in the love of truth—they have lost their charm for us: for that we are too experienced, too serious, too gay, too burned, too *deep.* We no longer believe that truth remains truth when the veils are withdrawn—we have lived enough not to believe this. Today we consider it a matter of decency not to wish to see everything naked, or to be present at everything, or to understand and "know" everything. *Tout comprendre—c'est tout mépriser.*[100]

"Is it true that God is present *everywhere?*" a little girl asked her mother; "I think that's indecent"—a hint for philosophers! One should have more respect for the bashfulness with which nature has hidden behind riddles and iridescent uncertainties. Perhaps truth is a woman who has reasons for not letting us see her reasons? Perhaps her name is—to speak Greek—*Baubo?*"[100a]

Oh, those Greeks! They knew how to live. What is required for that is to stop courageously at the surface, the fold, the skin, to adore appearance, to believe in forms, tones, words, in the whole *Olympus of appearance.* Those Greeks were superficial—*out of profundity.* And is not this precisely what we are again coming back to, we daredevils of the spirit who have climbed the highest and most dangerous peak of present thought and looked around from up there—we who have looked *down* from there? Are we not, precisely in this respect, Greeks? Adorers of forms, of tones, of words? And therefore—*artists?*

Translated by Walter Kaufmann

From *Ecce Homo: How One Becomes What One Is* (1888, published posthumously)

Thus Spoke Zarathustra: A Book for All and None

1.

Now I shall relate the history of *Zarathustra*. The fundamental conception of this work, the *idea of the eternal recurrence*, this highest formula of affirmation that is at all attainable, belongs in August 1881: it was penned on a sheet with the notation underneath, "six thousand feet beyond man and time." That day I was walking through the woods along the lake of Silvaplana; at a powerful pyramidal rock not far from Surlei I stopped.[101] It was then that this idea came to me.

If I reckon back a few months from this day, I find as an omen a sudden and profoundly decisive change in my taste, especially in music. Perhaps the whole of *Zarathustra* may be reckoned as music; certainly a rebirth of the art of *hearing* was among its preconditions. In a small mountain spa not far from Vicenza, Recoaro, where I spent the spring of 1881, I discovered together with my maestro and friend, Peter Gast,[102] who was also "reborn," that the phoenix of music flew past us with lighter and more brilliant feathers than it had ever displayed before. But if I reckon forward from that day to the sudden birth that occurred in February 1883 under the most improbable circumstances—the *finale* . . . was finished exactly in that sacred hour in which Richard Wagner died in Venice—we get eighteen months for the pregnancy. This figure of precisely eighteen months might suggest, at least to Buddhists, that I am really a female elephant.

My *gaya scienza*[103] belongs in the interval and contains a hundred signs of the proximity of something incomparable; in the end it even offers the beginning of *Zarathustra,* and in the penultimate section of the fourth book the basic idea of *Zarathustra.*

Something else also belongs in this interval: that *Hymn to Life* (for mixed choir and orchestra) whose score was published two years ago by E. W. Fritzsch in Leipzig—a perhaps not unimportant symptom of my condition during that year when the yes-saying pathos par excellence, which I call the tragic pathos, was alive in me to the highest degree. The time will come when it will be sung in my memory.

The text, to say this expressly because a misunderstanding has gained currency, is not by me: it is the amazing inspiration of a young Russian woman who was my friend at that time, Miss Lou von Salomé.[104] Whoever can find any meaning at all in the last words of this poem will guess why I preferred and admired it: they attain greatness. Pain is *not* considered an objection to life: "If you have no more happiness to give me, well then! *you still have suffering.*" Perhaps my music, too, attains greatness at this point. (Last note of the A-clarinet, C flat, not C: misprint.)

The following winter I stayed in that charming quiet bay of Rapallo which, not far from Genoa, is cut out between Chiavari and the foothills of Portofino. My health could have been better; the winter was cold and excessively rainy; my small *albergo,*[105] situated right at the shore so that the high sea made it impossible to sleep at night, was in just about every way the opposite of what one might wish for. In spite of this and almost in order to prove my proposition that everything decisive comes into being "in spite of," it was that winter and under these unfavorable circumstances that my *Zarathustra* came into being.

Mornings I would walk in a southerly direction on the splendid road to Zoagli, going up past pines with a magnificent view of the sea; in the afternoon, whenever my health permitted it, I walked around the whole bay from Santa Margherita all the way to Portofino. This place and this scenery came even closer to my heart because of the great love that the unforgettable German Emperor Frederick III felt for them; by chance, I was in this coastal region again in the fall of 1886 when he visited this small forgotten world of bliss for the last time.[106] It was on these two walks that the whole of *Zarathustra I* occurred to me,[107] and especially Zarathustra himself as a type: rather, he *overtook me.*[108]

2.

To understand this type, one must first become clear about his physiological presupposition: this is what I call the *great health.* I don't know how I could explain this concept better, more *personally,* than I have done it in one of the last sections of the fifth book of my *gaya scienza:*[109]

> Being new, nameless, hard to understand, we premature births of an as yet unproven future, we need for a new goal also a new means—namely, a new health, stronger, more seasoned, tougher, more audacious, and gayer than any previous health. Whoever has a soul that craves to have experienced the whole range of values and desiderata to date, and to have sailed around all the coasts of this ideal "Mediterranean"; whoever wants to know from the adventures of his own most authentic experience how a discoverer and conqueror of the ideal feels, and also an artist, a saint, a legislator, a sage, a scholar, a pious man, and one who stands divinely apart in the old style—needs one thing above everything else: the *great health*—that one does not merely have but also acquires continually, and must acquire, because one gives it up again and again, and must give it up.
>
> And now after we have long been on our way in this manner, we argonauts of the ideal, with more daring perhaps than is prudent, and have suffered shipwreck and damage often enough, but are, to repeat it, healthier than one likes to permit us, dangerously healthy, ever again healthy—it will seem to us as if, as a reward, we now confronted an as yet undiscovered country whose boundaries nobody has surveyed yet, something beyond all the lands and nooks of the ideal so far, a world so overrich in what is beautiful, strange, questionable, terrible, and divine that our curiosity as well as our craving to possess it has got beside itself—alas, now nothing will sate us anymore!
>
> After such vistas and with such a burning hunger in our conscience and science,[110] how could we still be satisfied with *present-day man?* It may be too bad, but it is inevitable that we find it difficult to remain serious when we look at his worthiest goals and hopes, and perhaps we do not even bother to look anymore.

Another ideal runs ahead of us, a strange, tempting, dangerous ideal to which we should not wish to persuade anybody
because we do not readily concede *the right to it* to anyone: the
ideal of a spirit who plays naively—that is, not deliberately but
from overflowing power and abundance—with all that was hitherto called holy, good, untouchable, divine; for whom those
supreme things that the people naturally accept as their value
standards, signify danger, decay, debasement, or at least recreation, blindness, and temporary self-oblivion; the ideal of a human, superhuman well-being and benevolence[111] that will often
appear *inhuman*—for example, when it confronts all earthly
seriousness so far, all solemnity in gesture, word, tone, eye,
morality, and task so far, as if it were their most incarnate and
involuntary parody—and in spite of all of this, it is perhaps
only with him that *great seriousness* really begins, that the real
question mark is posed for the first time, that the destiny of the
soul changes, the hand moves forward, the tragedy *begins*.

3.

Has anyone at the end of the nineteenth century a clear idea of
what poets of strong ages have called *inspiration?* If not, I will
describe it. If one had the slightest residue of superstition left in
one's system, one could hardly reject altogether the idea that one
is merely incarnation, merely mouthpiece, merely a medium of
overpowering forces. The concept of revelation—in the sense that
suddenly, with indescribable certainty and subtlety, something becomes *visible,* audible, something that shakes one to the last depths
and throws one down—that merely describes the facts. One hears,
one does not seek; one accepts, one does not ask who gives; like
lightning, a thought flashes up, with necessity, without hesitation
regarding its form—I never had any choice.

A rapture whose tremendous tension occasionally discharges itself in a flood of tears—now the pace quickens involuntarily, now
it becomes slow; one is altogether beside oneself, with the most
distinct consciousness of scores of subtle shudders and of one's
skin creeping[112] down to one's toes; a depth of happiness in which
even what is most painful and gloomy does not seem something
opposite but rather conditioned, provoked, a *necessary* color in
such a superabundance of light; an instinct for rhythmic relation-
ships that arches over wide spaces of forms—length, the need for

a rhythm with wide arches,[113] is almost the measure of the force of inspiration, a kind of compensation for its pressure and tension.

Everything happens involuntarily in the highest degree but as in a gale of a feeling of freedom, of absoluteness, of power, of divinity. The involuntariness of image and metaphor is strangest of all; one no longer has any notion of what is an image or a metaphor: everything offers itself as the nearest, most fitting, simplest expression. It actually seems, to allude to something Zarathustra says, as if the things themselves approached and offered themselves as metaphors ("Here all things come caressingly to your discourse and flatter you; for they want to ride on your back. On every metaphor you ride to every truth. Here the words and wordshrines of all being open up before you; here all being wishes to become word, all becoming wishes to learn from you how to speak").

This is *my* experience of inspiration; I do not doubt that one has to go back thousands of years in order to find anyone who could say to me, "it is mine as well."

4.

Afterwards I was sick for a few weeks in Genoa. Then came a melancholy spring in Rome where I put up with life—it was not easy. Fundamentally, this most indecent place on earth for the poet of *Zarathustra* distressed me exceedingly, and I had not chosen it voluntarily. I wanted to go to Aquila,[114] Rome's counterconcept, founded from hostility against Rome, as I shall one day found a place, in[115] memory of an atheist and enemy of the church *comme il faut,*[116] one of those most closely related to me, the great Hohenstaufen Emperor Frederick II. But some fatality was at work: I had to go back again. In the end I resigned myself to the Piazza Barberini, after my exertions to go to an *anti-Christian* environment had wearied me. I fear that in order to avoid bad odors as far as possible I once inquired at the Palazzo del Quirinale itself[117] whether they did not have a quiet room for a philosopher.

It was on a *loggia* high above that Piazza, from which one has a fine view of Rome and hears the *fontana* splashing far below, that the loneliest song was written that has ever been written, the "Night Song."[118] Around that time a melody of indescribable melancholy was always about me, and I found its refrain in the words, "dead from immortality."

That summer, back home at the holy spot where the first lightning of the *Zarathustra* idea had flashed for me, I found *Zarathustra II*. Ten days sufficed; in no case, neither for the first nor for the third and last,[119] did I require more. The next winter, under the halcyon sky of Nizza, which then shone into my life for the first time, I found *Zarathustra III*—and was finished. Scarcely a year for the whole of it.

Many concealed spots and heights in the landscape around Nizza are hallowed for me by unforgettable moments; that decisive passage which bears the title "On Old and New Tablets"[120] was composed on the most onerous ascent from the station to the marvelous Moorish eyrie, Eza—the suppleness of my muscles has always been greatest when my creative energies were flowing most abundantly. The *body* is inspired; let us keep the "soul" out of it. Often one could have seen me dance; in those days I could walk in the mountains for seven or eight hours without a trace of weariness. I slept well, I laughed much—my vigor and patience were perfect.

5.

Except for these ten-day works, the years during and above all *after* my *Zarathustra* were marked by distress without equal. One pays dearly for immortality: one has to die several times while still alive.

There is something I call the *rancune*[121] of what is great: everything great—a work, a deed—is no sooner accomplished than it turns *against* the man who did it. By doing it, he has become *weak*; he no longer endures his deed, he can no longer face it. Something one was never permitted to will lies *behind* one, something in which the knot in the destiny of humanity is tied—and now one labors *under* it!—It almost crushes one.—The *rancune* of what is great!

Then there is the gruesome silence one hears all around one. Solitude has seven skins; nothing penetrates them anymore. One comes to men, one greets friends—more desolation, no eye offers a greeting. At best, a kind of revolt. Such revolts I experienced, very different in degree but from almost everybody who was close to me. It seems nothing offends more deeply than suddenly letting others feel a distance; those *noble* natures who do not know how to live without reverence are rare.

Thirdly, there is the absurd sensitivity of the skin to small stings, a kind of helplessness against everything small. This seems to me to be due to the tremendous squandering of all defensive energies which is a presupposition of every *creative* deed, every deed that issues from one's most authentic, inmost, nethermost regions. Our *small* defensive capacities are thus, as it were, suspended; no energy is left for them.

In addition, I dare to hint that one digests less well, does not like to move, is all too susceptible to feeling chills as well as mistrust—mistrust that is in many instances merely an etiological blunder. In such a state I once sensed the proximity of a herd of cows even before I saw it, merely because milder and more philanthropic thoughts came back to me: *they* had warmth.

6.

This work stands altogether apart. Leaving aside the poets: perhaps nothing has ever been done from an equal excess of strength. My concept of the "Dionysian" here became a *supreme deed;* measured against that, all the rest of human activity seems poor and relative. That a Goethe, a Shakespeare, would be unable to breathe even for a moment in this tremendous passion and height, that Dante is, compared with Zarathustra, merely a believer and not one who first *creates* truth, a *world-governing* spirit, a destiny—that the poets of the Veda are priests and not even worthy of tying the shoelaces of a Zarathustra—that is the least thing and gives no idea of the distance, of the *azure* solitude in which this work lives. Zarathustra possesses an eternal right to say: "I draw circles around me and sacred boundaries; fewer and fewer men climb with me on ever higher mountains: I am building a mountain range out of ever more sacred mountains."[122]

Let anyone add up the spirit and good nature of all great souls: all of them together would not be capable of producing even one of Zarathustra's discourses. The ladder on which he ascends and descends[123] is tremendous; he has seen further, willed further, been *capable* further than any other human being. In every word he contradicts, this most yes-saying of all spirits; in him all opposites are blended into a new unity. The highest and the lowest energies of human nature, what is sweetest, most frivolous, and most terrible wells forth from one fount with immortal assurance. Until then one does not know what is height, what depth; one knows even less what truth is. There is no moment in this revelation of truth that has been anticipated or guessed by even *one* of the greatest.

There is no wisdom, no investigation of the soul, no art of speech before Zarathustra; what is nearest and most everyday, here speaks of unheard-of things. Maxims trembling with passion, eloquence become music, lightning bolts hurled forward into hitherto unfathomed futures. The most powerful capacity for metaphors that has existed so far is poor and mere child's play compared with this return of language to the nature of imagery.

And how Zarathustra descends and says to everyone what is most good-natured! How gently he handles even his antagonists, the priests, and suffers from them *with* them! Here man has been overcome at every moment; the concept of the "overman"[124] has here become the greatest reality—whatever was so far considered great in man lies *beneath* him at an infinite distance. The halcyon, the light feet, the omnipresence of malice and exuberance, and whatever else is typical of the type of Zarathustra—none of this has ever before been dreamed of as essential to greatness. Precisely in this width of space and this accessibility for what is contradictory, Zarathustra experiences himself as the *supreme type of all beings;* and once one hears how he defines this, one will refrain from seeking his simile:[125]

> The soul that has the longest ladder and can descend the deepest,
> the most comprehensive soul, which can run and stray and roam farthest within itself;
> the most necessary soul that plunges joyously into chance;
> the soul that, having being, dives into becoming; the soul that *has,* but *wants* to want and will;
> the soul that flees itself and catches up with itself in the widest circles;
> the wisest soul that folly exhorts most sweetly;
> the soul that loves itself most, in which all things have their sweep and countersweep and ebb and flood—[126]

But that is the concept of Dionysus himself.—Another consideration leads to the very same result. The psychological problem in the type of Zarathustra is how he that says *no* and *does no* to an unheard-of degree, to everything to which one has so far said *yes,* can nevertheless be the opposite of a *no*-saying spirit; how the spirit who bears the heaviest fate, a fatality of a task, can nevertheless be the lightest and most transcendent—Zarathustra is a dancer—how he that had the hardest, most terrible insight into reality, that has thought the "most abysmal idea," nevertheless does not consider it an objection to existence, not even to its eternal recurrence—but rather one reason more for being himself the eternal *yes* to all things, "the tremendous, unbounded saying *yes* and *amen*."[127]—"Into all abysses I still carry the blessings of my saying *yes.*"—*But this is the concept of Dionysus once again.*

7.

What language will such a spirit speak when he speaks to himself? The language of the *dithyramb.* I am the inventor of the dithyramb. Listen to how Zarathustra speaks to himself *before sunrise* (III, 18): such emerald happiness, such divine tenderness did not have a tongue before me. Even the deepest melancholy of such a Dionysus still turns into a dithyramb. To give some indication of this, I choose the "Night Song," the immortal lament at being condemned by the overabundance of light and power, by his sun-nature, not to love:

> Night has come; now all fountains speak more loudly.
> And my soul, too, is a fountain.
> Night has come; only now all the songs of lovers awaken.
> And my soul, too, is the song of a lover.
> Something unstilled, unstillable is within me; it wants to be voiced. A craving for love is within me; it speaks the language of love.
> Light am I; ah, that I were night! But this is my loneliness that I am girt with light.
> Ah, that I were dark and nocturnal! How I would suck at the breasts of light!
> And even you would I bless, you little sparkling stars and glowworms up there, and be overjoyed with your gifts of light.
> But I live in my own light; I drink back into myself the flames that break out of me.
> I do not know the happiness of those who receive; and I have often dreamed that stealing must be even more blessed than receiving.
> This is my poverty, that my hand never rests from giving; this is my envy, that I see waiting eyes and the lit-up nights of longing.
> Oh, wretchedness of all givers! Oh, darkening of my sun! Oh, craving to crave! Oh, ravenous hunger in satiation!

They receive from me, but do I touch their souls? There is a cleft between giving and receiving; and the narrowest cleft is the last to be bridged.

A hunger grows out of my beauty: I should like to hurt those for whom I shine; I should like to rob those to whom I give; thus do I hunger for malice.

To withdraw my hand when the other hand already reaches out to it; to linger like the waterfall, which lingers even while it plunges: thus do I hunger for malice.

Such revenge my fullness plots: such spite wells up out of my loneliness.

My happiness in giving died in giving; my virtue tired of itself in its overflow.

The danger of those who always give is that they lose their sense of shame; and the heart and hand of those who always mete out become callous from always meting out.

My eye no longer wells over at the shame of those who beg; my hand has grown too hard for the trembling of filled hands.

Where have the tears of my eyes gone and the down of my heart? Oh, the loneliness of all givers! Oh, the taciturnity of all who shine!

Many suns revolve in the void: to all that is dark they speak with their light—to me they are silent.

Oh, this is the enmity of the light against what shines: merciless it moves in its orbit.

Unjust in its heart against all that shines, cold against suns— thus moves every sun.

The suns fly like a storm in their orbits. They follow their inexorable will: that is their coldness.

Oh, it is only you, you dark ones, you nocturnal ones, who create warmth out of that which shines. It is only you who drink milk and refreshment out of the udders of light.

Alas, ice is all around me, my hand is burned by the ice. Alas, thirst is within me that languishes after your thirst.

Night has come: alas, that I must be light! And thirst for the nocturnal! And loneliness!

Night has come: now my craving breaks out of me like a well; to speak I crave.

Night has come; now all fountains speak more loudly. And my soul, too, is a fountain.

Night has come; now all the songs of lovers awaken. And my soul, too, is the song of a lover.

8.

Nothing like this has ever been written, felt, or *suffered:* thus suffers a god, a Dionysus. The answer to such a dithyramb of solar solitude in the light would be Ariadne.—Who besides me knows what Ariadne is!—For all such riddles nobody so far had any solution; I doubt that anybody even saw any riddles here.

Zarathustra once defines, quite strictly, his task—it is mine, too—and there is no mistaking his meaning: he says *yes* to the point of justifying, of redeeming even all of the past:

> I walk among men as among the fragments of the future—that future which I envisage.
>
> And this is all my creating and striving, that I create and carry together into One what is fragment and riddle and dreadful accident.
>
> And how could I bear to be a man if man were not also a creator and guesser of riddles and redeemer of accidents?
>
> *To redeem those who lived in the past* and to turn every 'it was' into a 'thus I willed it'—that alone should I call redemption.[128]

In another passage he defines as strictly as possible what alone "man" can be for him—*not* an object of love or, worse, pity—Zarathustra has mastered the *great nausea* over man, too: man is for him an un-form, a material, an ugly stone that needs a sculptor:

> *Willing* no more and *esteeming* no more and *creating* no more—oh, that this great weariness might always remain far from me!
>
> In knowledge, too, I feel only my will's joy in begetting and becoming; and if there is innocence in my knowledge, it is because the *will to beget* is in it.
>
> Away from God and gods this will has lured me; what could one create if gods—were there?
>
> But my fervent will to create impels me ever again toward man; thus is the hammer impelled toward the stone.
>
> O men, in the stone an image is sleeping, the image of images! Alas that it has to sleep in the hardest, ugliest stone!
>
> *Now my hammer rages cruelly against its prison.* Pieces of rock rain from the stone: what is that to me?
>
> I want to perfect it; for a shadow came to me—the stillest and lightest of all things once came to me.

The beauty of the overman came to me as a shadow. What are gods to me now?[129]

I stress a final point: the verse in italics furnishes the occasion. Among the conditions for a *Dionysian* task are, in a decisive way, the hardness of the hammer, the *joy even in destroying*. The imperative "become hard!," the most fundamental certainty *that all creators are hard,* is the distinctive mark of a Dionysian nature.

Translated by Walter Kaufmann
and R. J. Hollingdale

Genealogy of Morals: A Polemic

Regarding expression, intention, and the art of surprise, the three inquiries which constitute this *Genealogy* are perhaps uncannier than anything else written so far. Dionysus is, as is known, also the god of darkness.

Every time a beginning that is *calculated* to mislead: cool, scientific, even ironic, deliberately foreground, deliberately holding off. Gradually more unrest; sporadic lightning; very disagreeable truths are heard grumbling in the distance—until eventually a *tempo feroce* is attained in which everything rushes ahead in a tremendous tension. In the end, in the midst of perfectly gruesome detonations, a *new* truth becomes visible every time among thick clouds.

The truth of the *first* inquiry is the psychology of Christianity: the birth of Christianity out of the spirit of resentment, *not*, as people may believe, out of the "spirit"—a countermovement by its very nature, the great rebellion against the dominion of *noble* values.

The *second* inquiry offers the psychology of the *conscience*—which is *not*, as people may believe, "the voice of God in man": it is the instinct of cruelty that turns back after it can no longer discharge itself externally. Cruelty is here exposed for the first time as one of the most ancient and basic substrata of culture that simply cannot be imagined away.

The *third* inquiry offers the answer to the question whence the ascetic ideal, the priests' ideal, derives its tremendous *power* although it is the *harmful* ideal par excellence, a will to the end, an ideal of decadence. Answer: *not*, as people may believe, because

God is at work behind the priests but *faute de mieux*[130]—because it was the only ideal so far, because it had no rival. "For man would rather will even nothingness than *not* will."[131]—Above all, a *counterideal* was lacking—*until Zarathustra*.

I have been understood. Three decisive preliminary studies by a psychologist for a revaluation of all values.—This book contains the first psychology of the priest.

Translated by Walter Kaufmann
and R. J. Hollingdale

Why I Am a Destiny

1.

I know my fate. One day my name will be associated with the memory of something tremendous—a crisis without equal on earth, the most profound collision of conscience, a decision that was conjured up *against* everything that had been believed, demanded, hallowed so far. I am no man, I am dynamite.[132]—Yet for all that, there is nothing in me of a founder of a religion—religions are affairs of the rabble; I find it necessary to wash my hands after I have come into contact with religious people.—I *want* no "believers"; I think I am too malicious to believe in myself; I never speak to masses.—I have a terrible fear that one day I will be *canonized:* you will guess why I publish this book *before;* it shall prevent people from doing mischief with me.[133]

I do not want to be a saint; sooner even a buffoon.—Perhaps I am a buffoon.—Yet in spite of that—or rather *not* in spite of it, because so far nobody has been more mendacious than saints— the truth speaks out of me.—But my truth is *terrible;* for so far one has called *lies* truth.

Revaluation of all values: that is my formula for an act of supreme self-examination on the part of humanity, become flesh and genius in me. It is my fate that I have to be the first *decent* human being; that I know myself to stand in opposition to the mendaciousness of millennia.—I was the first to *discover* the truth by being the first to experience lies as lies—smelling them out.—My genius is in my nostrils.

I contradict as has never been contradicted before and am nevertheless the opposite of a *no*-saying spirit. I am a bringer of glad tidings like no one before me; I know tasks of such elevation that any notion of them has been lacking so far; only beginning with me are there hopes again. For all that, I am necessarily also the man of calamity. For when truth enters into a fight with the lies of millennia, we shall have upheavals, a convulsion of earthquakes, a moving of mountains and valleys the like of which has never been dreamed of. The concept of politics will have merged entirely with a war of spirits; all power structures of the old society will have been exploded—all of them are based on lies: there will be wars the like of which have never yet been seen on earth. It is only beginning with me that the earth knows *great politics*.

2.

You want a formula for such a destiny *become man?* That is to be found in my *Zarathustra:*

> And whoever wants to be a creator in good and evil, must first be an annihilator and break values.
> Thus the highest evil belongs to the greatest goodness; but this is—being creative.[134]

I am by far the most terrible human being that has existed so far; this does not preclude the possibility that I shall be the most beneficial. I know the pleasure in *destroying* to a degree that accords with my *powers* to destroy—in both respects I obey my Dionysian nature, which does not know how to separate doing *no* from saying *yes*. I am the first *immoralist:* that makes me the *annihilator* par excellence.

3.

I have not been asked, as I should have been asked, what the name of *Zarathustra* means in my mouth, the mouth of the first immoralist: for what constitutes the tremendous historical uniqueness of that Persian is just the opposite of this. Zarathustra was the first to consider the fight of good and evil the very wheel in the machinery of things: the transposition of morality into the metaphysical realm, as a force, cause, and end in itself, is *his* work. But this question itself is at bottom its own answer. Zarathustra created this most calamitous error, morality; consequently, he must also be the first to recognize it. Not only has he more experience in this matter, for a longer time, than any other thinker—after all, the whole of history is the refutation by experiment of the principle of the so-called "moral world order"—what is more important is that Zarathustra is more truthful than any other thinker. His doctrine, and his alone, posits truthfulness as the highest virtue; this means the opposite of the *cowardice* of the "idealist" who flees from reality; Zarathustra has more intestinal fortitude than all other thinkers taken together. To speak the truth and to *shoot well with arrows,* that is Persian virtue.[135]—Am I understood?— The self-overcoming of morality, out of truthfulness; the self-overcoming of the moralist, into his opposite—into me—that is what the name of Zarathustra means in my mouth.

4.

Fundamentally, my term *immoralist* involves two negations. For one, I negate a type of man that has so far been considered supreme: the good, the benevolent, the beneficent. And then I negate a type of morality that has become prevalent and predominant as morality itself—the morality of decadence or, more concretely, *Christian* morality. It would be permissible to consider the second contradiction the more decisive one, since I take the overestimation of goodness and benevolence on a large scale for a consequence of decadence, for a symptom of weakness, irreconcilable with an ascending, *yes*-saying life: negating *and destroying* are conditions of saying *yes.*

Let me tarry over the psychology of the good human being. To estimate what a type of man is worth, one must calculate the price paid for his preservation—one must know the conditions of his existence. The condition of the existence of the good is the *lie:* put differently, not *wanting* to see at any price how reality is constituted fundamentally—namely, not in such a way as to elicit benevolent instincts at all times, and even less in such a way as to tolerate at all times the interference of those who are myopically good-natured. To consider *distress* of all kinds as an objection, as something that must be *abolished,* is the *niaiserie*[136] par excellence and, on a large scale, a veritable disaster in its consequences, a nemesis of stupidity—almost as stupid as would be the desire to abolish bad weather—say, from pity for poor people.

In the great economy of the whole, the terrible aspects of reality (in affects, in desires, in the will to power) are to an incalculable degree more necessary than that form of petty happiness which people call "goodness"; one actually has to be quite lenient to accord the latter any place at all, considering that it presupposes an instinctive mendaciousness.[137] I shall have a major occasion to demonstrate how the historical consequences of *optimism,* this abortion of the *homines optimi,*[138] have been uncanny beyond measure. Zarathustra, who was the first to grasp that the optimist is just as decadent as the pessimist, and perhaps more harmful, says: *Good men never speak the truth.*[139] *False coasts and assurances the good have taught you; in the lies of the good you were hatched and huddled. Everything has been made fraudulent and has been twisted through and through by the good.*[140]

Fortunately, the world has not been designed with a view to such instincts that only good-natured herd animals could find their narrow happiness in it: to demand that all should become "good human beings," herd animals, blue-eyed, benevolent, "beautiful souls"—or as Mr. Herbert Spencer[141] would have it, altruistic—would deprive existence of its *great* character and would castrate men and reduce them to the level of wretched Chinese stagnation.[142]—*And this has been attempted!*—*Precisely this has been called morality.*

In this sense, Zarathustra calls the good, now "the last men," now the "beginning of the end"; above all, he considers them the most harmful type of man because they prevail at the expense of *truth* and at the expense of the *future:*

> The good are unable to *create;* they are always the beginning of the end;
> They crucify him who writes new values on new tablets; they sacrifice the future to *themselves*—they crucify the entire future of mankind.
> The good have always been the beginning of the end.
> And whatever harm those do who slander the world, *the harm done by the good is the most harmful harm.*[143]

5.

Zarathustra, the first psychologist of the good, is—consequently— a friend of the evil. When a decadent type of man ascended to the rank of the highest type, this could only happen at the expense of its countertype, the type of man that is strong and sure of life.

When the herd animal is irradiated by the glory of the purest virtue, the exceptional man must have been devaluated into evil. When mendaciousness at any price monopolizes the word "truth" for its perspective, the really truthful man is bound to be branded with the worst names. Zarathustra leaves no doubt at this point: he says that it was his insight precisely into the good, the "best," that made him shudder at man in general; that it was from *this* aversion that he grew wings "to soar off into distant futures"; he does not conceal the fact that *his* type of man, a relatively superhuman type, is superhuman precisely in its relation to the *good*—that the good and the just would call his overman *devil:*

> You highest men whom my eyes have seen, this is my doubt about you and my secret laughter: I guess that you would call my overman—devil.
>
> What is great is so alien to your souls that the overman would be terrifying to you in his goodness.[144]

It is here and nowhere else that one must make a start to comprehend what Zarathustra wants: this type of man that he conceives, conceives reality *as it is,* being strong enough to do so; this type is not estranged or removed from reality but is reality itself and exemplifies all that is terrible and questionable in it—*only in that way can man attain greatness.*

6.

There is yet another sense, however, in which I have chosen the word *immoralist* as a symbol and badge of honor for myself; I am proud of having this word which distinguishes me from the whole of humanity. Nobody yet has felt *Christian* morality to be *beneath* him; that requires a height, a view of distances, a hitherto altogether unheard-of psychological depth and profundity. Christian morality has been the Circe of all thinkers so far—they stood in her service.—Who before me climbed into the caverns from which the poisonous fumes of this type of ideal—*slander of the world*—are rising? Who even dared to suspect that they are caverns? Who among philosophers was a *psychologist* at all before me, and not rather the opposite, a "higher swindler" and "idealist"? There was no psychology at all before me.—To be the first here may be a curse; it is at any rate a destiny: *for one is also the first to despise.—* *Nausea* at man is my danger.

7.

Have I been understood?—What defines me, what sets me apart from the whole rest of humanity is that I *uncovered* Christian morality. That is why I needed a word that had the meaning of a provocation for everybody. That to this they did not open their eyes earlier, I regard as the greatest uncleanliness that humanity has on its conscience; as self-deception become instinctive; as a fundamental will *not* to see any event, any causality, any reality; as counterfeiting *in psychologicis* to the point of criminality. Blindness to Christianity is the crime par excellence—the crime *against life.*

The millennia, the nations, the first and the last, the philosophers and old women—excepting five, six moments in history, and me as the seventh—at this point all of them are worthy of each other. The Christian has so far been *the* "moral being"—a matchless curiosity—and *as* the "moral being" he was more absurd, mendacious, vain, frivolous, and *more disadvantageous for himself* than ever the greatest despiser of humanity could imagine in his dreams. Christian morality—the most malignant form of the will to lie, the real Circe of humanity—that which *corrupted* humanity. It is *not* error as error that horrifies me at this sight—not the lack, for thousands of years, of "good will," discipline, decency, courage in matters of the spirit, revealed by its victory: it is the lack of nature, it is the utterly gruesome fact that *antinature* itself received the highest honors as morality and was fixed over humanity as law and categorical imperative.—To blunder to such an extent, not as individuals, not as people, but as humanity!—That one taught men to despise the very first instincts of life; that one mendaciously invented a "soul," a "spirit" to ruin the body; that one taught men to experience the presupposition of life, sexuality, as something unclean; that one looks for the evil principle in what is most profoundly necessary for growth, in *severe* self-love[145] (this very word constitutes slander); that, conversely, one regards the typical signs of decline and contradiction of the instincts, the "selfless," the loss of a center of gravity, "depersonalization": and "neighbor love" (*addiction* to the neighbor)[146] as the *higher* value—what am I saying?—the *absolute* value!

What? Is humanity itself decadent? Was it always?—What is certain is that it has been *taught* only decadence values as supreme values. The morality that would un-self man is the morality of decline par excellence—the fact, "I am declining," transposed into the imperative, "all of you *ought* to decline"—and not only into the imperative.—This only morality that has been taught so far, that of un-selfing, reveals a will to the end; fundamentally, it *negates* life.

This would still leave open the possibility that not humanity is degenerating but only that parasitical type of man—that of the *priest*—which has used morality to raise itself mendaciously to the position of determining human values—finding in Christian morality the means to come to *power.*—Indeed, this is *my* insight: the teachers, the leaders of humanity, theologians all of them, were also all of them, decadents: *hence* the revaluation of all values into hostility to life, *hence* morality—

Definition of morality: Morality—the idiosyncrasy of decadents, with the ulterior motive *of revenging oneself against life*—and *successfully.* I attach value to this definition.

8.

Have I been understood?—I have not said one word here that I did not say five years ago through the mouth of Zarathustra.

The uncovering of Christian morality is an event without parallel, a real catastrophe. He who enlightens us about it is a *force majeure,* a destiny—he breaks the history of mankind in two. One lives *before* him, or one lives *after* him.

The lightning bolt of truth struck precisely what was highest so far: let whoever comprehends *what* has here been destroyed see whether anything is left in his hands. Everything that has hitherto been called "truth" has been recognized as the most harmful, insidious, and subterranean form of lie; the holy pretext of "improving" mankind, as the ruse for sucking the blood of life itself. Morality as *vampirism.*

Whoever uncovers morality also uncovers the disvalue of all values that are and have been believed; he no longer sees anything venerable in the most venerated types of man, even in those pronounced holy; he considers them the most calamitous type of abortion—calamitous *because they exerted such fascination.*

The concept of "God" invented as a counterconcept of life—everything harmful, poisonous, slanderous, the whole hostility unto death against life synthesized in this concept in a gruesome unity! The concept of the "beyond," the "true world" invented in order to devaluate the only world there is—in order to retain no goal, no reason, no task for our earthly reality! The concept of the "soul," the "spirit," finally even *"immortal* soul," invented in order to despise the body, to make it sick, "holy"; to oppose with a ghastly carelessness everything that deserves to be taken seriously in life, the questions of nourishment, abode, spiritual diet, treatment of the sick, cleanliness, and weather.

In place of health, the "salvation of the soul"—that is, a *folie circulaire*[147] between penitential convulsions and hysteria about redemption. The concept of "sin" invented along with the torture instrument that belongs with it, the concept of "free will," in order to confuse the instincts, to make mistrust of the instincts second nature. In the concept of the "selfless," the "self-denier," the distinctive sign of decadence, *feeling attracted* by what is harmful, being unable to find any longer what profits one, self-destruction is turned into the sign of value itself, into "duty," into "holiness," into what is "divine" in man. Finally—this is what is most terrible of all—the concept of the *good* man signifies that one sides with all that is weak, sick, failure, suffering from itself—*all that ought to perish*: the principle of *selection* is crossed—an ideal is fabricated from the contradiction against the proud and well-developed human being who says *yes,* who is sure of the future, who guarantees the future—and he is now called *evil.*—And all this was believed, *as morality!—Ecrasez l'infâme!*[148]—

9.

Have I been understood?—*Dionysus versus the Crucified.*—

Translated by Walter Kaufmann
and R. J. Hollingdale

From *The Antichrist: Curse upon Christianity* (1888)[149]

48.

Has the famous story that stands at the beginning of the Bible really been understood? the story of God's hellish fear of *science?* It has not been understood. This priestly book par excellence begins, as is fitting, with the great inner difficulty of the priest: he knows only one great danger, *consequently* "God" knows only one great danger.

The old God, all "spirit," all high priest, all perfection, takes a stroll in his garden; but he is bored. Against boredom even gods struggle in vain. What does he do? He invents man—man is entertaining. But lo and behold! Man, too, is bored. God's compassion with the sole distress that distinguishes all paradises knows no limits: soon he creates other animals as well. God's *first* mistake: man did not find the animals entertaining; he ruled over them, he did not even want to be "animal." Consequently God created woman. And indeed, that was the end of boredom—but of other things, too! Woman was God's *second* mistake. "Woman is by nature a snake, Heve"[150]—every priest knows that; "from woman comes *all* calamity in the world"—every priest knows that, too. "*Consequently,* it is from her, too, that *science* comes." Only from woman did man learn to taste the tree of knowledge.

What had happened? The old God was seized with hellish fear. Man himself had turned out to be his *greatest* mistake; he had created a rival for himself; science makes man *godlike*—it is all over with priests and gods when man becomes scientific. *Moral:* science is the forbidden as such—it alone is forbidden. Science is the *first* sin, the seed of all sin, the *original* sin. *This alone is morality.* "Thou shalt not know"—the rest follows.

God's hellish fear did not prevent him from being clever. How does one *resist* science? This became his main problem for a long time. Answer: out of paradise with man! Happiness, idleness give rise to ideas—all ideas are bad ideas. Man *shall* not think. And the "priest-as-such" invents distress, death, the mortal danger of pregnancy, every kind of misery, old age, trouble, and, above all, *sickness*—all means in the fight against science. Distress does not *permit* man to think. And yet—horrible!—the edifice of knowledge begins to tower, heaven-storming, suggesting twilight to the gods. What is to be done? The old God invents *war*, he divides the peoples, he fixes it so men will annihilate each other (priests have always required wars). War—among other things, a great disrupter of science! Incredible! Knowledge, the *emancipation from the priest,* continues to grow in spite of wars. And the old God makes a final decision: "Man has become scientific—*there is no other way, he has to be drowned.*"

Translated by Walter Kaufmann

From the so-called *Will to Power* (Summer 1883–Spring/Summer 1888)

417. *(Summer 1883/Winter 1883–84)*[151]

*M*y first solution: Dionysian wisdom.—Dionysian: temporary identification with the principle of life (including the voluptuousness of the martyr). *Joy in the destruction of the noblest* and at the sight of their[152] progressive ruin: *as joy in what is coming and lies in the future, which triumphs over existing things, however good.*[153]

My innovations.—Further development of pessimism: pessimism of the *intellect*; critique of *morality,* disintegration of the last consolation. Knowledge of the signs of *decay:* every action veiled with delusion; culture isolated, unjust, therefore strong.

1. My *endeavor to oppose* decay and increasing weakness of personality. I sought a new *center.*

2. Impossibility of this endeavor *recognized.*

3. *Thereupon I advanced further down the road of disintegration*—where I *found new sources of strength* for *individuals. We have to be destroyers!*—*I realized* that the state of *disintegration,* in which *individual natures can perfect themselves as never before*—is an image and *isolated example of existence in general.*

Theory of chance; the soul [is] *a being which selects and feeds,* utterly prudent and creative *all the time* (this *creative* force: usually overlooked! conceived as *"passive"* only). I recognized the *active force,* that which is creative, in the midst of what is accidental—chance is itself *only the clash of creative impulses.*[154]

To the paralyzing sense of general disintegration and incompleteness I *opposed* the *eternal recurrence*.

29. *(Winter 1883–84)*

—[155]Deep down: not knowing whither. *Emptiness*. Attempt to get over it by intoxication: intoxication as music; intoxication as cruelty in the tragic enjoyment of the destruction of the noblest; intoxication as blind enthusiasm for single *human beings* or *ages* (as hatred, etc.).—Attempt to work insensibly, as an instrument of science. Opening one's eyes to the many small enjoyments; e.g., also in the quest of knowledge. Modesty toward oneself; resignation to generalizing about oneself, to a pathos; mysticism, the voluptuous *enjoyment* of eternal emptiness; art for its own sake, *"le fait,"* "pure knowledge" as ways of narcotizing the disgust with *oneself;* some kind or other of continual work, *any* stupid little fanaticism; the medley of all means—sickness owing to general immoderation. (Debauchery kills enjoyment.)

1. Weakness of the will as a result.
2. Extreme pride and the humiliation of petty weakness *felt* in contrast.

594. *(Winter 1883–84)*

Science—this has been hitherto a way of putting an end to the complete confusion in which things exist, by hypotheses that "explain" everything—so it has come from the intellect's dislike of chaos.—This same dislike seizes me when I consider *myself:* I should like to form an image of the inner world, too, by means of some *schema,* and thus triumph over intellectual confusion. Morality has been a *simplification* of this kind: it taught that man was *known, familiar.*[156]—Now we have destroyed morality—we have again become *completely obscure* to ourselves! I know that I know nothing *of myself.* Physics proves to be a boon for the heart: science (as the way to knowledge) acquires a new charm after morality has been eliminated—and *because* it is *here alone* that we find consistency, we have to construct our life so as to preserve it. This yields a sort of *practical reflection* on the *conditions of our existence* as men of knowledge.

1029. *(Spring 1884)*

I have forced knowledge to confront such terrible images that any "Epicurean delight" is out of the question. Only Dionysian joy is sufficient: *I have been the first to discover the tragic.* The Greeks, thanks to their moralistic superficiality, misunderstood it. Even resignation is *not* a lesson of tragedy, but a misunderstanding of it! Yearning for nothingness is a *denial* of tragic wisdom, its opposite!

420. (Summer/Fall 1884)

I do not wish to persuade anyone to philosophy: it is inevitable, it is perhaps also desirable, that the philosopher should be a *rare* plant. I find nothing more repugnant than didactic praise of philosophy, as one finds it in Senecca, or worse, Cicero. Philosophy has little to do with virtue. Permit me to say that the scholar and scientist,[157] too, are fundamentally different from the philosopher.—What I desire is that the genuine concept of the philosopher should not utterly perish in Germany. There are so many half-baked creatures of all kinds in Germany who would be glad to conceal their ill-constitutedness beneath so noble a name.

91. (June/July 1885)

On German Pessimism.—The increase of darkness,[158] the pessimistic coloring, comes necessarily in the wake of the Enlightenment. As early as around 1770, the decline of cheerfulness began to be noticed; women, with that feminine instinct which always sides with virtue, supposed that immorality was the cause. Galiani[159] was right on the mark; he cited Voltaire's verse:

> *Un monstre gai vaut mieux*
> *Qu'un sentimental ennuyeux.*[160]

When I believe now that I am a few centuries ahead in Enlightenment not only of Voltaire but even of Galiani, who was far profounder—how far must I have got in the increase of darkness! And this is really the case, and I bewared in time, with some sort of regret, of the German and Christian narrowness and inconsequence[161] of pessimism à la Schopenhauer or, worse, Leopardi, and sought out the most quintessential forms (Asia). Among those thinkers who develop pessimism further I do not include Eduard von Hartmann,[162] whom I'd far sooner lump with "agreeable literature" ... But in order to endure this type of extreme pessimism (it can be perceived here and there in my *Birth of Tragedy*) and to live alone "without God and morality" I had to invent a counterpart for myself. Perhaps I know best why man alone laughs: he alone suffers so deeply that he *had* to invent laughter. The unhappy and melancholy animal is, as fitting, the most cheerful.

1067. *(June/July 1885)*

And do you know what "the world" is to me? Shall I show it to you in my mirror? This world: a monster of energy, without beginning, without end; a firm, iron magnitude of force that does not grow bigger or smaller, that does not expend itself but only transforms itself; as a whole, of unalterable size, a household without expenses or losses, but likewise without increase or income; enclosed by "nothingness" as by a boundary; not something blurry or wasted, not something endlessly extended, but set in a definite space as a definite force, and not a space that might be "empty" here or there, but rather as force throughout, as a play of forces and waves of forces, at the same time one and "many," increasing here and at the same time decreasing there; a sea of forces flowing and rushing together, eternally changing, eternally flooding back, with tremendous years of recurrence, with an ebb and a flood of its forms; out of the simplest forms striving toward the most complex, out of the stillest, most rigid, coldest forms toward the hottest, most turbulent, most self-contradictory, and then again returning home to the simple out of this abundance, out of the play of contradictions back to the joy of concord, affirming itself even in this uniformity of its courses and its years, blessing itself as that which must return eternally, as a becoming that knows no satiety, no disgust, no weariness: this, my *Dionysian* world of the eternally self-creating, the eternally self-destroying, this mystery world of the twofold voluptuous delight, my "beyond good and evil," without goal, unless the joy of the circle is itself a goal; without will, unless a ring feels good will toward itself—do you want a *name* for this world? A *solution* for all its riddles? A *light* for you, too, you best-concealed, strongest, most intrepid, most midnightly men?—*This world is the will to power—and nothing besides!* And you yourselves are also this will to power—and nothing besides![163]

1051. *(August/September 1885)*[164]

The highest and most illustrious human joys, in which existence celebrates its own transfiguration, come, as is fitting, only to the rarest and best-constituted men; and even to these only when they themselves and their ancestors have lived long, preparatory lives directed to this goal, and not even in the knowledge of this goal. Then an overflowing wealth of the most multifarious forces and the most dexterous power of "free willing" and lordly command dwell amicably together in one man; the spirit is then as much at home in the senses as the senses are at home in the spirit; and whatever takes place in the spirit must enkindle a subtle extraordinary happiness and play in the senses. And also the other way around! Consider this reverse process in the case of Hafiz; even Goethe, however much more faintly,[165] gives us an idea of this occurrence. It is probable that with such perfect and well-constituted men the most sensual functions are finally transfigured by a symbol-intoxication of the highest spirituality: they experience a kind of *deification of the body* in themselves and are as distant as possible from the ascetic philosophy of the proposition "God is a spirit"—and this shows clearly that the ascetic is the "ill-constituted man," who calls good only one thing in himself and indeed something that judges and condemns—and also calls it "God."

From that height of joy where man feels himself[166] to be altogether a deified form and a self-justification of nature, down to the joy of healthy peasants and healthy half-human animals, this whole long, tremendous light and color scale of *happiness,* the Greeks, not without the grateful shudder of him who is initiated into a mystery, not without much caution and pious silence, called by the divine name: *Dionysus.*—What do any latter-day men, the children of an invalid, multifarious, sick, strange mother, know of the *range* of Greek happiness; what *could* they know of it! Whence would the slaves of "modern ideas" derive a right to Dionysian festivals![167]

When the Greek body and the Greek soul "bloomed," and not in conditions of morbid exaltation and madness, there arose that mysterious symbol of the highest world-affirmation and transfiguration of existence that has yet been attained on earth. Here we have a *standard* by which everything that has grown up since is found too short, too poor, too narrow. One only needs to pronounce the word "Dionysus" in the presence of the best latter-day names and things, in the presence of Goethe perhaps, or Beethoven, or Shakespeare, or Raphael—at once we feel that our best things and moments have been *judged*. Dionysus is a *judge!*—Have I been understood?

There can be no doubt that the Greeks sought to interpret the ultimate mysteries "of the destiny of the soul" and everything they knew concerning education and purification, above all concerning the immovable order of rank and inequality of value between man and man, on the basis of their Dionysian experiences; here is the great depth, the great silence, in all matters Greek—*one does not know the Greeks* as long as this hidden subterranean entrance lies blocked as with rubble. Importunate scholar's eyes will never see anything in these things, however much scholarship still has to be employed in this excavation. Even the noble zeal of such friends of antiquity as Goethe and Winckelmann here has something un-permitted, even immodest about it.

To wait and to prepare oneself; to await the emergence of new sources; to prepare oneself in solitude for strange faces and voices; to wash one's soul ever cleaner from the marketplace dust and noise of this age; to *overcome* everything Christian through some-thing supra-Christian, and not merely to put it aside—for the Christian doctrine was the counterdoctrine to the Dionysian; to rediscover the South in oneself and to spread out above oneself a bright, glittering, mysterious southern sky; to reconquer southern health and hidden powerfulness of soul; step by step to become more comprehensive, more supranational, more European, more supra-European, more Oriental, finally more *Greek*—for the Greek was the first great union and synthesis of everything Oriental, and on that account the *inception* of the European soul, the discovery of *our "new world"*: whoever lives under such imperatives, who knows what *he* may not encounter one day? Perhaps—a *new day!*

606. *(Fall 1885/Fall 1886)*
Ultimately, man finds in things nothing but what he himself has imported into them: the finding is called science, the importing—art, religion, love, pride. Even if these should be children's games, one should carry on with both and be well-disposed toward both[168]—some should find in this way; others—*we* others!—should so import![169]

616. *(Fall 1885/Fall 1886)*
That the *value of the world* lies in our interpretation (—that other interpretations than merely human ones are perhaps somewhere

possible—); that previous interpretations have been perspective valuations by virtue of which we can survive in life, i.e., in the will to power, for the growth of power; that every *elevation of man* brings with it the overcoming of narrower interpretations; that every strengthening and increase of power opens up new perspectives and means believing in new horizons—this idea permeates my writings. The world with which *we are concerned* is false, i.e., is not a fact but a fiction and approximation[170] on the basis of a meager sum of observations; it is "in flux," as something in a state of becoming, as a falsehood always changing but never getting near the truth: for—there is no "truth."

1049. (Fall 1885/Fall 1886)

Apollo's deception: the eternity of beautiful form; the aristocratic legislation, *"thus shall it be forever!"*

Dionysus: sensuality and cruelty. Transitoriness could be interpreted as enjoyment of productive and destructive force, as continual creation.

677. (Winter 1886/Spring 1887)
In What Way Interpretations of the World
Are Symptoms of a Ruling Drive

The *artistic* view of the world: to sit down to contemplate life. But any analysis of the aesthetic outlook is lacking: its reduction to cruelty, a feeling of security, playing the judge and standing outside, etc. One must examine the artist himself, and his psychology (critique of the drive to play as a release of force, a pleasure in change, in impressing one's soul on something, the absolute egoism of the artist, etc.). What drives he sublimates.

The *scientific* view of the world: critique of the psychological need for science. The desire to make comprehensible; the desire to make practical, useful, exploitable—in what way anti-aesthetic. Only value, what can be counted and calculated. How an average type of man seeks to gain the upper hand in this way. Dreadful when even *history* is appropriated in this way—the realm of the superior, of those who judge. What drives they sublimate!

The *religious* view of the world: critique of the religious man. He is *not* necessarily the moral man, but the man of powerful exaltations and deep depressions who interprets the former with gratitude or suspicion and does not derive them from *himself*

(—nor the latter, either). Essentially the man who feels himself "unfree," who sublimates his moods, his instincts of subjection.

The *moral* view of the world: The feelings of a social order of rank are projected into the universe: irremovability, law, classification and coordination,[171] because they are valued the highest, are also *sought* in the highest places—above the universe or behind the universe. . . .[172]

What is *common to all:* the ruling drives want to be viewed also as the *highest courts of value in general, indeed as creative and ruling powers.* It is clear that these drives either oppose or subject each other (sometimes also join together synthetically) or alternate in dominating. Their profound antagonism is so great, however, that where they *all* seek satisfaction, a man of profound *mediocrity* must result.[173]

544. (Fall 1887)

Increase in "dissimulation" proportionate to the rising *order of rank* of creatures. It seems to be lacking in the inorganic world; cunning begins in the organic world: plants are already masters of it. The highest human beings, such as Caesar, Napoleon (Stendhal's remark on him),[174] also the higher races (Italians), the Greeks (Odysseus); craftiness belongs to the *essence* of the enhancement of man—Problem of the actor. My Dionysus ideal—The perspective of all organic functions, all the strongest instincts of life: the force in all life that *wills* error; error as the precondition even of thought. Before there is "thought" there must have been "invention";[175] the *construction*[176] of identical cases, of the *appearance* of sameness, is more primitive than the *knowledge* of sameness.

1005. (Fall 1887)

Around 1876 I was terrified to see all I had desired hitherto *compromised,* as I grasped which way Wagner was going now; and I was bound very closely to him by all the bonds of a profound identity of needs, by gratitude, by his irreplaceability and the absolute privation I saw before me.

At the same time I seemed to myself irrevocably *incarcerated* in my philology and teaching—in an accident and makeshift of my life: I no longer knew how to extricate myself, and was weary, spent, used up.

At the same time I grasped that my instinct went into the opposite direction from Schopenhauer's: toward a justification of life, even at its most terrible, ambiguous, and mendacious; for this I had the formula "Dionysian."

Against the theory that an "in-itself of things" must necessarily be good, blissful, true, and one, Schopenhauer's interpretation of the "in-itself" as will was an essential step; but he did not understand how to *deify* this will: he remained entangled in the moral-Christian ideal. Schopenhauer was still so much subject to the dominion of Christian values that, as soon as the thing-in-itself was no longer "God" for him, he had to see it as bad, stupid, absolutely reprehensible. He failed to grasp that there can be an infinite variety of ways of being different, even of being god.—A curse on that bigoted duality: "good and evil."

71. (Fall 1887; revised Summer 1888)
"Modernity" in the perspective of the metaphor of nourishment and digestion.—

Sensibility immensely more irritable (—dressed up moralistically as the increase in *pity*—); the abundance of disparate impressions greater than ever: *cosmopolitanism* in foods, literatures, newspapers, forms, tastes, even landscapes. The *tempo* of this influx *prestissimo;* the impressions erase each other; one instinctively resists taking in anything, taking anything *deeply,* to "digest" anything; a *weakening* of the power to digest results from this. A kind of *adaptation* to this flood of impressions takes place: men unlearn spontaneous action, *they merely react* to stimuli from outside. *They spend their strength* partly in *assimilating* things, partly in *defense,* partly in *opposition. Profound weakening of spontaneity:* the historian, critic, analyst, the interpreter, the observer, the collector, the reader—all of them *reactive* talents: all science!

Artificial *change*[177] of one's nature into a "mirror"; interested but, as it were, merely epidermically interested; a fundamental coolness, a balance, a fixed *low* temperature closely underneath the thin surface on which warmth, movement, "tempest," and the play of waves are encountered.

Opposition of *external* mobility and a certain *deep heaviness and weariness.*

852. (Fall 1887; revised Summer 1888)
The tragic artist.[178]—It is a question of *strength* (of an individual or of a people), *whether* and *where* the judgment "beautiful" is

applied. The feeling of plenitude, of *dammed-up strength* (which permits one to meet with courage and good-humor much that makes the weakling *shudder*)—the feeling of *power* applies the judgment "beautiful" even to things and conditions that the instinct of impotence can only find *hateful* and "ugly." The nose for what we could more or less deal with if it confronted us in the flesh—as danger, problem, temptation—this determines even our aesthetic *yes*. ("That is beautiful" is an *affirmation*.)

From this it appears that, broadly speaking, a *preference for questionable and terrifying things* is a symptom of *strength*; while a taste for the *pretty and dainty* belongs to the weak and delicate. *Pleasure* in tragedy characterizes *strong* ages and natures: their *non plus ultra* is perhaps the *divina commedia*. It is the *heroic* spirits who say *yes* to themselves in tragic cruelty: they are hard enough to experience suffering as a *pleasure*.

Supposing, on the other hand, that the weak desire to enjoy an art that is not meant for them; what will they do to make tragedy palatable for themselves? They will interpret *their own value feelings* into it; e.g., the "triumph of the moral world order" or the doctrine of the "worthlessness of existence" or the invitation to resignation (—or half-medicinal, half-moral discharges of affects à la Aristotle).[179] Finally: the *art of the terrifying,* insofar as it excites the nerves, can be esteemed by the weak and exhausted as a stimulant: that, for example, is the reason Wagnerian art is esteemed today. It is a sign of one's *feeling of power and well-being* how much one can acknowledge the terrifying and questionable character of things; and *whether* one needs some sort of "solution" at the end.

This type of *artists' pessimism* is precisely the *opposite of that religio-moral pessimism* that suffers from the "corruption" of man and the riddle of existence—and by all means craves a solution, or at least a hope for a solution. The suffering, desperate, self-mistrustful, in a word the sick, have at all times had need of entrancing *visions* to endure life (*this* is the origin of the concept "blessedness"). A related case: the artists of decadence, who basically have a *nihilistic* attitude toward life, take *refuge* in the *beauty of form*—in those *select* things in which nature has become perfect, in which it is indifferently *great* and *beautiful*. . .(—"Love of beauty" can therefore be something other than the *ability* to *see* the beautiful, *create* the beautiful; it can be an expression of the very *inability* to do so.)

Those imposing artists who let a *harmony* sound forth from every conflict are those who bestow upon things their own power and self-redemption: they express their innermost experience in the symbolism of every work of art they produce—their creativity is gratitude for their existence.

The *profundity of the tragic artist* lies in this, that his aesthetic instinct surveys the more remote consequences, that he does not halt short-windedly at what is closest at hand, that he affirms the *large-scale economy* which justifies the *terrifying,* the *evil,* the *questionable*—and more than merely justifies them.

68. (Spring 1888)[180]

Why everything turns into histrionics.—Modern man lacks: the sure instinct (consequence of a *long homogeneous form of activity* of one kind of man); the inability to achieve anything *perfect* is merely a consequence of this: as an individual one can never make up for lost schooling.[181]

That which creates a morality, a code of laws, the profound instinct that only *automatism* makes possible perfection in life and creation.

But now we have reached the opposite point; indeed, we *wanted* to reach it: the most extreme consciousness, the ability of man and history to see through themselves. With this we are practically as far as possible from perfection in being, doing, and willing: our desire, even our will for knowledge is a symptom of a tremendous decadence. We strive for the opposite of that which *strong races, strong natures* want—understanding is an *ending.*—

That science is possible in the sense that is cultivated today is proof that all elementary instincts, life's instincts of *self-defense* and *protection*, no longer function. We no longer collect, we squander the capital of our ancestors, even in the way in which we *gain knowledge.*—

432/433. (Spring 1888)

The problem of Socrates.—The two antitheses: the *tragic* disposition, the *Socratic* disposition—measured according to the law of life.

To what extent the Socratic disposition is a phenomenon of decadence: to what extent, however, a robust health and a strength is still exhibited in the whole *habitus,* in the dialectics, efficiency, and self-discipline of the scientific man (—the health of the plebeian; his wickedness, *esprit frondeur*,[182] his cunning, his *canaille au fond*[183] are held in check by shrewdness; "ugly").

Making ugly: self-mockery, dialectical dryness, shrewdness as *tyrant* in opposition to a "tyrant" (instinct). Everything is exaggerated, eccentric, caricature in Socrates, a *buffo* with the instincts of Voltaire. He discovers a new form of *agon;*[184] he is the first fencing master to the leading circles of Athens; he represents nothing but the *highest form of shrewdness:* he calls it "virtue" (—he divined it to be *deliverance:* he was not shrewd from choice, it was *de rigueur*[185]); to have oneself under control, so as to go into battle with reasons and not with affects (—the cunning of Spinoza—the unraveling of the errors caused by affects);—to discover that one can capture anyone in whom one produces affects, that affects proceed illogically; practice in self-mockery, so as to damage the feeling of rancor at its roots.

I try to understand from what partial and idiosyncratic states the Socratic problem is to be derived: his equalization of reason = virtue = happiness. It was with this absurdity of a doctrine of identity that he cast a spell: the philosophers of antiquity never freed themselves [from this fascination]—

Problem of Socrates. Shrewdness, clarity, severity, and logicality as weapons against the *ferocity of the drives.* These must be dangerous and threaten destruction; otherwise there would be no sense in developing *shrewdness* to the point of making it into a tyrant. *To make a tyrant* of shrewdness—but *for that* the drives must be tyrants. This is the problem.—In those days it was a very timely problem. Reason became = virtue = happiness.

Absolute lack of objective interest: hatred for science; the idiosyncrasy of feeling oneself as a problem. Socrates' acoustic hallucination: morbid element. When the spirit is rich and independent it most resists any preoccupation with morality. How came it that Socrates was a *monomaniac in regard to morality?*—In emergencies, "practical" philosophy steps at once to the fore. Morality and religion as chief interests are signs of an emergency.

Solution: The Greek philosophers rest on the same fundamental facts of inner experience as Socrates: five steps from excess, from anarchy, from intemperance—all men of decadence. They see in him a physician. *Solution:* The ferocity and anarchy of the instincts in the case of Socrates is a *symptom of decadence.* Likewise, the superfetation of logic and of clarity of reason. Both are abnormalities, both belong together. Logic as will to power, to self-mastery, to "happiness."

Critique. Decadence betrays itself in this preoccupation with "happiness" (i.e., with "salvation of the soul," i.e., to feel *one's condition* as a *danger*). The fanaticism of the interest in "happiness" indicates the pathological nature of the hidden cause:[186] it was a life-or-death interest. *To be reasonable or* perish was the *alternative* before which they all stood. The moralism of the Greek philosophers indicates that they felt themselves to be *in danger*—

444. (Spring 1888)

Problem of the philosopher *and the* man of science.—*Type on the rise:* strength in tranquillity, in the relative indifference and difficulty to react. The great affects, *all of them,* and wonderfully aiding each other.—Influence of age; depressive habits (staying-at-home, à la Kant), overwork; insufficient nourishment of the brain; reading. More essentially: whether a tendency toward generalities is not already a symptom of decadence; objectivity as *dispersion of the will*[187] (—to be *able* to remain so *distant*—). This presupposes a great *adiaphory*[188] in regard to the powerful drives: a kind of isolation, exceptional stance, resistance in regard to the normal drives.

Type: separation from the *homeland;* farther and farther afield; increasing exoticism; the old imperatives become dumb—; moreover, this continual questioning "whether?" ("happiness") is a sign of disengagement from forms of organization, of a breaking loose.

Problem: whether the man of science is more of a symptom of decadence than the philosopher:—he is not disengaged as a *whole,* only a *part* of him is absolutely dedicated to knowledge, trained to one niche and perspective—here he needs *all* the virtues of a strong race and health, great severity, manliness, shrewdness; here one might speak of division of labor and training,[189] all very much for the benefit of the whole and possible only on a very high scale of culture. The man of science is a symptom more of a higher multiplicity of culture than of its weariness. The scholar of decadence is a *bad* scholar. While the philosopher of decadence has counted, hitherto at least, as the typical philosopher.[190]

799. (Spring 1888)

In the Dionysian intoxication there is sexuality and voluptuousness: they are not lacking in the Apollonian. There must also be a difference in tempo in the two conditions—*The extreme calm in certain sensations of intoxication* (more strictly: the retardation of the feelings of time and space) likes to be reflected in a vision of the calmest gestures and types of soul. The classical style is essentially a representation of this calm, simplification, abbreviation, concentration—the *highest feeling of power* is concentrated in the classical type. To react slowly; a great consciousness; no feeling of struggle . . .[191]

816. (Spring 1888)

Compared with the *artist,* the appearance of the *scientific* man is indeed a sign of a certain damming up and lowering of the level of life (—but also of *strengthening, severity, hardness, will power*).

In what way falsity, indifference to truth, and utility may be signs of youth, of "childishness," in an artist—Their habitual manner, their unreasonableness, their ignorance about themselves, their indifference to eternal values, their seriousness in "play"—their lack of dignity; buffoon and god side by side; saint and *canaille*— Imitation as an instinct, commanding . . .[192] *Artists of ascending life—artists of declining life: do they not belong to all phases?—Yes.*

821. (Spring 1888)

Pessimism in art?[193]—The artist gradually comes to love for their own sake the means that reveal a state of intoxication: extreme subtlety and splendor of color, definiteness of line, nuances of tone: the *distinct* where otherwise, under normal conditions, any distinctness is lacking. All distinct things, all nuances, in that they recall these extreme enhancements of strength that intoxication produces, awaken this feeling of intoxication by association:[194] the effect of works of art is to *excite the state that creates art*— intoxication.

What is essential in art remains its *perfection* of existence, its production of perfection and plenitude; art is essentially *affirmation, blessing, deification of existence*—What does a *pessimistic art* signify? Is it not a *contradiction?*—Yes.—Schopenhauer is *wrong* when he says that certain works of art serve pessimism. Tragedy does *not* teach "resignation"—To represent terrible and questionable things is in itself an instinct for power and magnificence in an artist: he does not fear them—There is no such thing as pessimistic art—Art affirms. Job affirms.—But Zola? But de Goncourt? The things they display are ugly; but *that* they display them comes from their *pleasure in the ugly*—No use [in denying it!] If you think otherwise, you're deceiving yourselves.—How redeeming is Dostoevski!

1050. *(Spring 1888)*

Birth of Tragedy.[195]—These two natural forces of art[196] are opposed to each other by Nietzsche as the Dionysian and the Apollonian: he maintains that ... The word "Dionysian" expresses: an urge to unity, a reaching out beyond personality, the everyday, society, reality; an abyss of forgetting; a passionate-painful overflowing into darker, fuller, more floating states; an ecstatic affirmation of the total character of life as that which, ever changing, remains the same, just as powerful, just as blissful; the great pantheistic sharing of joy and sorrow that sanctifies and calls good even the most terrible and questionable qualities of life; the eternal will to procreation, to fruitfulness, to eternity; the feeling of the necessary unity of creation and destruction.[197]

The word "Apollonian" expresses: the urge to perfect self-sufficiency,[198] to the typical "individual," to all that simplifies, distinguishes, makes strong, clear, unambiguous, typical: freedom under the law.

The further development of art is as necessarily tied to the antagonism between these two forces as the further development of mankind is to that between the sexes. Plenitude of power and moderation, the highest form of self-affirmation in a cool, noble, severe beauty: the Apollonianism of the Hellenic will.

The origin of tragedy and comedy as [man's] *seeing*, in a state of total ecstasy, the *presence* of a divine type, as a sharing in the experience of the local legend, of the [divine] visit, the miracle, the act of founding, the "drama."[199]

This antithesis of the Dionysian and the Apollonian within the Greek soul is one of the great riddles to which Nietzsche felt himself drawn when considering the nature of the Greeks. Basically, Nietzsche was concerned with nothing except to guess why precisely Greek Apollonianism had to grow out of a Dionysian substratum; why the Dionysian Greek needed to become Apollonian; that is, to break his will to the terrible, the multifarious, uncertain, frightful, upon a will to measure, to simplicity, to submission to rule and concept. The immoderate, disorderly Asiatic lies at his roots: the bravery of the Greek consists in his struggle with his Asiaticism; beauty is not given to him, as little as is logic or the naturalness of customs—it is conquered, willed, won by struggle—it is his victory.[200]

1052. *(Spring 1888)*

The two types: Dionysus *and the* Crucified.[201]—To determine:[202] whether the typical *religious* man [is] a form of decadence (the great innovators are one and all morbid and epileptic); but are we not here omitting one type of religious man, the *pagan?* Is the pagan cult not a form of thanksgiving and affirmation of life? Ought not its highest representative to be an apology for, and deification of, life? The type of a well-constituted and ecstatically overflowing spirit—the type of a spirit[203] that takes into itself and *redeems*—the contradictions and questionable aspects of existence?

It is here I set the *Dionysus* of the Greeks: the religious affirmation of life, life whole and not denied or in part; (typical—that the sexual act arouses profundity, mystery, reverence).

Dionysus versus the "Crucified": there you have the antithesis. It is *not* a difference in regard to their martyrdom—it is a difference in the meaning of it. Life itself, its eternal fruitfulness and recurrence, creates torment, destruction, the will to annihilation. In the other case, suffering—the "Crucified as the innocent one"—counts as an objection to this life, as a formula for its condemnation.—One surmises that the problem is that of the meaning of suffering: whether a Christian meaning or a tragic meaning. In the former case, suffering is supposed to be the path to a blessed existence; in the latter case, being is seen as *blessed*[204] *enough* to justify even a monstrous amount of suffering. The tragic man affirms even the harshest suffering: he is sufficiently strong, rich, and capable of deifying to do so. The Christian denies even the happiest lot on earth; he is sufficiently weak, poor, disinherited to suffer from life in whatever form he meets it. The "god on the cross" is a curse on life, a signal to seek redemption from life; Dionysus cut to pieces is a *promise* of life: it will be eternally reborn and return home from destruction.

1041. *(Spring/Summer 1888)*

How I recognize my equals.[205]—Philosophy, as I have hitherto understood and lived it, is a voluntary quest for even the cursed and wicked sides of existence. From the long experience I gained from such a wandering through ice and desert, I learned to view differently all that had hitherto philosophized: the *hidden* history of philosophy, the psychology of its great names, came to light for me. "How much truth can a spirit *endure,* how much truth does a spirit *dare?*"—this became for me the real standard of value. Error is *cowardice*—every achievement of knowledge is a consequence of courage, of severity toward oneself, of cleanliness toward oneself— Such an experimental philosophy as I live anticipates experimentally even the possibilities of fundamental nihilism; but this does not mean that it must halt at a negation, a *no,* a will to negation. It wants rather to cross over to the opposite of this—to a *Dionysian affirmation* of the world as it is, without subtraction, exception, or selection—it wants the eternal circulation:—the same things, the same logic and illogic of entanglements. The highest state a philosopher can attain: to stand in a Dionysian relationship to existence—my formula for this is *amor fati.*

It is part of this state to perceive not merely the necessity of those sides of existence hitherto denied, but their desirability; and not their desirability merely in relation to the sides hitherto affirmed (perhaps as their complement or precondition), but for their own sake, as the more powerful, more faithful, *truer* sides of existence, in which its will finds clearer expression.

It is also part of this state to depreciate that side of existence which alone has been affirmed hitherto; to perceive the origin of this valuation and how little a Dionysian value standard for existence is obliged to it: I pulled up and perceived *what* it really was that here affirmed (on the one hand, the instinct of the suffering; on the other, the instinct of the herd; and thirdly, the instinct of the majority as opposed to the exceptions—).

Thus I guessed to what extent a stronger type of man would necessarily have to conceive the elevation and enhancement of man as taking place in another direction: *higher beings,* beyond good and evil, beyond those values which cannot deny their origin in the sphere of suffering, the herd, and the majority—I sought in history the beginnings of this construction of reverse ideals (the concepts "pagan," "classical," "noble" newly discovered and expounded—).

Translated by Walter Kaufmann
and R. J. Hollingdale

Notes

PART I

1. An allusion to Friedrich Schiller's lines in the prologue to his *Wallensteins Lager:* "He that has satisfied the best minds of the time has lived for all times."
2. In the arts.
3. The profane crowd.
4. When Nietzsche died in 1900, Stefan George wrote a poem entitled "Nietzsche" that ends: "... it should have sung, not spoken, this new soul."
5. *Die Welt als Wille und Vorstellung,* ed. Julius Frauenstädt (Leipzig: F. A. Brockhaus, 1873).
6. Nietzsche's coinage.
7. The allusion is to the time of Goethe, when Germany, at her cultural zenith, was at her political nadir.
8. From Goethe's *Faust,* part 2, lines 7438ff.
9. "On the Higher Man," sections 17–20, quoted by Nietzsche with omissions.
10. Nietzsche uses the somewhat odd term "petrifaction" *(Petrefakt).*
11. In the first edition: "... an opposition of style: two different tendencies run parallel in it, for the most part in conflict; and they ..." Most of the changes in the revision of 1874 are as slight as this, and therefore not included in the following pages.
12. First edition: "... until eventually, at the moment of the flowering of the Hellenic 'will,' they appear fused to generate together the art form of Attic tragedy."
13. *Schein* has been rendered in these pages sometimes as "illusion" and sometimes as "mere appearance."
14. Allusion to a poem by Goethe which begins: *"Wär nicht das Auge sonnenhaft, / Die Sonne könnt' es nie erblicken ..."*
15. The Sanskrit word *māyā* is usually translated as "illusion."
16. This reference, like subsequent references to the same work, is Nietzsche's own and refers to the edition of 1873, edited by Julius Frauenstädt (see n. 5).
17. Principle of individuation.
18. A Babylonian festival that lasted five days and was marked by general license. During this time slaves are said to have ruled their masters, and a criminal was given all royal rights before he was put to death at the end of the festival.
19. In German, "the prodigal son" is *der verlorene Sohn* ("the lost son").
20. An allusion to Friedrich Schiller's hymn "An die Freude" ("To Joy"), used by Beethoven in the final movement of his Ninth Symphony.
21. Quotation from Schiller's hymn.

22. *Sentimentalisch* (not *sentimental*): an allusion to Schiller's influential contrast of *naiv* poetry with his own *sentimentalische Dichtung.*

23. Cf. Sophocles, *Oedipus at Colonus*, lines 1224ff.

24. Fate.

25. An allusion to Homer's *Odyssey* 11, lines 489ff.

26. Sparta.

27. The German term is *ahnungsvoll.*

28. An early Greek poet whose dates are disputed. He mentions an eclipse that some believe to be the one of 711 B.C., others that of 648 B.C. His mother was a slave, and he was killed in battle.

29. Literally, *interesselos,* a Kantian concept adopted by Schopenhauer.

30. Lines 677ff.

31. An anthology of German folk songs published in 1806–8, edited by Achim von Arnim (1781–1831) and his brother-in-law, Clemens Brentano (1778–1842). The title means "The Boy's Magic Horn."

32. Middle of the seventh century B.C.; Terpander, a poet, was born in Lesbos and lived in Sparta.

33. One of the leading spirits of the early German romantic movement, especially renowned for his translations of about half of Shakespeare's plays.

34. *Aufgehoben:* one of Hegel's favorite words, which can also mean "lifted up" or "preserved."

35. *Erscheinungswelt.*

36. "The Greek theater appears to have been originally designed for the performance of dithyrambic choruses in honour of Dionysus. The center of it was the *orchēstrā* (dancing place), a circular space, in the middle of which stood the *thumelē,* or altar of the god. Round more than half of the *orchēstrā,* forming a kind of horseshoe, was the *theātron* (seeing place) proper, circular tiers of seats, generally cut out of the side of a hill . . . . Behind the orchestra and facing the audience was the *skēnē,* called "scene" in . . . translation, originally a wooden structure, a façade with three doors, through which, when the drama had developed from the dithyrambic chorus, the actors made their entrances" (*The Oxford Companion to Classical Literature,* ed. Sir Paul Harvey, revised edition, 1946, pp. 422f.).

37. *Der "idealische Zuschauer."*

38. *. . . der einzige Schauer ist, der Schauer der Visionswelt der Szene.* The word *Schauer* could also mean "shudder," the shudder of holy awe; and while this is certainly not the primary meaning intended here, it enters into the coloring of the sentence.

39. *Übersehen,* like overlook, can mean both "survey" and "ignore."

40. Quoted from Goethe's *Faust,* part 1, lines 505–7.

41. Lion and human. Actually, the Sphinx also has wings in ancient Greek representations.

42. Memnon's Column was an ancient name given to one of the two colossal statues of the pharaoh Amenophis III, across the river from Karnak. When the first rays of the sun struck the weathered statue in the morning, it is said to have produced a musical sound—a phenomenon that stopped when an earthquake damaged the statue.

43. After his emancipation from Wagner, Nietzsche came to consider the terms "Aryan" and "Semitic" more problematic.

44. *Der Frevel.*

45. *Die Sünde.*

46. Goethe's *Faust,* part 1, lines 3982–85.

47. Allusion to Goethe's *Faust,* part 1, line 409.

48. Those initiated into the mysteries.

49. Again, Nietzsche's term is *ahnungsvoll.*

50. Truth.

51. The chief representative of the so-called Old Comedy was Aristophanes (about 448–380 B.C.). "The New Comedy began to prevail about 336; its characteristic features are the representation of contemporary life by means of imaginary persons drawn from it, the development of plot and character, the substitution of humor for wit, and the introduction of romantic love as a theme. It resembles the tragedy of Euripides (the *Ion* for example) more than the comedy of Aristophanes. Of the chorus, no more remains than a band of musicians and dancers whose performances punctuate intervals in the play. The New Comedy is in fact an obvious progenitor of the modern drama. But the moral standard is surprisingly low...." (*The Oxford Companion to Classical Literature,* p. 116).

52. Lines 937ff. Aristophanes also lampoons Euripides in *The Acharnians* and in *Thesmophoriazousae.*

53. Quotation from a six-line poem of the young Goethe, entitled "Grabschrift" ("Epitaph").

54. *Selbstgenügsamkeit.*

55. The Greek word is translated as "understanding" *(Verstand)* in the preceding sentence. The quotation is not to be found in precisely this form in the extant fragments.

56. Aristotle, *Metaphysics* 984b (A, end of chap. 3).

57. *Volksverführer* (der Gegenwart), which also implies "seducers and corrupters of the people."

58. Goethe's *Faust,* part 1, lines 1607–11.

59. Christian Fürchtegott Gellert, a well-known 18th-century poet.

60. Handmaid.

61. Aristotle had called Euripides "the most tragic of the poets" (*Poetics* 1453a). Although Nietzsche has more feeling for poetry—and for tragedy—than Aristotle did, this estimate seems fairer than Nietzsche's conception of Euripides as the most optimistic. Surely, Euripides did not believe that "he who is virtuous is happy"— on the contrary—and the superabundance of dialectical fireworks in his tragedies, though it does dissipate the tragic emotion, usually illustrates the futility of reason, its inability to prevent tragedy.

62. Lynceus, one of the Argonauts, was so sharp-sighted that he could see through the earth and distinguish objects almost ten miles away.

63. The best commentary on this contrast is found in section 4 of Nietzsche's preface to *The Gay Science.* Here he takes issue with those who "want by all means to unveil, uncover . . . We no longer believe that truth remains truth when the veils are withdrawn." We have learned "to stop courageously at the surface, the fold, the skin, to adore appearance, to believe in forms, tones, words, in the whole Olympus of appearance. Those Greeks were superficial—*out of profundity.* . . . *Are we not, precisely in this respect, Greeks? Adorers of forms, of tones, of words? And therefore—artists?*"

64. "Not the truth in whose possession any man is, or thinks he is, but the honest effort he has made to find out the truth, is what constitutes the worth of a man. For it is not through the possession but through the inquiry after truth that his powers expand, and in this alone consists his ever-growing perfection. Possession makes one calm, lazy, proud—

"If God had locked up all truth in his right hand, and in his left the unique, ever-live striving for truth, albeit with the addition that I should always and eternally err, and he said to me, 'Choose!'—I should humbly clasp his left hand, saying 'Father, give! Pure truth is after all for thee alone!'"

This celebrated passage is found at the end of the first section of *Eine Duplik* (a reply of the accused to the rejoinder of his accuser), 1778.

65. Often rendered, not quite adequately, as "temperance."

66. "Before the middle of his existence" presumably alludes to the beginning of Dante's *Inferno*, not, like this translation, to Milton's sonnet on his blindness.

67. In Nietzsche's text, knowledge is insatiable, not merely the hunger for it.

68. *Umschlagen*, another Hegelian term (cf. "has turned into tragic resignation" in the preceding paragraph).

69. Nietzsche uses the derogatory term *Wagnerei*.

70. Literally, *Leichenbitterparfüm* (*Leichenbitter*, "inviter to a funeral").

71. *Aufgehoben*: a term Hegel liked especially because in ordinary German it can mean "canceled," "preserved," and "lifted up."

72. *Gutheißen, gut heißen.*

73. In the final section of the book.

74. In *Twilight*: "guessed to be."

75. In *Twilight*: "understood." Nietzsche is referring to Aristotle's conception of catharsis (*Poetics* 6, 1449b).

76. *Richard Wagner in Bayreuth*. The next three paragraphs refer to this book.

77. *The Will to Power*, section 853. Title and text combine three different entries from Nietzsche's notebooks, but they all refer to *The Birth of Tragedy*.

78. The quotation is not exact.

PART II

1. Nietzsche says simply *das Größte*.

2. Literally, *von Diamant*.

3. Heraclitus.

4. Nietzsche has *Menschen mit fühlenden Brüsten* and *Larve*, allusions to Friedrich Schiller's ballad "Der Taucher."

5. An allusion to Mephisto's disdainful words about Gretchen in Goethe's *Faust*.

6. Nietzsche uses the more general term *erstarren*.

7. The German poet Lessing had been married for just a little over one year to Eva König. A son was born and died the same day, and the mother's life was despaired of. In a letter to his friend Eschenburg the poet wrote ". . . and I lost him so unwillingly, this son! For he had so much understanding! so much understanding! Do not suppose that the few hours of fatherhood have made me an ape of a father! I know what I say. Was it not understanding, that they had to drag him into the world with a pair of forceps? that he so soon suspected the evil of this world? Was it not understanding, that he seized the first opportunity to get away from it?"

8. War of all against all.

9. In German "the tree"—*der Baum*—is masculine.

10. In German "the plant"—*die Pflanze*—is feminine.

11. Hidden quality.

12. A literal translation of Nietzsche's *Schildzeichen* ("devices") might prove to be misleading.

PART III

1. *Begriffsbeben*.

2. The ugliest and most scurrilous of the Greeks before Troy.

3. Queen of the Amazons.

4. *Auktorität.*

5. "Know thyself."

6. The German term *Übel*, used throughout this paragraph, is ambiguous; it can denote both "evil" and "misfortune."

7. Nietzsche's term for "phases" is *Jahresringe,* "annual rings."

8. *Vorstufe.*

9. *Jedermanns-Freund.*

10. Nietzsche has *der . . . geistige und seelische Horizont.*

11. *Vergröberung.*

12. See n. 3.

13. Nietzsche has *die Geistig-Weichlichen.*

14. Nietzsche has *zum schönsten Schein umbilden.*

14a. To be excited by nothing; equanimity.

15. Literally, *Taschenspieler,* i.e. "sleight of hand artist."

16. An allusion to Klärchen's song in Goethe's *Egmont,* act 3, scene 2.

17. Literally, *die Sitte der Sittlichkeit.*

18. See Aristotle's *Poetics,* chap. 6, 1449b.

19. Love based on pleasure.

20. Love based on vanity.

21. Having purchased a manuscript of the hitherto unpublished first five books of Tacitus's *Annals* (later divided into six) as well as a copy of a printed volume that contained the last six books and the first five books of Tacitus's *History,* Pope Leo X "determined to give to the world as complete an edition as possible; for which purpose he entrusted the manuscript to the younger Filippo Beroaldo, with directions to correct the text, and to superintend the printing of it in an elegant and useful form. In order to reward the editor for his trouble on this occasion, Leo proposed to grant him an exclusive privilege for the reprinting and sale of the work: and . . . the brief in which this privilege is conceded contains a kind of justification on the part of the pontiff for devoting so much of his attention to the promotion of profane learning.

"We have considered those pursuits as not the least important which lead to the promotion of literature and useful arts; for we have been accustomed even from our early years to think that nothing more excellent or more useful has been given by the Creator to mankind, if we except only the knowledge and true worship of Himself, than these studies, which not only lead to the ornament and guidance of human life, but are applicable and useful to every particular situation; in adversity consolatory, in prosperity pleasing and honorable; insomuch, that without them we should be deprived of all the grace of life and all the polish of society" (William Roscoe, *The Life and Pontificate of Leo the Tenth,* 5th ed., London: 1846, vol. 1, p. 355f.).

It will be noted that Nietzsche's "quotation" is rather free, and that the pope did not really keep silent about "the knowledge and true worship" of God. But these criticisms do not undermine Nietzsche's point, which he actually understates.

21a. Eternal repose for God; "requiem."

22. The passage in Horace to which Nietzsche alludes is *Ars Poetica,* lines 191f., where the point is that no god should be introduced (i.e., no *deus ex machina*) unless the knot is such that no one else could untie it.

23. I am, therefore I think: I think, therefore I am. The second half of this statement is quoted from Descartes, who made this formulation famous.

24. Love of fate.

25. Socrates's last words imply that he has been cured of a disease, for Asclepius is the god of medicine.

26. *Das größte Schwergewicht.* Literally, the noun means "heavyweight," and this term is actually used to designate the heaviest class in boxing; but it is also commonly used for "main emphasis" or "stress."

27. The tragedy begins.

28. Lake Urmi, or Urmia, is a lake in northwestern Iran between the massif of Ararat, whose highest peak rises to almost 17,000 feet, and Mount Sabalan, which is over 15,000 feet. The original readers of *The Gay Science* might well be put in mind of the historical Zarathustra, the founder of the religion of ancient Iran, who is also known as Zoroaster. The ancient Greeks thought he had lived 6,000 years before Xerxes invaded Greece in the fifth century B.C.; some recent scholars have dated him around 1,000 B.C., but most scholars now consider him a contemporary of the prophet Jeremiah and believe that Zarathustra's religious reforms, around 600 B.C., helped to trigger the Persian conquest of the Babylonian empire.

29. In German, the last word of this section is *Untergang;* and here the German word is *untergehen,* emphasized in the original. There is no English equivalent for *untergehen* (literally, "going under"). The German verb is used for the setting of the sun, for drowning, for sinking, and, above all, for perishing.

30. This Greek word (sing. *polytropos*) is applied to Odysseus in the first line of the *Odyssey.* Its meaning ranges from "much-turned" to "much-traveled," "versatile," "wily," and "manifold."

31. Nietzsche's term *Heiland* for both "healer" and "savior" is, of course, fraught with ambiguities, all the more so since it is put in quotation marks.

32. Literally, *Haß des Mißratenen, Entbehrenden, Schlechtweggekommenen* (Nietzsche uses the singular).

33. My own and my quintessence.

34. *Sensualisten:* cf. the reference to Condillac and the sensualists near the beginning of section 370.

35. In the twelfth canto of the *Odyssey,* Odysseus stops the ears of his companions with wax to keep them from hearing the Sirens' dangerously seductive song as their ship approaches the Sirens' island, and he has himself bound to the mast.

36. Intellectual love of God.

37. *Großgezüchtet: züchten* means "to breed, grow, or cultivate animals, plants, or qualities." Nietzsche uses the word frequently, and it is often rendered by "cultivate."

38. Nietzsche's coinage, initially introduced by him in *Human, All-Too-Human* (1878).

39. Contradiction between the noun and the adjective.

40. Holy simplicity!

41. "To be a good philosopher, one must be dry, clear, without illusion. A banker who has made a fortune has one character trait that is needed for making discoveries in philosophy, that is to say, for seeing clearly into what is."

42. *Winkel* has been translated here and elsewhere as "nook"; but it can also mean "angle," which would make sense here, though not in many of the other passages.

43. Freethinkers.

44. "Plato in front and Plato behind, in the middle Chimaera." Cf. *Iliad,* 6:181, where Chimaera is described: "Lion in front and serpent behind, in the middle a goat."

45. "Neither god nor master."

45a. Giuseppe Balsamo alias Count Alessandro di Cagliostro (1743–95), Italian adventurer and impostor.

46. *Störendsten, zerstörendsten.*

47. *Entsinnlichten.*

48. An allusion to the conception of Spinoza as "God-intoxicated."
49. *"Geblüt."*
50. *Um zu verbergen, was man bei sich birgt.*
51. *Ein Abgrund hinter jedem Grunde, unter jeder "Begründung."*
52. Literally, *Falte der Lockung.* German *Falte* means both "fold" and "wrinkle."
53. *Geistigkeit,* otherwise translated as "intellectuality."
54. Although "firstborn" is plural in the original *(Erstlinge),* the reference is to *The Birth of Tragedy.*
55. *"Wir Menschen sind—menschlicher."*
56. Paul Rée (1849–1901) had been a friend of Nietzsche's. He was the author of *The Origin of the Moral Sensations* (1877), to which Nietzsche refers.
57. "On Reading and Writing."
58. Literally, *bei . . . Verstimmten.* Nietzsche is playing on the ambiguity of the word *verstimmt,* which can mean both "out of tune" and "ill-humored."
59. Newest lust for glory.
60. Horror of a vacuum.
61. Instrument of the devil.
62. The philosophical animal.
63. Socrates appears in Aristophanes' comedy *The Clouds.*
64. Let the world perish, but let there be philosophy, the philosopher, *me!*
65. *Wissenschaft* does not refer only, or primarily, to the natural sciences, and when Nietzsche refers to scholars later in this section, he is by no means changing the subject. It seems best to call attention to this while using "science" to translate *Wissenschaft.*
66. *Braves und bescheidnes Arbeitervolk.*
67. *Arbeiter.*
67a. Self-deprecation.
68. *Eckensteherischer,* a Neitzschean neologism based on *Eckensteher,* which literally means "one who stands at a corner." Thus, Nietzsche's coinage implies "idle" and "loafing," even "beggarly"; in addition, however, he plays on the double meaning of *Ecke,* suggesting the connotation: "in a corner," i.e., "remote" and "insignificant."
69. *Rangabfolge der Wesen.*
70. Ximénès Doudan (1800–1872), a French critic, contributed to the *Journal des Débats* and was the author of the posthumously published *Mélanges et lettres* (1876–77; "Mixed Writings and Letters"), *Lettres* (1879; "Letters"), and *Pensées et fragments, suivis des révolutions du goût* (1881; "Thoughts and Fragments, and the Revolutions of Taste").
71. The habit of admiring the unintelligible instead of staying quite simply in the unknown.
72. Elegance of the syllogism.
73. *Widerwillen.*
74. *Lieber will noch der Mensch* das Nichts *wollen, als* nicht *wollen.*
75. *Ein Musikanten-Problem,* which can also mean "a problem for musicians."
76. *Heiland.*
77. Consensus of the sages.
78. A monstrous face, a monstrous mind.
79. Contest.
79a. Mandatory, indispensable.
80. Under the aspect of the eternal.
81. A pre-Socratic school of Greek philosophers, named after the city of Elea.
82. Self-caused.

83. The most real being.
84. That is, Kantian.
85. Zarathustra begins.
86. See n. 83.
86a. Gaius Sallustius Crispus (ca. 86–35/34 B.C.), Roman historian.
87. Nietzsche adds a somewhat redundant *auf dem Grunde,* "at the bottom" (but see n. 93).
88. More enduring than bronze.
89. Literally: *In gewissen Sprachen ist das, was hier erreicht ist, nicht einmal zu wollen.*
90. Varro's satire on the model of Menippus the Cynic.
91. A German silliness.
92. *Biedermännerei.*
93. Nietzsche has only *auf dem Grunde.*
94. *Desgleichen deutete ich mir . . . zurecht . . . .*
95. Nietzsche has *Heiland* only.
96. Flaubert is always hateful; the man is nothing, the work is all.
97. Love of fate.
98. Based on the expression *jemandem ein X für ein U* [i.e., V] *vormachen,* which means "to deceive" (the reference is to Roman numerals).
99. Allusion to Friedrich Schiller's poem "Das verschleierte Bild zu Sais."
100. To understand everything is to despise everything.
100a. Figure from Greek mythology who exposes herself indecently.
101. Near Sils-Maria, in the Upper Engadine.
102. 1854–1918; his real name was Heinrich Köselitz.
103. *The Gay Science.*
104. The writer Lou Andreas-Salomé (1861–1937) who was also a friend of Sigmund Freud and Rainer Maria Rilke.
105. Hotel.
106. When the first emperor of the Second *Reich,* Wilhelm I, died at ninety-one on 9 March 1888, his much more liberal son, Friedrich III, succeeded him; but Friedrich died of cancer after a hundred days, and was succeeded by his son, the last German kaiser, Wilhelm II.
107. *Fiel mir . . . ein.*
108. *Überfiel mich.*
109. Section 382.
110. *In Wissen und Gewissen.*
111. *Wohlseins und Wohlwollens.*
112. "One's skin creeping": *Überrieselungen* conjures up a slightly different image—as if water trickled over us.
113. "Arches over" and "wide arches" are in the original *überspannt* and *weitgespannt,* and the word for tension at the end of the sentence and also a little earlier is *Spannung.*
114. A town fifty miles northeast of Rome, founded as a bulwark against the power of the papacy by Conrad, son of Emperor Frederick II (1194–1250).
115. The translator reads *zur* ("in") where the German editions have *die* ("the"). On closer scrutiny, however, this emendation—though not wrong—reveals itself as unnecessary.
116. As he should be.
117. Before 1870 this had been a papal residence; after 1870 it was the residence of the king of Italy.
118. The ninth chapter of *Zarathustra II.*

119. Nietzsche had published only parts 1, 2, and 3, at first separately and then, in 1887, in one volume. Part 4, written in Nizza and Mentone the next winter (early in 1885), was printed privately in 1885.
120. The twelfth chapter of *Zarathustra III.*
121. Rancor.
122. *Zarathustra III,* "On Old and New Tablets," section 19.
123. Genesis 28:12.
124. *Übermensch,* usually rendered as "superman."
125. *Nach seinem Gleichnis zu suchen.*
126. "On Old and New Tablets," section 19.
127. Cf. *Zarathustra III,* "The Seven Seals (Or: The Yes and Amen Song)."
128. *Zarathustra II,* "On Redemption."
129. *Zarathustra II,* "Upon the Blessed Isles."
130. Lacking something better.
131. An almost exact quotation of the last words of the book, found also—again a little differently—near the end of the first section of the third inquiry.
132. This had been said of Nietzsche in the *Berner Bund* (16–17 September 1886), in J. V. Widmann's review of *Beyond Good and Evil.*
133. But *Ecce Homo* was not published until 1908, and at Nietzsche's funeral in 1900 Peter Gast proclaimed: "Holy be thy name to all coming generations."
134. Cf. *Zarathustra II,* "On Self-Overcoming."
135. Cf. *Zarathustra I,* "On the Thousand and One Goals."
136. Folly, stupidity, silliness.
137. *Instinkt-Verlogenheit.* Nietzsche's neologism is ambiguous; it could also mean "mendaciousness with regard to the (true or real) instincts" (see Sections 7, 8).
138. Best men.
139. Quoted from *Zarathustra III,* "On Old and New Tablets," section 7.
140. Ibid., Section 28.
141. English philosopher (1820–1903).
142. *Eine armselige Chineserei.*
143. Both quotations are from section 26 of "On Old and New Tablets."
144. All three quotations, beginning with "to soar off," come from *Zarathustra II,* "On Human Prudence."
145. *Selbstsucht:* the word is pejorative, like "selfishness."
146. *Nächstenliebe* and *Nächstensucht,* respectively.
147. Manic-depressive insanity.
148. Voltaire's motto—"Crush the infamous one!"—in his fight against the church.
149. *Antichrist* means both *the* Antichrist and "the anti-Christian."
150. Although Nietzsche seems to have in mind a well-known etymology of the Hebrew *Havvah* ("Eva" in German), not one of the Hebrew words for snake resembles this name. Genesis 3:20 links the name with life, and the only other verse in which it figures is Genesis 4:1.
151. The so-called *Will to Power* here combines two separate entries from Nietzsche's notebooks, rearranging the first and omitting a sizable portion of the second (cf. *KGW* VII/1, pp. 344f. and 703f.).
152. Nietzsche uses the singular.
153. End of first entry.
154. This entire paragraph was left out in the so-called *Will to Power.*
155. A heading which reads *The ways of self-narcotization* was added in the so-called *Will to Power.*
156. *Als erkannt, als bekannt.*
157. "Scholar and scientist": *der wissenschaftliche Mensch.*

158. *Verdüsterung.*
159. Ferdinando Galiani (1728–1787), Italian economist.
160. "A gay monster is worth more / Than a sentimental bore." Nietzsche omitted this couplet, but did quote it elsewhere in his notebooks.
161. *Folge-Unrichtigkeit.*
162. 1842–1906. German philosopher and author of a *Philosophie des Unbewußten* (1868).
163. In an earlier version, Nietzsche speaks of his "Dionysian riddle" *(Dionysos-Rätsel)* of the world, indeed of his "Dionysian mirror" *(Dionysos-Spiegel)* to which one has to hold up one's own mirror (cf. note to *KGW* VII/3, pp. 338f.).
164. The so-called *Will to Power* again combines two separate entries (cf. *KGW* VII/3, pp. 414ff.).
165. *Wie sehr auch schon im abgeschwächten Bilde.*
166. *Wo der Mensch sich selber und sich ganz und gar . . . fühlt . . . .*
167. End of first entry.
168. *Guter Mut zu beiden,* which also means "resoluteness with regard to both."
169. The entry in Nietzsche's notebook consists of two—largely identical and partly fragmentary—paragraphs. They have been edited accordingly. For the German original, see *KGW* VIII/1, p. 151.
170. *Ausdichtung und Rundung.*
171. *Einordnung und Gleichordnung.*
172. The sentence breaks off: *"ebenso—"*
173. Literally, "must be imagined."
174. Nietzsche copied a passage from Stendhal's *Vie de Napoléon* (preface, p. xv) into another notebook: *Une croyance presque instinctive chez moi, c'est que tout homme puissant ment, quand il parle, et à plus forte raison, quand il écrit* ("An almost instinctive belief on my part that every powerful man lies when he speaks and even more when he writes").
175. *Bevor "gedacht" wird, muß schon "gedichtet" worden sein.* Nietzsche means to stress the quasi-poetic function of the imagination.
176. *Zurechtbilden.*
177. *Zurechtmachung,* "rearrangement."
178. Nietzsche has only *Aesthetica;* the above title, taken from one of the lists of sections in his notebooks, was substituted in the so-called *Will to Power.*
179. Cf. Aristotle's conception of catharsis: *Poetics,* 1449b ff.
180. Once again, the so-called *Will to Power* offers a combination of two separate entries; cf. *KGW* VIII/3, pp. 180, 190.
181. End of first entry.
182. Censorious spirit.
183. Plebeian at bottom.
184. See n. 79.
185. See n. 79a.
186. Literally, *Pathologie des Untergrundes,* "pathology of the substratum."
187. *Willens-Disgregation* ("disgregation," in analogy to "congregation").
188. Indifference.
189. *Dressur.*
190. Another translation would be: "While hitherto the philosopher of decadence has counted at least as the typical philosopher."
191. Fragmentary.
192. Nietzsche inserted *Die bejahenden* [Künstler], *die Niedergangs-Künstler,* "the affirming [artists], the artists of declining life."
193. Actually, the entry begins with the elliptic note, *Gegenbewegung der Kunst* ("countermovement of art," or "art—as a countermovement").

194. Literally, *rückwärts* ("retroactively," or "in retrospect").

195. Again, Nietzsche's entry begins with a laconic and almost identical note; it reads, *Gegenbewegung* Kunst, "countermovement *art.*" Both this note and the title are missing in the so-called *Will to Power,* as is the fragmentary sentence which follows.

196. *Kunst-Naturgewalten.*

197. *Einheitsgefühl von der Notwendigkeit des Schaffens und Vernichtens.*

198. *Für-sich-sein.*

199. This entire paragraph was left out in the so-called *Will to Power.*

200. On subsequent pages, a whole series of similar drafts can be found; some of them are again in the third person.

201. This entry is preceded by the words *Gegenbewegung: Religion* ("countermovement: religion").

202. Nietzsche's term is *festzuhalten*; but the entire sentence is fragmentary and elliptic, and therefore has to be edited.

203. Erroneously, Nietzsche repeated *Typus,* "type."

204. *Selig* means, as before, both "blessed" and "blissful."

205. The so-called *Will to Power* has *my new path to a "yes"* from an earlier entry (Fall 1887) (cf. *KGW* VIII/3, pp. 288f. and VIII/2, p. 121).

SOURCES OF THE SELECTIONS

Part I

1. *The Birth of Tragedy; or, Greekness and Pessimism* (§§ 1–15). Taken from: Nietzsche, Friedrich. *The Birth of Tragedy* and *The Case of Wagner.* Translated, with Commentary, by Walter Kaufmann. New York: Vintage Books, 1967, pp. 17–98.
2. "The Birth of Tragedy" from *Ecce Homo: How One Becomes What One Is.* Taken from: Nietzsche, Friedrich. *On the Genealogy of Morals* and *Ecce Homo.* Edited, with Commentary, by Walter Kaufmann. New York: Vintage Books, 1969, pp. 270–75.
3. "Art in the 'Birth of Tragedy'" from the so-called *Will to Power.* Taken from: Nietzsche, Friedrich. *The Will to Power.* Translated by Walter Kaufmann and R. J. Hollingdale. Edited, with Commentary, by Walter Kaufmann. New York: Random House, 1967, pp. 451–53 (§ 853).

Part II

4. "On the Pathos of Truth" from *Five Prefaces to Five Unwritten Books.* Translated by Bruce Armstrong.
5. "On Truth and Falsity in Their Extramoral Sense." Taken from: Nietzsche, Friedrich. *Early Greek Philosophy & Other Essays.* Translated by Maximilian A. Mügge. New York: Russell & Russell 1964. (= Levy, Oscar, ed. *The Complete Works of Friedrich Nietzsche.* Volume 2), pp. 173–92.

Part III

6. From "On the Use and Disadvantage of History for Life" from *Untimely Meditations.* Taken from: Nietzsche, Friedrich. *Thoughts Out of Season*, Part 2. Translated by Adrian Collins. New York: Russell & Russell, 1964 (= Levy, Oscar, ed. *The Complete Works of Friedrich Nietzsche.* Volume 5), pp. 95–96.
7. From "Schopenhauer as Educator" from *Untimely Meditations and Related Writings.* Taken from: Nietzsche, Friedrich. *Schopenhauer as Educator.* Translated by J. W. Hillesheim and Malcolm R. Simpson. Chicago: Gateway Editions / Henry Regnery, 1965, p. 71.
8. From the fragmentary notes for *The Battle between Science and Wisdom.* Translated by Anthony M. Ludovici.
9. From "Richard Wagner in Bayreuth" from *Untimely Meditations and Related Writings.* Taken from: Nietzsche, Friedrich. *Thoughts Out of Season*, Part 1.

Translated by Anthony M. Ludovici. New York: Russell & Russell, 1964. (=Levy, Oscar, ed. *The Complete Works of Friedrich Nietzsche*. Volume 4), pp. 128–31, 172–73.

10. From *Human, All-Too-Human: A Book for Free Spirits*. Taken from: Nietzsche, Friedrich. *Human, All-Too-Human: A Book for Free Spirits*, Part 1. Translated by Helen Zimmern. New York: Russell & Russell, 1964 (=Levy, Oscar, ed. *The Complete Works of Friedrich Nietzsche*. Volume 6): "Of First and Last Things": §1, 2, 6, 7, 26, 28, 33, 34. "Concerning the History of Moral Sentiments": §38, 102. "The Religious Life": §108, 126. "From the Soul of Artists and Authors": §165, 212, 222, 223. "Signs of Higher and Lower Culture": §244, 251, 261, 272, 276, 278. "Man in Society": §361. "Man Alone by Himself": §635.

11. From *Human, All-Too-Human: Mixed Opinions and Maxims*. Taken from: Nietzsche, Friedrich. *Human, All-Too-Human: A Book for Free Spirits*, Part 2. Translated by Paul V. Cohn. New York: Russell & Russell, 1964. (=Levy, Oscar, ed. *The Complete Works of Friedrich Nietzsche*. Volume 7): §90, 98, 99, 100, 205, 221.

12. From *Human, All-Too-Human II: The Wanderer and His Shadow*. Taken from same as 11: §6, 16, 72, 86, 313, 315.

13. From *Dawn: Thoughts about Morality as a Prejudice*. Taken from: Nietzsche, Friedrich. *The Dawn of Day*. Translated by J. M. Kennedy. New York: Russell & Russell, 1964 (=Levy, Oscar, ed. *The Complete Works of Friedrich Nietzsche*. Volume 9): §6, 41, 144, 270, 327, 328, 433, 547.

14. From *The Gay Science*. Taken from: Nietzsche, Friedrich. *The Gay Science*. Translated, with Commentary, by Walter Kaufmann. New York: Vintage Books, 1974: Books I–III: §7, 11, 12, 37, 46, 80, 107, 123, 125, 153. "Sanctus Januarius": §276, 293, 328, 340, 341, 342. "We Fearless Ones": §344, 370, 372, 373.

15. *From Beyond Good and Evil: Prelude to a Philosophy of the Future*. Taken from: Nietzsche, Friedrich. *Beyond Good and Evil: Prelude to a Philosophy of the Future*. Translated, with Commentary, by Walter Kaufmann. New York: Vintage Books, 1966: Preface. "On the Prejudices of Philosophers": §6, 16, 20. "The Free Spirit": §24, 39, 41, 44. "Maxims and Interludes": §80, 155. "Concerning the Natural History of Morals": §190, 191, 202. "We Scholars": §205, 206, 211, 213. "What Is Noble?": §289, 292, 295.

16. From *On the Genealogy of Morals: A Polemic*. Taken from same as 2: Preface: §7. "What Is the Meaning of Ascetic Ideals?": §1, 7, 23, 25, 28.

17. From *The Case of Wagner: A Musician's Problem*. Taken from same as 1: Preface.

18. From *Twilight of the Idols: Or How One Philosophizes with a Hammer*. Taken from: Nietzsche, Friedrich. *The Portable Nietzsche*. Selected and Translated, with an Introduction, Prefaces, and Notes by Walter Kaufmann. New York: Viking Press, 1968: "Maxims and Arrows": §11. "The Problem of Socrates," pp. 473–479. "'Reason' in Philosophy," pp. 479–484. "How the 'True World' Finally Became a Fable," pp. 485–486. "Skirmishes of an Untimely Man": §10, 19, 24, 49. "What I Owe to the Ancients," pp. 556–563.

19. From *Nietzsche contra Wagner: From the Files of a Psychologist*. Taken from same as 18: "We Antipodes," pp. 669–671. Epilogue, pp. 680, 683.

20. From *Ecce Homo: How One Becomes What One Is*. Taken from same as 2: "Thus Spoke Zarathustra," pp. 295–309. "Genealogy of Morals," pp. 312–313. "Why I Am a Destiny," pp. 326–335.

21. From *The Antichrist: Curse upon Christianity*. Taken from same as 18: §48.

22. From the so-called *Will to Power*. Taken from same as 3: §417, 29, 594, 1029, 420, 91, 1067, 1051, 606, 616, 1049, 677, 544, 1005, 71, 852, 68, 432/433, 444, 799, 816, 821, 1050, 1052, 1041.

ACKNOWLEDGMENTS

Every reasonable effort has been made to locate the owners to rights to previously published translations printed here. We gratefully acknowledge permission to reprint the following material:

Permission to reprint from the *Complete Works of Friedrich Nietzsche,* edited by Oscar Levy, has been granted by George Allen & Unwin Ltd.

From *The Portable Nietzsche,* selected and translated by Walter Kaufmann. Copyright 1954 by the Viking Press, Inc. Copyright © renewed 1982 by Viking Penguin Inc. Reprinted by permission of the publisher, Viking Penguin, a division of Penguin Books USA Inc.

From *The Birth of Tragedy and the Case of Wagner* by Friedrich Nietzsche, trans. with comment. by Walter Kaufmann. Copyright © 1967 by Random House, Inc. Reprinted by permission of Random House, Inc.

From *On the Genealogy of Morals and Ecce Homo* by Friedrich Nietzsche, trans. by Walter Kaufmann. Copyright © 1967 by Random House, Inc. Reprinted by permission of Random House, Inc.

From *Beyond Good and Evil* by Friedrich Nietzsche, trans. and Preface by Walter Kaufmann. Copyright © by 1966 by Random House, Inc. Reprinted by permission of Random House, Inc.

From *The Will to Power* by Friedrich Nietzsche, trans. and edited by Walter Kaufmann. Copyright © 1967 by Walter Kaufmann. Reprinted by permission of Random House, Inc.

THE GERMAN LIBRARY
in 100 Volumes

Wolfram von Eschenbach
Parzival
Edited by André Lefevere

Gottfried von Strassburg
Tristan and Isolde
Edited and Revised by
    Francis G. Gentry
Foreword by C. Stephen Jaeger

German Medieval Tales
Edited by Francis G. Gentry
Foreword by Thomas Berger

German Mystical Writings
Edited by Karen J. Campbell
Foreword by Carol Zaleski

German Humanism and Reformation
Edited by Reinhard P. Becker
Foreword by Roland Bainton

Immanuel Kant
Philosophical Writings
Edited by Ernst Behler
Foreword by René Wellek

Friedrich Schiller
*Plays: Intrigue and Love
    and Don Carlos*
Edited by Walter Hinderer
Foreword by Gordon Craig

Friedrich Schiller
Wallenstein and Mary Stuart
Edited by Walter Hinderer

Johann Wolfgang von Goethe
*The Sufferings of Young Werther
and Elective Affinities*
Edited by Victor Lange
Forewords by Thomas Mann

German Romantic Criticism
Edited by A. Leslie Willson
Foreword by Ernst Behler

Friedrich Hölderlin
Hyperion and Selected Poems
Edited by Eric L. Santner

Philosophy of German Idealism
Edited by Ernst Behler

G. W. F. Hegel
*Encyclopedia of the Philosophical
    Sciences in Outline and Critical
    Writings*
Edited by Ernst Behler

Heinrich von Kleist
Plays
Edited by Walter Hinderer
Foreword by E. L. Doctorow

E. T. A. Hoffmann
Tales
Edited by Victor Lange

Georg Büchner
Complete Works and Letters
Edited by Walter Hinderer and
    Henry J. Schmidt

German Fairy Tales
Edited by Helmut Brackert and
    Volkmar Sander
Foreword by Bruno Bettelheim

German Literary Fairy Tales
Edited by Frank G. Ryder and
    Robert M. Browning
Introduction by Gordon Birrell
Foreword by John Gardner

F. Grillparzer, J. H. Nestroy,
    F. Hebbel
Nineteenth Century German Plays
Edited by Egon Schwarz in
    collaboration with
    Hannelore M. Spence

Heinrich Heine
Poetry and Prose
Edited by Jost Hermand and
 Robert C. Holub
Foreword by Alfred Kazin

Heinrich von Kleist and Jean Paul
German Romantic Novellas
Edited by Frank G. Ryder and
 Robert M. Browning
Foreword by John Simon

German Romantic Stories
Edited by Frank Ryder
Introduction by Gordon Birrell

German Poetry from 1750 to 1900
Edited by Robert M. Browning
Foreword by Michael Hamburger

Karl Marx, Friedrich Engels, August
 Bebel, and Others
*German Essays on Socialism
 in the Nineteenth Century*
Edited by Frank Mecklenburg
 and Manfred Stassen

Wilhelm Raabe
Novels
Edited by Volkmar Sander
Foreword by Joel Agee

Theodor Fontane
Short Novels and Other Writings
Edited by Peter Demetz
Foreword by Peter Gay

Gerhart Hauptmann
Plays
Edited by Reinhold Grimm and
 Caroline Molina y Vedia

Rainer Maria Rilke
Prose and Poetry
Edited by Egon Schwarz
Foreword by Howard Nemerov

Robert Musil
Selected Writings
Edited by Burton Pike
Foreword by Joel Agee

Essays on German Theater
Edited by Margaret Herzfeld-Sander
Foreword by Martin Esslin

Hermann Hesse
*Siddhartha, Demian,
 and Other Writings*
Edited by Egon Schwarz
 in collaboration with Ingrid Fry

Friedrich Dürrenmatt
Plays and Essays
Edited by Volkmar Sander
Foreword by Martin Esslin

Max Frisch
Novels, Plays, Essays
Edited by Rolf Kieser
Foreword by Peter Demetz

Gottfried Benn
Prose, Essays, Poems
Edited by Volkmar Sander
Foreword by E. B. Ashton
Introduction by Reinhard
 Paul Becker

German Essays on Art History
Edited by Gert Schiff

German Radio Plays
Edited by Everett Frost and Margaret
 Herzfeld-Sander

Hans Magnus Enzensberger
Critical Essays
Edited by Reinhold Grimm and
 Bruce Armstrong
Foreword by John Simon

All volumes available in hardcover and paperback editions at your bookstore or
from the publisher. For more information on The German Library write to: The
Continuum Publishing Company, 370 Lexington Avenue, New York, NY 10017.